The Mystery of Music

Also by this author

Kosegarten : The Turbulent Life and Times of a Northern German Poet
(Peter Lang, New York, 2004).
*Kosegarten's Cultural Legacy : Aesthetics, Religion, Literature, Art, and
Music* (Peter Lang, New York, 2005).

The Mystery of Music

An Exploration Centered on the Lives of Thirty Ancient Musicians

Lewis M. Holmes

CEK PUBLISHING LLC
BURLINGTON, VERMONT

ISBN: 978-0-692-19787-5

Library of Congress Control Number: 2018911576

1. World music. 2. Music history – ancient music. 3. Biography of musicians. 4. Ethnomusicology. 5. Music and human evolution.

2018
CEK Publishing LLC
Burlington, Vermont

CREDITS AND PERMISSIONS

All efforts have been made to contact copyright owners of cited materials. The author would be glad to hear of anybody who has not been duly acknowledged, so that he can make the proper attribution.

CONTENTS

All day and night, music,
a quiet, bright
reedsong. If it
fades, we fade.

— Rūmī 1207–1273 CE

PREFACE

My appreciation of music is, I suppose, typical for a mature adult. I have preferences that mostly were instilled during childhood and dislikes that mostly relate to recent innovation.

Personally, I like classical, ethnic, and melodic music but dislike twelve-tone and rap. I rank acoustic over electronic sound and moderate over loud volume.

Friends of mine have radically different musical tastes. One friend loves jazz; another, rock; a third, European music of the fifteenth century; and so on.

Almost without exception, however, everyone I know does like music in one form or another. That is what this book is about. It is not about individual differences in taste, which would also be an interesting subject to explore, but rather about fundamentals: Why do human beings like music? What does it do for us? How has it become part of our being?

In the third edition of his *Study of Ethnomusicology* (2015, University of Illinois Press), Bruno Nettl writes: "Of the many domains of culture, music would perhaps seem to be one of the least necessary" (p. 262). This thought, or a variation on it, had occurred to me also, before I started writing this book, and it gnawed at my consciousness. We do not need music in order to put a roof over our heads and food on our tables (unless we survive as professional musicians). Pretty songs do not keep dangerous animals at bay or protect us from our enemies. Music may be useful in attracting mates, but the deaf are able to couple in the absence of sound. And yet, as Nettl completes his observation about the necessity of music, "we know of no culture that does not have it" (*ibid.*).

I had the idea that reporting on the lives of ancient musicians might provide clues about music's "necessity." After all, individual patrons or communities in the distant past had been willing to support practitioners of this art and must, therefore, have felt that their music was worth having. By examining the lives of ancient musicians, I hoped to discover what they did that their audiences found important or even necessary.

Of course, instead of delving into history, I could have taken the lives of contemporary musicians as my subject. However, there are advantages to probing into the distant past. Life in earlier civilizations seems to have been lived at a more basic level than at present, and information gleaned from the study of ancient musicians might therefore reflect more closely the fundamentals of human existence. The avoidance of bias resulting from personal musical tastes—such as, for example, a dislike of rap or a preference for jazz—is another potential advantage of historical studies.

At the center of this study are thirty musicians from various regions of the world. Biographical sketches, or 'profiles,' of these individuals have been prepared and collected in Chapter 3. Falling under my operational definition of musician are instrumentalists, singers, and composers. Dancers and choreographers are not included, even though movement is often linked to music participation. The reason for the exclusion is to focus the discussion: Singers and instrumentalists always create musical sound, but they do not always move about; dancers always move about, but they do not always create musical sound.

Chapter 3 includes an analysis of the societal functions of the profiled musicians. It makes use of an ethnomusicological framework, the relevance of which is described in Appendix A. The broader implications of the present study are explored in Chapter 4, where examples from the profiles have been integrated into a discussion of the origin and development of human musicality.

Although the profiled musicians lived many centuries ago, many of the music cultures in which they flourished have had a lasting effect on subsequent musical practices. Early musical developments in Japan, China, India, Mesopotamia, the Islamic Empire, and Christianized Rome—to name but a few examples—have given rise to traditions that retain their relevance even to the present day.

Acknowledgments

This book has been made possible by the aid and advice of numerous individuals. John Curtis Franklin, professor of Classics at the University of Vermont, pointed me to the Ancient Near East. He suggested both subjects and sources, and he provided crucial input for several of the profiled musicians. Wolfgang Mieder, professor of German and Folklore at the University of Vermont, shared his extensive knowledge of the minnesinger Walther von der Vogelweide. Charles Benn, formerly of the University of Hawaii, responded to queries about the Tang Emperor Xuanzong and his concubine Yang Guifei, and he directed me to information on the 'Entertainment District' in Chang'an. Barbara Ruch, director of the Institute for Medieval Japanese Studies at Columbia University, offered the names of two female musicians. An Xin in

Beijing and Jie Yuxi in Xi'an assisted with the Chinese language and sources. Johannes Holeschofsky located valuable material for me in the library of the University of Vienna. In Rome, Mauro Crocenzi translated from the Italian and sent me texts that were unavailable on this side to the Atlantic Ocean. My wife Madelyn Holmes read the entire book and suggested countless significant improvements.

My thanks go to all these people, and especially to Madelyn for her continuing personal encouragement and substantive scholarly support. True to her vocation, she convinced me of the importance of historical context. Readers will find that it enlivens and deepens the text.

Burlington, Vermont
October 1, 2018

CHAPTER ONE

The Question of Music

Since the dawn of history, people have considered music a special, even mysterious, art and wondered about its provenance and functions. Through the ages, many great scholars have addressed these matters. This chapter provides a brief overview of their efforts and serves as background and introduction to the rest of the book.

In the early civilizations, music was often associated with important deities and legendary figures. They were said to have invented musical instruments and revealed musical secrets to human beings (Lewis 1992). This aspect of the history is discussed below under the heading **Mythology**.

Acoustical experiments and philosophical discourses succeeded mythology. Prominent examples of both these approaches have been documented in ancient China and Greece (Anderson & Mathieson 2001; Liang 1985: 35–36, 65; Thrasher et al. 2001; West 1992: 167 & 233–245). These are discussed below under the heading **Protoscience and Early Philosophy.**

Throughout the European Renaissance, Enlightenment, and Modern periods, scholars in Europe and elsewhere elaborated on the earlier interpretations (see concise reviews by Deutsch et al. 2001: 527–532; Kaden, Giese, & Schrammek 1997: 1620–1625; Rösing & Bruhn 1997: 1552–1567). These developments are outlined below under the heading **Later Efforts and Enlightenment.**

Despite wide-ranging efforts, human musicality remains, even today, a subject for continued speculation and research. Investigations of musical behavior have grown increasingly sophisticated. Specialists have attempted—among other things—to link music with evolutionary processes (Morley 2013; Radocy & Boyle 2012; cf. Thompson 2015: 17–44), to establish the effects of music on the human psyche (as described by Deutsch et al. 2001; Hallam, Cross, & Thaut 2016; Rösing & Bruhn 1997; Thompson 2015), and to pinpoint regions within the brain that respond to musical stimulation (see, e.g., Cameron & Grahn 2016; Koelsch 2012; Trainor & Zatorre 2016). For more on this subject, see the section below labeled **Recent Work**.

Scholars have recently emphasized a particular characteristic of musical behavior known as entrainment, which will be described toward the end of this chapter. Entrainment will be revisited in Chapter 4. A deeper understanding of the societal functions of musicians and their art, which emerges out of the profiles in Chapter 3, will sharpen the outlines of this somewhat obscure concept. See the section below labeled **Musical Entrainment**.

Mythology

The association of music with the gods seems to have been almost universal in the ancient civilizations. Here examples are provided from five of the regions treated in this book.

In **China**, the goddess Nüwa was said to have created humankind. She and her brother Fuxi, a *yin-yang* pair, originated musical instruments: His were the vessel flute *xun* and long zithers known as *guqin* and *se*; hers was the *shenghuang*, a reed mouth-organ or instrument resembling a jew's harp (Liang 1985: 35–36).

In **India**, the god Shiva together with Vishnu's avatar Krishna and Brahma's consort Sarasvatī are connected with music: Shiva played the *dumru* hourglass drum in his Dance of Creation; Krishna charmed the *gopī* cowherdesses with his *bansari* flute (present work: Chapter 3, "Jayadeva"); and Sarasvatī, who was considered to be the patroness of music, played the stringed instrument known as a *veena* (Lewis 1992: 1100–1110).

In **Egypt**, a great many important deities, including Amun, Isis, and Osiris, had musical associations. The cow goddess Hathor has been described as the goddess of love, music, and dance, while her son Ihy is said to have presided over the musical art. Bes, who served as a guardian during childbirth, and Thoth, whom the Greeks called Hermes, also were musical deities for the ancient Egyptians (Lewis 1992: 208–213 & 847–853).

In **Greece**, Hermes was considered to have invented the lyre, which he gave to the god Apollo, who became so closely associated with the instrument that *citharode* (lyre-player) was his epithet (Anderson 1997: 177; Lewis 1992: 332). That Apollo also sang can be inferred from an anecdote in which he bested the *aulete* (reed-piper) Marsyas in a contest (Wilson 2004: 274–277). The goddess Athena invented and then rejected the *aulos* (Wilson 2004: 275), while Pan is said to have formed the first shepherd's pipe (Lewis 1992: 332).

In **Western Asia**, the Sumerians considered the love goddess Nina (a.k.a. Inanna) to be the patroness of music; elsewhere, this goddess took on still other names, including Ishtar, Astarte, and Ashtoreth (Lewis 1992: 419; 616). A Hurrian/Hittite legend has Ishtar attempting through music and sex appeal to subdue a stone monster (*ibid.*, p. 420), and according to a recent, tentative interpretation of the image on an ancient clay seal, she played harp for the powerful god Ea (Franklin 2015: 92). Another aspect of ancient practice made the association of music with the gods of Western Asia even more immediate: the instruments themselves, and particularly lyres, were treated as divinities (Franklin 2005 & 2015).

Protoscience and Early Philosophy

As early scholars moved beyond the limitations of mythology, they gained insights into the physics of musical sound production and control of pitches. By the seventh century BCE, or possibly even earlier, Chinese 'musicologists' had discovered the so-called 'cycle of fifths' for generating a pentatonic scale. This procedure is documented in a treatise on music and agronomy ascribed to Master Guan Zhong, who died ca. 645 BCE. Making repeated use of a ratio of small numbers, 2:3, to move from tone to tone, the cycle of fifths epitomizes an ancient Chinese ideal of cosmological harmony, with two representing the earth and three, the heavens (Liang 1985: 65). The Greek philosopher/mathematician Pythagoras (ca. 570–495 BCE) and his adherents also favored numerical interpretations of music. They defined pitch intervals in terms of mathematical ratios and used instruments such as a special monochord in their experimental investigations of consonance and dissonance. Like the Chinese, Pythagoreans extended musical numerology into the heavenly realm, with their "harmony of the spheres" providing a famous example (West 1992: 167 & 233–245).

The Chinese sage Confucius (551–479 BCE), who lived during the so-called Spring and Autumn period (770–476 BCE) of the Eastern Zhou dynasty, considered 'appropriate' music to be conducive to individual morality and societal well-being. At this time, the existence of governmental institutions of music testifies to the importance that rulers attached to this art. Confucius explained his morality-related characterizations of music through historical examples that would have been clear to his contemporaries: He praised '*Shao*' music and denounced the music of the state of Zheng, which, he said, encouraged licentiousness. This contrast established categories of 'proper music' (*yayue*) and 'vernacular music' (*suyue*) that persisted throughout much of Chinese imperial history (Thrasher et al. 2001: 638). The *Yueji* ("Record of Music") chapter in the ancient Chinese *Book of Rites*, the preserved form of which dates from a few centuries after Confucius's death, quotes the master on this subject:

> Confucius said: "When you come to a state, you can easily discover in which (kind of) subjects (the inhabitants) had been instructed … if they are magnanimous, charitable, mild, and virtuous, they have been taught according to the [*Yueji*]. […] If they are magnanimous, charitable, mild, and virtuous and show not inclination toward excess, their knowledge of music is profound" (Kaufmann 1976: 55).

Even an inappropriate choice for the fundamental pitch of the musical scale could create confusion, annihilation, and disaster in the state, according to the *Yueji* (*ibid.*, p.33). To ensure peace and stability, many Chinese rulers adjusted pitch standards when they ascended to the throne (Thrasher et al. 2001: 638).

In Athens of the fifth century BCE, a prominent intellectual called Damon (dates unknown) composed an essay on music for presentation to the Areopagus Council, in which he asserts that musical modes and rhythms possess ethical qualities. He urged that the state become involved in music regulation and education and that boys be taught melodies that imbue "manliness, self-control, and even-handedness" (West 1992: 246–247). The philosopher Plato (ca. 429–347 BCE) took up and expanded on Damon's ideas, and those of the Pythagoreans and Sophists, to depict music in a way that closely resembles the views expressed by Confucius in China. Plato described the importance of a proper musical education in the following terms:

> [M]usical education is the most important, [because] rhythm and attunement are what most penetrate the inner soul and grasp it most powerfully, bringing good order, and make a person well-regulated if he is educated correctly and the opposite if he is not (*The Republic* 3: 401d; cited by West 1992: 248).

In discussing musical forms and instrumentation, Plato showed a clear preference for the traditional. Only the Dorian and Phrygian modes were to be allowed in his ideal city state (West 1992: 105), and novelty was to be avoided (Wong 1998: 112). With respect to instrumentation, Plato took account primarily of the *aulos* (reed pipe) and lyre. The former had a reputation for creating an "exciting and orgiastic effect," whereas the latter was Apollo's instrument and therefore consistent with Plato's conservative views on propriety (Anderson & Mathieson 2001). In the fifth and fourth centuries BCE, performers on the aulos were exploiting its tonal flexibility to move beyond the limitations of traditional music (West 1992: 356–372). Plato banned this instrument from his ideal state (Anderson & Mathieson 2001).

Attempts aimed at encouraging 'good' music and banning 'bad' music have recurred through the centuries. Early in the Christian era, the Fathers of the Roman Catholic Church accepted hymn-singing in their religious services but warned against musical entertainment (Anderson & Mathieson 2001). Starting in the seventh century CE, Islamic societies exhibited complex and frequently negative attitudes to music (Shiloah 1994: 701–709), causing musicians to tread a cautious path (present work: Chapter 3, "Musicians of India" and "Musicians of Western Asia CE," *passim*). Around 1700 CE, when both Pietism and Orthodox Lutheranism thrived in Germany, the city authorities in Leipzig subjected several types of secular music to regulation by law (Kevorkian 2007: 140). During the 1920s and 1930s, when jazz became popular in the USA, it was widely criticized as immoral and disruptive (Merriam 1964: 242; cf. present work: Appendix B). In the 1990s, another African-American genre, rap music, became the target for similar condemnation (Rose 1994: 124–145; Toop 2001; Toop, Cheney, & Kajikawa 2017).

Some twentieth-century governments pursued policies of musical correctness. The authorities in Nazi Germany favored the works of "Aryan" composers of the nineteenth century, while promulgating vague music standards and suppressing the activities of Jews and minority musicians (Potter 2001). In the Soviet Union, application of the concept of 'socialist realism in music' profoundly impacted compositional efforts and overturned the lives of dissenting practitioners (Krebs 1970: 51–60; Powell & Bartlett 2001; Robinson 2012: 276–277). During the Cultural Revolution in China (ca. 1966–1976), a small number of exemplary works—operas, ballets, symphonies, and piano pieces—functioned as models to which all musical activity should conform (Mittler 2012: 36; Thrasher et al. 2001: 650); other approaches to music were silenced, and their practioners, persecuted (Thrasher et al. 2001: 648–649, 660, 662, & *passim*). The sinologist Barbara Mittler associates such "dictatorship over 'correct sounds'" during the Cultural Revolution with the writings of Confucius and discussions of music in the Chinese Classics (2012: 97).

Later Efforts and Enlightenment

After Confucius and Plato's lifetimes, and right up to the present, efforts to understand musical behavior and its implications for individuals and society have consistently attracted attention. The many scholars involved in such efforts include philosophers, archeologists, psychologists, physiologists, sociologists, neurologists, acoustical scientists, ethnomusicologists, and music theorists (for summary overviews of the history, see, e.g., Deutsch et al. 2001: 527–532; Kaden, Giese, & Schrammek 1997: 1620–1625; Rösing & Bruhn 1997: 1552–1567).

A notable marker was put down in 1761 CE, when Jean-Jacques Rousseau completed his *Essay on the Origin of Languages* (Rousseau & Scott 1998: 289–332). In this work, Rousseau depicts music as a cultural phenomenon that grew out of gatherings at the watering spots in southern settlements:

> There were formed the first ties between families; there the first meetings between the two sexes took place. Young girls came to fetch water for the household, young men came to water their herds. There […] from the pure crystal of the fountains came the first fires of love (p. 314).

Rousseau writes that "the liveliness of the agreeable passions" (p. 315) inspired the inhabitants to speak, and argues that melody emerged out of the tuneful cadences of their spoken words.

Rousseau's idyllic presentation is important for linking music with language and for associating both with human courtship, ideas that re-emerged a century later in *Descent of Man*, from 1871, by Charles Darwin. Darwin's conclusions about musical behavior resemble Rousseau's, with the important exception that for Darwin, language derives from music, rather than the other way around.

Darwin acknowledges the difficulty of understanding the origins of human musicality:

> As neither the enjoyment nor the capacity of producing musical notes are faculties of the least use to man in reference to his daily habits of life, they must be ranked amongst the most *mysterious* with which he is endowed (Darwin 2004 [1871]: 636, emphasis added).

He rises to the challenge of trying to clear up the mystery. Surveying in detail the mating habits of other fauna, and especially the behavoir of songbirds, he suggests that the musical embellishment of mating calls may have provided our ancestors with a reproductive advantage during courtship. Because other animals produce "musical notes and rhythms," whereas "articulate speech is […] the highest" of the human arts, Darwin rejects the idea that music "developed from the tones used in impassioned speech." Instead, he asserts "that the rhythms and cadences of oratory are derived from previously developed musical powers" (p. 638).

Recent Work

Recent scholars have categorized musicality as either a product of human evolution or as something that people acquire from their cultures. However, several aspects of human musicality argue against the latter possibility. First, with some exceptions (Stevens & Byron 2016), many music systems of the world share a number of common elements: They treat the octave as a privileged interval; they form scales of discrete pitches; they incorporate unequal intervals within the scales; they are timed to repetitive pulses; they associate music and dance; and they adhere to a tonal center (e.g., the dominant in European music or the drone in the music of South Asia). Secondly, archeological artifacts such as the remnants of ancient bone flutes show that music is not a recent cultural development, but rather has been practiced for tens of thousands of years. In addition, certain types of music such as lullabies are identifiable across cultural boundaries, and infants can discriminate between consonance and dissonance soon after birth. Finally, neuro-imaging techniques have shown that the evolved brain contains modular regions that respond to musical sounds (Thompson 2015: 14 & 20–21; Tillmann 2013).

With respect to evolutionary treatments of musical behavior, Darwin's sexual-selection theory continues to be viewed with considerable respect (cf. Morley 2013: 285–289; Radocy & Boyle 2012: 32–33; Thompson 2015: 21–23). The association of music and dancing with courtship is well known and will not be explored further in the present work. Evolutionary theorists have, however, also proposed other models for the acquisition of music.

Morley (2013) describes four types of potentially selective benefits of musical behavior that may have contributed to human evolution. In addition to considering the role of music in attracting mates, he discusses the survival benefits of bonding individuals into groups, of signaling group cohesion and cooperation, and of supporting the development of cognitive versatility (pp. 279–294).

Radocy and Boyle (2013) list six theories of musical evolution (pp. 31–37). These theories relate to musilanguage (an imagined early tonal system out of which both music and language evolved); sexual-selection; synchronous-chorusing (a means of attracting mates from a distance); mother-infant interactions (involving both rhythmic movements and a form of modulated speech that is sometimes labeled 'motherese'), together with the beginnings of family (when lullabies were presumably first sung); music as an adaptive social force (promotion of group identification, cohesion, and social-bonding); and music in a biological perspective (music as an autonomous human function).

Thompson (2015) divides adaptationist theories of musical evolution into two categories, based on whether the theories model reproductive or survival benefits. The former involve extensions of Darwin's sexual-selection approach. The broader survival grouping includes theories that emphasize the nurturement of social bonds, the entrainment of coordinated movements, the promotion of emotional bonding, the enhancement of cognitive and social skills, and the engagement of others for the purpose of attuning to and influencing their affective states (pp. 20–33). Thompson also discusses non-adaptationist accounts, which base their considerations on the repurposing, or 'exaptation,' of previously adopted traits (pp. 33–37).

Musical Entrainment

During the past quarter-century, or so, the characteristic of music participation known as 'entrainment' has attracted a good deal of scholarly attention. Entrainment can be thought of in the simplest of terms as the quality of music that gets us moving to a beat. Without using the actual expression, the historian William H. McNeill (1997) introduces entrainment and discusses its role in human evolution, religion, and warfare, in a book titled *Keeping Together in Time*. He asserts that the practice of "moving rhythmically while giving voice together" (p. 152), such as occurs, for example, in military drill and communal dancing, arouses "euphoric fellow feeling" (p. 2) and is "the surest, most speedy, and efficacious way of creating and sustaining [...] communities" (p. 152). Strengthened emotional bonds would have facilitated growth in the size of early human bands, he argues, "with immediate advantages for mutual protection and the expansion of territory at the expense both of competing species and of smaller bands [...] that did not learn to dance." Cooperative hunting would have become more efficient, larger animals could have been taken, and females could share more widely in the nurturing of their young (p. 27).

More formally, the archeologist and evolutionist Iain Morley characterizes entrainment as "the coordination of [vocal and corporeal] gestures with an internally or externally generated pulse" (2013: 314) or, again, as "the timing of our own sound production and movement with either an internally generated pulse or with the percept of a pulse within an externally generated stimulus" (p. 243). Entrainment has been described recently as being as important as vocal utterance as a source of musical behavior (Clayton 2016: 51). Cameron and Grahn (2016), who have undertaken neuro-imaging studies of the phenomenon, note that "the tendency to move in synchrony with rhythm arises without training" (p. 357). Stevens and Byron (2016) write that "temporal entrainment" is one of "the basic, domain-general processes" that qualify as universals in music (p. 26).

Musical entrainment will be considered further in Chapter 4. Examples drawn from the profiles in Chapter 3 and elsewhere will illustrate the importance of this phenomenon in historical situations and attest to the likelihood of its role in the evolution of human musicality.

References Cited

Anderson, Warren D. 1997. *Music and Musicians in Ancient Greece.* Ithaca: Cornell University Press.

Anderson, Warren, and Thomas J. Mathieson. 2001. Plato [Platon]. In *The New Grove Dictionary of Music and Musicians*, edited by S. Sadie and J. Tyrrell. London: Macmillan Publishers Ltd.

Cameron, Daniel J., and Jessica A. Grahn. 2016. The Neuroscience of Rhythm. In *The Oxford Handbook of Music*

Psychology. Oxford Library of Psychology, edited by S. Hallam, I. Cross and M. Thaut. Oxford: Oxford University Press.

Clayton, Martin. 2016. The Social and Personal Functions of Music in Cross-Cultural Perspective. In *The Oxford Handbook of Music Psychology. Oxford Library of Psychology*, edited by S. Hallam, I. Cross and M. Thaut. Oxford: Oxford University Press.

Darwin, Charles; with an introduction by James Moore and Adrian Desmond. 2004 [1871]. *The Descent of Man, and Selection in Relation to Sex*. London: Penguin Books.

Deutsch, Diana, et al. 2001. Psychology of Music. In *The New Grove Dictionary of Music and Musicians*, edited by S. Sadie and J. Tyrrell. New York: Grove.

Franklin, John Curtis. 2005. Lyre Gods of the Bronze Age Musical Koine. *Journal of Ancient Near East Religions* 6:39–70.

———. 2015. *Kinyras: The Divine Lyre. With a Study of Balang Gods by Wolfgang Heimpel and Illustrations by Glynnis Fawkes. 1st ed, Hellenic Studies Series*. Washington, D.C.: Center for Hellenic Studies.

Hallam, Susan, Ian Cross, and Michael Thaut. 2016. *The Oxford Handbook of Music Psychology*. 2nd ed, Oxford Library of Psychology. Oxford: Oxford University Press.

Kaden, Christian, Dietlef Giese, and Bernhard Schrammek. 1997. Musiksoziologie. In *Die Musik in Geschichte und Gegenwart. Allgemeine Enzyklopädie der Musik begründet von Friedrich Blume. Sachteil in neun Bänden*, edited by L. Finscher. Kassel - Basel - London - New York - Prag / Stuttgart - Weimar: Bärenreiter-Verlag / Metzler.

Kaufmann, Walter. 1976. *Musical References in the Chinese Classics*, Detroit Monographs in Musicology. Detroit: Information Coordinators.

Kevorkian, Tanya. 2007. *Baroque Piety: Religion, Society, and Music in Leipzig, 1650–1750*. Aldershot & Burlington: Ashgate.

Koelsch, Stefan. 2012. *Brain and Music*. Chichester: Wiley-Blackwell.

Krebs, Stanley Dale. 1970. *Soviet Composers and the Development of Soviet Music*. New York: W. W. Norton.

Lewis, Thomas P. 1992. *The Pro/Am Book of Music and Mythology*. 1st ed. 2 vols. White Plains: Pro/Am Music Resources.

Liang Mingyue. 1985. *Music of the Billion: An Introduction to Chinese Musical Culture*. New York: Heinrichshofen.

McNeill, William Hardy. 1995. *Keeping Together in Time: Dance and Drill in Human History*. Cambridge: Harvard University Press.

Merriam, Alan P. 1964. *The Anthropology of Music*. Evanston: Northwestern University Press.

Mittler, Barbara. 2012. *A Continuous Revolution: Making Sense of Cultural Revolution Culture*, Harvard East Asian Monographs. Cambridge: Harvard University Asia Center.

Morley, Iain. 2013. *The Prehistory of Music: Human Evolution, Archaeology, and the Origins of Musicality*. 1st ed. Oxford: Oxford University Press.

Potter, Pamela M. 2001. Nazism. In *The New Grove Dictionary of Music and Musicians*, edited by S. Sadie and J. Tyrrell. New York: Grove.

Powell, Jonathan, and Rosamund Bartlett. 2001. Russian Federation: 4. The 20th Century. In *The New Grove Dictionary of Music and Musicians*, edited by S. Sadie and J. Tyrrell. London: Macmillan Publishers Ltd.

Radocy, Rudolf E., and J. David Boyle. *2012. Psychological Foundations of Musical Behavior*. 5th ed. Springfield: Charles C Thomas, Publisher, LTD.

Robinson, Harlow. 2012. Music. In *The Cambridge Companion to Modern Russian Culture*, edited by N. Rzhevsky. Cambridge & New York: Cambridge University Press.

Rose, Tricia. 1994. *Black Noise: Rap Music and Black Culture in Contemporary America*. Hanover & London: Wesleyan University Press; published by University Press of New England.

Rösing, Helmut, and Herbert Bruhn. 1997. Musikpsychologie. In *Die Musik in Geschichte und Gegenwart. Allgemeine Enzyklopädie der Musik begründet von Friedrich Blume*. Sachteil in neun Bänden, edited by L. Finscher. Kassel - Basel - London - New York - Prag / Stuttgart - Weimar: Bärenreiter-Verlag / Metzler.

Rousseau, Jean-Jacques, and John T. Scott. 1998. *Essay on the Origin of Languages and Writings Related to Music, The Collected Writings of Rousseau, Vol. 7*. Hanover: University Press of New England.

Shiloah, Amnon. 1994. Arabische Musik. In *Die Musik in Geschichte und Gegenwart. Sachteil*, edited by F. Blume and L. Finscher. Kassel: Bärenreiter; Stuttgart: Metzler.

Stevens, Catherine J., and Tim Byron. 2016. Universals in Music Processing: Entrainment, Acquiring Expectations, and Learning. In *The Oxford Handbook of Music Psychology. Oxford Library of Psychology*, edited by S. Hallam, I. Cross and M. Thaut. Oxford: Oxford University Press.

Thompson, William Forde. 2015. *Music, Thought, and Feeling: Understanding the Psychology of Music*. 2nd ed. New York & Oxford: Oxford University Press.

Thrasher, Alan R., et al. 2001. China, People's Republic of. In *The New Grove Dictionary of Music and Musicians*, edited by S. Sadie and J. Tyrrell, Vol. 5: 631–695. London: Macmillan Publishers Ltd.

Tillmann, Barbara. 2013. La musique: un langage universel? In *Le cerveau mélomane*, edited by E. Bigand. Paris: Belin.

Toop, David. 2001. Rap. In *The New Grove Dictionary of Music and Musicians*, edited by S. Sadie and J. Tyrrell. London: Macmillan Publishers Ltd.

Toop, David, Charise Cheney, and Loren Kajikawa. 2017. Rap. *Grove Music Online. Oxford Music Online*, accessed May 25, 2017, http://www.oxfordmusiconline.com/subscriber/article/grove/music/2225387.

Trainor, Laurel J., and Robert J. Zatorre. 2016. The Neurobiology of Musical Expectations from Perception to Emotion. In *The Oxford Handbook of Music Psychology. Oxford Library of Psychology*, edited by S. Hallam, I. Cross and M. Thaut. Oxford: Oxford University Press.

West, M. L. 1992. *Ancient Greek Music*. Oxford: Clarendon Press.

Wilson, Olly. 1985. The Association of Movement and Music as a Manifestation of a Black Conceptual Approach to Music-Making. In *More Than Dancing: Essays on Afro-American Music and Musicians: Contributions in Afro-American and African Studies*, edited by I. V. Jackson. Westport: Greenwood Press.

Wilson, Peter. 2004. Athenian Strings. In *Music and the Muses: The Culture of 'Mousike' in the Classical Athenian City*, edited by P. Murray and P. Wilson. Oxford & New York: Oxford University Press.

Wong, Marina. 1998. A Comparison between the Philosophies of Confucius and Plato as Applied to Music Education. *The Journal of Aesthetic Education* 32 (3):109–112.

Further Reading

Bigand, Emmanuel. 2013. *Le cerveau mélomane*. Paris: Belin.

Blaukopf, Kurt. 1992. *Musical Life in a Changing Society: Aspects of Music Sociology*. Translated by D. Marinelli. Revised ed. Portland: Amadeus Press. Original edition, *Musik im Wandel der Gesellschaft*.1982.

Bunt, Leslie. 2001. Music Therapy. In *The New Grove Dictionary of Music and Musicians*, edited by S. Sadie and J. Tyrrell. New York: Grove.

Hagen, Edward H., and Gregory A. Bryant. 2003. Music and Dance as a Coalition Signaling System. *Human Nature* 14 (1):21–51.

Levinson, Jerrold. 2015. *Musical Concerns: Essays in Philosophy of Music*. 1st ed. Oxford & New York: Oxford University Press.

Mahns, Wolfgang. 1997. Musiktherapie. In *Die Musik in Geschichte und Gegenwart. Allgemeine Enzyklopädie der Musik begründet von Friedrich Blume. Sachteil in neun Bänden*, edited by L. Finscher. Kassel - Basel - London - New York - Prag / Stuttgart - Weimar: Bärenreiter-Verlag / Metzler.

Perlovsky, Leonid I. 2017. *Music, Passion, and Cognitive Function*. London: Academic Press.

Shepherd, John, and Kyle Devine. 2017. Sociology of Music. In *Grove Music Online. Oxford Music Online*: Oxford University Press. Web. 26 Jan. 2017. http://www.oxfordmusiconline.com/subscriber/article/grove/music/A2242526.

———, eds. 2015. *The Routledge Reader on the Sociology of Music*. New York & London: Routledge.

Tan Siu-Lan, Peter Pfordresher, and Rom Harré. 2010. *Psychology of Music: From Sound to Significance*. Hove & New York: Psychology Press.

CHAPTER TWO

Selection and Presentation

To select musicians for profiling, I turned to the scholarly literature, focusing far back in time. I also covered as a broad a range of early societies and locations as possible, in an attempt to capture the general characteristics of musical behavior, rather than those that might pertain only to a particular region or society.

During the initial phases of the project, it became apparent that relevant information could be found about early musicians in many different locations: between Iberia and Mali in the West and China and Japan in the East—in other words, throughout a wide swath of regions, cultures, and societies. Fortunately, useful studies were available in English, French, and German. Working from primary sources would have required facility in a dozen or more languages.

My underlying wish was to explore the lives of early musicians in circumstances that differed markedly from those of the present. Because social organization took root and matured at different times in different places, even musicians who lived many years apart from one another could satisfy this criterion. For inclusion in this book, a Malian from the thirteenth century CE (present work: Chapter 7, "Dugha") is no less suitable than an Egyptian from the thirteenth century BCE (present work: Chapter 3, "Ra-ia").

I searched first for subjects from the beginnings of civilization. In Mesopotamia and Egypt, this societal stage (as characterized by the existence of written languages, cities, and monumental structures) is thought to have started around 3000 BCE. The Egyptian flutist **Ipi (fl. ca. 2600 BCE)** and the Akkadian priestess-composer **Enheduanna (fl. ca. 2300 BCE)**, both of whom are profiled in Chapter 3, lived just several hundred years later.

Enheduanna acquired her position of *en*-priestess shortly after her father, Sargon the Great, founded the Akkadian Empire in ca. 2330 BCE. Many other musicians in my study also practiced the musical arts soon after the creation of historically significant new political and religious alignments. These individuals include the lyre-playing psalmist **David of Bethlehem (1040–970 BCE)**, who unified and strengthened the Kingdom of Israel and Judah during his lifetime; **Li Yannian (fl. ca. 100 BCE)**, who served as a court musician under the Han emperor Wudi (r. 141–87 BCE), approximately one century after the unification of China; the piper **Tigellius (ca. 54 BCE–39 CE)**, who played for the leading political circles at the start of the Roman Empire; **Bishop Ambrose of Milan (339–397 CE)**, who helped to establish liturgical hymnody during the century in which Christianity became a state religion; the lutenist and singer **Jamīla (d. ca. 715 CE)**, who was revered by her audiences in Medina during the first century of the Islamic Empire; the singer and composer **Ziryāb (ca. 790–850 CE)**, who brought Middle-Eastern musical practices to the recently founded, independent Emirate of Córdoba on the Iberian Peninsula; the *djeli* (or 'griot') **Balla Fasséké Kouyaté (fl. ca. 1230 CE)**, who sang for and advised the founding ruler Sundiata of the Mali Empire; the poet-composer **Amīr Khusrau Delhavī (1253–1325 CE)**, who brought Persian and Arabian songs into India during the first century of the Delhi Sultanate; and the blind lutenist and singer **Akashi no Kakuichi (ca. 1300–1371 CE)**, who composed his epic *Tale of the Heike* during the second century of the military, shogunate form of government in Japan, which prevailed until the mid-1800s.

Of course, the limited availability of source materials from the past has restricted my choice of subjects. The lives of individual *aulētrides*, who performed at symposia in Athens (Anderson 1997: 143–144), street entertainers, who plied their trade in Rome (Baudot 1973: 66–70), and *asobi*, who entertained on river boats in Japan (Goodwin 2007: 21–27), to name but a few examples, have passed into history unrecorded. As anonymity may have been the rule, rather than the exception, for the musicians of antiquity, I cannot claim that the individuals who are profiled in Chapter 3 form a *representative* cohort of musicians of the past. Their lives are, however, *illustrative* of the variety to be found among the lives of such individuals.

Although biographical information is more readily available about rich and powerful men than about women and members of the lower classes, I have made an effort to seek out subjects from the latter two groups for inclusion together with upper-class males. Thus, alongside profiles of **King David** of Israel, **Emperor Nero (37–68; r. 54–68 CE)** of Rome, and **Emperor Xuanzong (685–762; r. 712–756 CE)** of China, readers will also find profiles of an Egyptian trumpeter named **Peripatjauemope (fl. ca. 1080 BCE)**, a professional Greek citharode named **Stratonicus (ca. 410–360 BCE)**, and a European troubadour named **Marcabru (fl. ca. 1130–1150 CE)**, all of whom were without independent means of support. Among the profiled female musicians, the differences in social status are similarly great. **Enheduanna** was a princess in Mesopotamia, and **Yang Guifei (719–756 CE)** was for a time probably the most powerful woman in China, whereas both **Otomae (1085–1169 CE)** in Japan and **Jamīla (d. ca. 715 CE)** in the Islamic Empire had more lowly origins. Lowest of all was the Tang-dynasty prostitute **Fu Niang (fl. ca. 880 CE)**, who had to sing while entertaining her clients.

Arrangement of the Profiles

Even though the profiled musicians' lives form part of the grand history of the world, their circumstances, and their musical traditions, were influenced by their societies. The profiles have therefore been grouped according to region, and the regions have been listed alphabetically: China, Egypt, Europe, etc. Within each grouping, the musicians' names appear in chronological order.

The number of profiled musicians from Western Asia is comparatively large, reflecting in part the long recorded history of music in this area of the world. For clarity, and to mark the shift in music sensibilities associated with the rise of Islam in the seventh century CE, the Western Asian musicians have been separated into two groups, Western Asia BCE and Western Asia CE.

Identifying Musical Functions

The profiles contain a wealth of information about music in ancient societies. To highlight this information, the activities of the profiled musicians have been categorized with the help of a list of ten functions of music, which the anthropologist Allen P. Merriam formulated in the 1960s (Merriam 1964: 219–227):

> The function of emotional expression
> The function of aesthetic enjoyment
> The function of entertainment

The function of communication
The function of symbolic representation
The function of physical response
The function of enforcing conformity to social norms
The function of validation of social institutions and religious rituals
The function of contribution to the continuity and stability of culture
The function of contribution to the integration of society

These functions and reactions of other specialists to them are discussed in Appendix B, where their relevance to the present study is also established. The musical functions for each of the profiled musicians are identified in brief introductions to the regional groupings.

All the profiled musicians flourished in the distant past. Merriam developed his list of musical functions by reference to musicological studies in the nineteenth and twentieth centuries CE. It is not clear *a priori* that his functions should adequately describe the activities of ancient musicians. After all, many salient features of music have changed enormously during the intervening period. One of the aims of the present study is to determine the suitability of Merriam's functions to historical studies, for this can provide an indication of the extent to which musical functionality has remained constant through the years. Changes in functionality might indicate dependence on evolving societal influences, whereas constancy would suggest a deeper connection to the fundamentals of human nature.

References Cited

Anderson, Warren D. 1997. *Music and Musicians in Ancient Greece.* Ithaca: Cornell University Press.

Baudot, Alain. 1973. *Musiciens romains de l'antiquité.* Montréal: Presses de l'Université de Montréal.

Goodwin, Janet R. 2007. *Selling Songs and Smiles: The Sex Trade in Heian and Kamakura Japan.* Honolulu: University of Hawai'i Press.

Merriam, Alan P. 1964. *The Anthropology of Music.* Evanston: Northwestern University Press.

CHAPTER THREE

Profiles

Musicians of China

Very early in the history of China, state institutions of music were actively supporting the Confucian concept, that 'proper music' (*yayue*) was conducive to peace and morality in the public sphere (cf. present work: Chapter 1). This perception impacted the lives of the musicians profiled in this section, who were active during the important Han (206 BCE–220 CE) and Tang (618–907 CE) dynasties of ancient imperial China.

In 112 BCE, the Han emperor Wudi (r. 141–87 BCE) reorganized and expanded the operations of his Imperial Music Bureau. He appointed the musician **Li Yannian (fl. ca. 100 BCE)** to be its director. In this capacity, Li collected popular songs and adapted them to court, religious, and secular functions. He appropriated folk music and dance for use in nocturnal cultic sacrifices. One of Li's nonreligious compositions, "The Beauty Song," which may have referred to his sister, survived to become a central motif in a Chinese movie of the year 2003, *House of Flying Daggers*.

The multifaceted Tang emperor **Xuanzong (685–762; r. 712–756 CE)** made notable contributions in the field of music. He streamlined the state's musical institutions and reorganized ethnic music ensembles. In a more personal sphere, he led the elite Pear Garden performers in pieces that he himself arranged or composed.

The profiles of two female musicians of the Tang are included in the present section. Imperial concubine **Yang Guifei (719–756 CE)** shared Emperor Xuanzong's passion for music before their life together ended in tragedy. The courtesan **Fu Niang (fl. ca. 880 CE)** sang and most likely also played *pipa* (lute) for her clients.

∞

Six of Merriam's ten functions of music can be associated with these musicians:

THE FUNCTION OF EMOTIONAL EXPRESSION

At the terrible conclusion of a glorious reign in China, **Emperor Xuanzong** lost both his throne and his imperial consort Yang Guifei, whom he adored. The dynasty survived, weakened, as did Xuanzong. A broken man, he spent the rest of his days as Retired Emperor, mourning his losses. In these final years, he seems to have felt compelled to express his sadness in music. He composed a song about a military defeat. Playing flute, he accompanied a Pear Garden singer in the "Song of Liang Prefecture," which Yang Guifei had composed. He wept when listening to the "Song of the Bell in the Misty Rain" and also at the close of a performance by a dancer who had been one of Yang Guifei's favorites.

THE FUNCTION OF AESTHETIC ENJOYMENT

Emperor Xuanzong modified the musical aesthetic by merging 'foreign' musicians and music into the imperial musical establishment. He composed and directed the performance of innovative secular music.

THE FUNCTION OF ENTERTAINMENT

In Han-dynasty China, the singer and composer **Li Yannian** entertained for Emperor Wu. The Tang emperor **Xuanzong** let courtiers enjoy performances of his Pear Garden Troupe; creating beautiful music even without an audience also clearly gave him pleasure. Xuanzong's imperial consort **Yang Guifei** contributed to court entertainment by playing lute and stone chimes in the Pear Garden orchestra. Far lower on the social scale were courtesans such as **Fu Niang**, who worked in the entertainment quarter of the capital Chang'an. Fu Niang was required to sing songs and play drinking games to entertain her clients.

THE FUNCTION OF PHYSICAL RESPONSE

Yang Guifei was a singer and dancer, as well as an instrumentalist. Moving to music, she danced two well-known numbers of the Tang era, *Huxuan wu* ("Whirling Barbarian Dance") and *Nishang yuyi qu* ("Music of the Rainbow Feather Dress"). The latter piece was performed when she officially entered Emperor Xuanzong's harem.

THE FUNCTION OF VALIDATION OF SOCIAL INSTITUTIONS AND RELIGIOUS RITUALS

Li Yannian adapted melodies for use in ritualistic sacrifices, and, as a court musician, he performed in courtly entertainments, as mentioned earlier. These activities helped to validate religious rituals and contributed to imperial pomp-and-circumstance, respectively. In addition, as director of the Imperial Bureau of Music, Li encouraged the performance of 'proper music' during state functions and rituals, as it was believed that this would improve the moral fiber of the population and serve as an aid to good governance. Many years later, **Emperor Xuanzong** reorganized this bureau. He expanded its operations and brought in new forms of music. His innovations made the bureau more imposing, helping to ensure for state music a continuing role in validating the central institutions of the empire.

THE FUNCTION OF CONTRIBUTION TO THE CONTINUITY AND STABILITY OF CULTURE

As head of the Imperial Music Bureau, **Li Yannian** oversaw the collection of popular music and its adaptation to court, religious, and secular functions. His efforts and those of the bureau provided a basis for continuity in the development of Chinese music and literature. Li's own *Beauty Song* retained a presence in popular culture for two millennia. **Emperor Xuanzong** revitalized the imperial music establishment, ensuring its extended relevance as a musical guide to the continuity of Chinese culture. His own *Music of the Rainbow Feather Dress* was so greatly admired that its title later became a metaphor for exquisite music.

Li Yannian (fl. ca. 100 BCE)

Li Yannian came from a musical family in ancient Zhongshan, which lay southwest of Beijing, China, in a region now known as Hebei Province. A singer, composer, and sometime court musician, Li's personal and public lives careered between brilliant success and base tragedy (Pan Ku 1974: 247–251; Sima Qian & Watson 1993: II422–423). He served an emperor known as Wudi, who reigned over the Western Han Empire between 141 and 87 BCE from his capital at Chang'an (now Xi'an) in central China (Keay 2009: 128–155).

In Chinese, the name Wudi (武帝) means 'martial emperor,' which is an appropriate label for this ruler, even though he did not personally lead his troops in battle. His half-century reign saw incessant, and mostly successful, campaigning in border regions, particularly against the Xiongnu in the north, but also against other powers in the east, west, and south. The territory controlled by the Han peaked in size around 90 BCE; imperial China would not grow significantly larger before the time of the Tang dynasty, some eight centuries later. Wudi recruited capable government officials; increased taxes; invested in transportation infrastructure; improved flood control on the Yellow River; established state monopolies of iron, salt, and liquor; and mobilized convicts, slaves, conscripts, and *corvée* laborers "on a massive scale" (Keay 2009: 129–130 & 143; Sima Qian & Watson 1993: IIxiii).

In addition to overseeing such matters of state, Wudi also took a strong interest in literary, musical, and liturgical developments. During his reign, imperial patronage of the arts was "at its zenith" (Birrell 1993: 29). In his personal life, he found women with artistic skills especially attractive (*ibid.*, p. 26). These aspects of Wudi's makeup proved a boon to the musician Li Yannian.

The story of Li Yannian's professional life, as it has been passed down to us, begins with a terrible punishment. For some (presumably serious) crime, the musician was castrated and relegated to a lowly position in the royal kennels (Birrell 1993: 29; Sima Qian & Watson 1993: II422). In spite of this setback, Li's musical talent later took him literally out of the dog house and led subsequently to his appointment as head of the Imperial Music Bureau. He became prominent at court and an intimate of the emperor (Sima Qian & Watson 1993: I334 & II423). The fact that Wudi found Li's talented sister irresistibly beautiful could only have helped in his rise.

During the Han dynasty, castration was sometimes imposed on men who had been convicted of a serious crime but did not have the means to buy their way out of the punishment (Loewe 1986: 200). In an odd coincidence, Sima Qian, the 'grand historian' whose works provide most of our information about Li Yannian, also suffered this terrible mutilation. Sima had spoken out unwisely in defense of a friend, a general named Li Ling, who had surrendered his troops in a hopeless situation during a campaign against the Xiongnu (Sima Qian & Watson 1993: IIxi–xii). In another odd coincidence, the general in overall charge of this campaign was Li Guangli, who was Li Yannian's older brother. Later, this general also surrendered to the Xiongnu (Luo Yunhun 2000; Pan Ku 1974: 251).

Even as a dog keeper, it seems, Li was called upon to perform songs at court. One of his compositions, known as "The Beauty Song," describes a woman of breathtaking appeal:

> Beautiful lady in a northern land,
> standing alone, none in the world like her,

> a single glance and she upsets a city,
> a second glance, she upsets the state!

> Not that I don't know she upsets states and cities,
> but one so lovely you'll never find again! (Pan Ku 1974: 247)

Intrigued, the emperor wondered aloud if such a lovely creature could possibly exist. Wudi's sister, Princess Pingyang, told her brother that a talented young dancer in her retinue might merit such praise. Apparently Wudi agreed, for he took the young woman as his fourth wife or concubine (*ibid.*, pp. 247–248; Luo Yunhun 2000).

The young woman was Li Yannian's sister, who became known as Lady Li. However, this fetching account of how she came to the emperor's attention, which was recorded by the Chinese historian Ban Gu (a.k.a. Pan Ku) in the first century CE, is possibly a romanticized version of the events. Li Yannian's contemporary Sima Qian writes simply that Princess Pingyang introduced the future Lady Li because she was a good dancer. The emperor took a liking to her and brought her into the palace, "at the same time summoning Li Yannian to an audience and appointing him to a higher post" (Sima Qian & Watson 1993: II422; cf. Birrell 1993: 29 & 181 n.6).

In either of these scenarios, Li Yannian's ascendancy paralleled that of his sister. Two other brothers also could improve their stations: Li Ji, who acquired a court function that has not been recorded, and Li Guangli, who was made a general and later enfeoffed as the Marquis of Hexi (Luo Yunhun 2000). For her part, Lady Li became such a favorite before she passed away that the emperor awarded her posthumously the title of empress (Pan Ku 1974: 248).

The Imperial Music Bureau, which Li Yannian came to direct, was a uniquely Chinese institution. It grew out of long-standing Confucian tradition, according to which the performance of music of a certain quality—'proper' music or *yayue*—during state functions and rituals would improve the moral fiber of the population and serve as an aid to good governance. Music was therefore considered to be important to the well-being of the state (Thrasher et al. 2001: 631 & 635–636).

The Imperial Music Bureau is believed to have been in existence since the start of the Han in 206 BCE and may have been established during the short-lived previous dynasty known as the Qin (Kamatani 1996; Wilhelm 1978: 125). Wudi reorganized and expanded its operations in 112 BCE with Li Yannian as director. Musicians in this institution collected popular songs and adapted them to court, religious, and secular functions. To a degree their activities anticipated efforts undertaken 1900 years later in Germany, when folk music and literature were collected and studied at the instigation of the philosopher Johann Gottfried von Herder (Birrell 1993: 15). Although it is known that Wudi increased the number of vice-directors to three in 104 BCE, the overall size of the bureau during his reign has not been established. Later on, just before the Imperial Music Bureau was disbanded temporarily in 7 BCE, there were 829 employees (Kamatani 1996: 51).

Wudi was both superstitious and desirous of attaining life after death. He had the idea to better his chances for an eternal existence by improving religious services. In particular he proposed adapting the music and dances from the religious services of commoners for performance during his nocturnal sacrifices to Heaven and Earth. Percussion accompaniment of singing would be augmented through the addition of strings—Chinese zithers and harps. Li Yannian was adept at composing; he may even have suggested these changes to the emperor, and in any case he suc-

cessfully undertook the musical tasks (Birrell 1993: 30–31; Kamatani 1996: 37–41; Sima Qian & Watson 1993: II40).

For use in the sacrifices, Li set to music 19 poems by the renowned poet Sima Xiangru. In addition to arranging folk songs,
he also adapted a piece that a Chinese emissary named Zhang Qian had brought back from Central Asia. The meaning of the Chinese title of this piece, 摩诃兜勒, is somewhat obscure today; it
may have signified "the great piece of the Tocharians," an
ancient ethnic group that resided in Xinjiang. The identification
of both title and composer is exceptional in the early history of
Chinese music (An Xin 2012: private communication).

Li's efforts and those of the bureau he headed had a lasting influence on Chinese music and literature. *Yuefu shi* (Music Bureau
poetry) became known as a genre of writing. The *Anthology of Yuefu
Poetry* of ca. 1100 CE, as compiled by Guo Maoqian, contains
some 5290 song texts (Birrell 1993: 8–9). The scholar Joseph R.
Allen points out that in a poem titled "The Boatman's Song,"
sixth-century poet Xiao Gang makes explicit reference to Li Yannian, who may himself have composed a poem of the same name
(1992: pp. 120–124). And Li's music continues to resonate into the
twenty-first century: "The Beauty Song" that he wrote is a central
motif in the blockbuster Chinese movie *House of Flying Daggers*
from the year 2003.

Li's ascendancy was based both on his beautiful singing voice
and his talent as a composer and arranger. Directly or indirectly,
erotic elements also underlay his success. As the favorite concubine of the emperor, his sister helped her siblings to secure high
positions (Sima Qian & Watson 1993: II246) and tried to shield
them from intrigues at court (Pan Ku 1974: 248–249). Moreover,
according to an analysis by Bret Hinsch, Li himself may have been
exploited by the emperor for sexual purposes (1990: 42–44). Sima

Qian writes of the musician: "Day and night he was by the emperor's side" (Sima Qian & Watson 1993: II423).

Li and his relatives were denied the joys of a live-happily-ever-after existence. Lady Li gave birth to a child, a boy who was named Liu Bo, but then she contracted a serious illness and died. According to the historian Ban Gu, Li Yannian and Li Ji became involved improperly with the women of the court, and both brothers were executed for the offense (Pan Ku 1974: 251). However, a twentieth-century scholar ascribes their elimination to political infighting between the Li family and that of the former Empress Wei (Loewe 1986: 177–178; cf. Keay 2009: 149). Li Guangli's wife and children were executed after he had surrendered to the Xiongnu (*ibid.*; cf. Pan Ku 1974: 251).

Lady Li's son Liu Bo received the title Prince of Chengyi. His son Liu He was named emperor in 74 BCE, but he proved so incompetent that he was impeached and dismissed after only 27 days (Luo Yunhun 2000: 65; cf. Loewe 1986: Table 6, p. 176).

References Cited

Allen, Joseph Roe. 1992. *In the Voice of Others : Chinese Music Bureau Poetry, Michigan Monographs in Chinese Studies.* Ann Arbor, Mich.: Center for Chinese Studies, University of Michigan.

Birrell, Anne. 1993. *Popular Songs and Ballads of Han China.* Pbk. ed. Honolulu: University of Hawaii Press.

Hinsch, Bret. 1990. *Passions of the Cut Sleeve: The Male Homosexual Tradition in China.* Berkeley: University of California Press.

Kamatani, Takeshi. 1996. The Early Bureau of Music (Yüeh-fu). *Acta Asiatica: Bulletin of the Institute of Eastern Culture* 70:37–53.

Keay, John. 2009. *China: A History.* New York: Basic Books.

Loewe, Michael. 1986. The Former Han Dynasty. In *The Cambridge History of China. Volume 1, The Ch'in and Han Empires, 221 B.C. - A.D. 220*, edited by D. Twitchett and M. Loewe. Cambridge: Cambridge University Press.

Luo Yunhun. 2000. Queen Xiaowu (transl. by Tan Mingxia). In *Notable Women of China: Shang Dynasty to the Early Twentieth Century*, edited by B. B. Peterson. Armonk: M. E. Sharpe.

Pan Ku. 1974. *Courtier and Commoner in Ancient China; Selections From the History of the Former Han*. Translated by B. Watson. New York: Columbia University Press.

Sima Qian and Burton Watson. 1993. *Records of the Grand Historian. Han Dynasty*. Rev. ed. 2 vols, *Records of Civilization, Sources and Studies*. New York: Renditions-Columbia University Press.

Thrasher, Alan R., et al. 2001. China, People's Republic of. In *The New Grove Dictionary of Music and Musicians*, edited by S. Sadie and J. Tyrrell. New York: Grove.

Wilhelm, Hellmut. 1978. The Bureau of Music in Western Han. In *Society and History: Essays in Honor of Karl August Wittfogel*, edited by G. L. Ulmen. The Hague - Paris - New York: Mouton.

Further Reading

Ban Gu and Pan Chao. *The History of the Former Han Dynasty*. Translated by H. H. Dubs. Baltimore: Waverly Press 1938–1955.

Gimm, Martin, and Liu Jingshu. 1995. China. In *Die Musik in Geschichte und Gegenwart. Sachteil*, edited by F. Blume and L. Finscher. Kassel: Bärenreiter; Stuttgart: Metzler.

Kern, Martin. 2010. Tropes of Music and Poetry: From Wudi (r. 141–87 BCE) to ca 100 CE. In *China's Early Empires: A*

Re-Appraisal, edited by M. Nylan and M. Loewe. Cambridge: Cambridge University Press.

Liang Mingyue. 1985. Music of the Billion: An Introduction to Chinese Musical Culture. New York: Heinrichshofen.

Ssu-ma Ch'ien and Burton Watson. 1961. *Records of the Grand Historian of China*. 2 vols, *Records of Civilization: Sources and Studies*. New York: Columbia University Press.

Emperor Xuanzong (685–762; r. 712–756 CE)

Emperor Xuanzong of the Tang dynasty reigned over China from 712 to 756 CE, a period of more than four decades. Historians rank the early years of his rule, which are known as the *Kaiyuan* era (713–741), as among the most glorious in all Chinese history. China was prosperous and widely respected; many people enjoyed a comparatively peaceful existence; and the capital Chang'an (now Xi'an)—then the world's largest and probably most cosmopolitan city—maintained a glittering cultural life of poets, artists, and musicians. In later years, however, Xuanzong withdrew from active leadership, and the regime faltered. His reign ended in a series of tragedies (Benn 2002; Keay 2009: 267–273; Twitchett 1978).

Emperor Xuanzong had important qualities of a strong leader: ambition, determination, and political acumen. Other personal attributes allowed him to excel in the cultural sphere. He patronized talented writers and artists. He wrote poetry, painted calligraphy, and became deeply versed in Daoism and Tantric Buddhism. He made notable contributions in the field of music. He acquired the sobriquet *tang minghuang*, the 'brilliant emperor of the Tang' (Embree, Lewis, & Bulliet 1988: IV68).

Xuanzong began life in the year 685 in Luoyang, the secondary, eastern capital of the Tang dynasty. He was the third son of Emperor Ruizong (r.684–690 & 710–712), a member of the royal Li clan, from whom the child received the name Li Longji. Ruizong was emperor in name only, for his mother, the Empress Consort Wu, held the actual reins of power (Twichett 1978: 334).

Li Longji was a favorite of the empress consort. When he was five years old, he danced for her during a banquet in the palace (Benn 2002: 166)—anticipating, perhaps, his later predilection for musical entertainment. However, his personal situation worsened: In 688, some princes of the Li clan had staged a rebellion, which was put down in a series of purges. In 690, Empress Consort Wu forced Emperor Ruizong to abdicate, freeing the way for her personally to ascend to the throne. In 693, she had Li Longji's mother, Lady Dou, executed on trumped-up charges (*ibid.*).

Li Longji survived Empress Wu's reign, which ended in 705, and he managed to thrive during the tumultuous years that followed. Three different men served as emperor between 705 and 712, when Li Longji took over the office. Two of Empress Wu's sons, the emperors Zhongzong (r. 684 & 705–710) and Ruizong, both of whom she had forced to abdicate during her lifetime, ruled once again in near succession. Their reigns were separated by a brief interlude: In 710, Zhongzong was poisoned by his empress consort, and after this, his youngest son served briefly as Emperor Shang (Twitchett 1978: 334–345).

Emperor Shang's reign lasted only sixteen days before Li Longji and his aunt, Princess Taiping (665– 713), managed to put Ruizong in his place. Li Longji served as a chief minister in the new government. He was named as heir-apparent and then, in 711, as regent with limited powers. Although Ruizong abdicated in favor of him in 712, Princess Taiping continued to exercise enormous influence. When the new emperor heard that she and her accomplices were planning a coup, he had them killed and forced her to commit suicide. At the age of 28 years, Li Longji—now Emperor Xuanzong—had climbed to the pinnacle of power (*ibid.*).

Emperor Xuanzong immediately set in motion a broad array of civil and military reforms. He worked to eliminate corruption, improve infrastructure and the delivery of food, make government more efficient, increase state revenues, and secure the borders of the empire. Early in his reign, he also reformed the state's musical institutions. Music was taken seriously by the rulers of China, because of the country's strong Confucian tradition, which ascribed to the art both metaphysical and socio-political significance (Lai & Mok 1985: 37). Refined music, in contrast to secular music, was thought to promote good government and to encourage harmonious relations within society (Thrasher et al. 2001: 638; Wiant [1965?]: 11–13). Such concepts underlay the establishment and maintenance through many years of state-sponsored musical institutions.

In implementing his music reforms, Xuanzong built on the work of his predecessors. Emperor Wendi (r. 581–604) had placed sacred and banquet music under a state Bureau of High Music, into which an office for secular music was later merged. A Teaching Authority (*Jiaofang*) was put in charge of courtly entertainment, and an Authority of Drummers and Blowers administered processional music for religious holidays (Gimm & Liu 1995: 722).

The *Jiaofang* selected and trained female and male singers as well as instrumentalists, dancers, and show artists. In 714, under Emperor Xuanzong, it was expanded to encompass multiple separate divisions: an Inner *Jiaofang* situated within the northern palace; an Outer *Jiaofang*, with two branches in the western capital Chang'an and two others in the eastern capital Luoyang; the Court of the Refreshing Springtime, in the eastern part of the middle palace complex in Chang'an, which housed the best female musicians; and the famous Pear Garden (*Lìyuán*) in the north of Chang'an, whose performers interpreted solo and choral music with elegant vocal, dance, and instrumental art. In addition, there were organizations subsidiary to the Pear Garden in both capitals: the Special Teaching Institute of the Pear Garden in Chang'an, with ca. 1000 members, and the New Institute of the Pear Garden in Luoyang, consisting of ca. 1500 persons (Gimm & Liu 1995: 722–723; Liang 1985: 104–105). At the peak of the Tang dynasty, tens of thousands of musicians, dancers, entertainers, teachers, and administrators were attached to the state's music institutions (Gimm & Liu 1995: 722; Liang 1985: 97; Sun, Luo, Zi, Li, Liu, & Zhang 1999: 28).

Xuanzong's organizational efforts had a lasting effect on the quality of Chinese music. With the expansion of Chinese power and influence, many ethnic musical ensembles had come to Chang'an, sent either as tribute or under other conditions. When Xuanzong took office, the capital was home to ten such divisions of 'foreign' music. His administration merged them together with Chinese musicians into just two divisions: The Division of Standing Music and The Division of Sitting Music. The 60–180 members in the former grouping had a core repertory of eight pieces for outdoor performance. The latter, with a dozen members, performed six pieces indoors. This restructuring formalized a process of sincretization that invigorated traditional Chinese music through the introduction of new instrumentation, melodies, and rhythms (Embree, Lewis, & Bulliet 1988: III: 58 & IV:68; Gimm & Liu 1995:726; Lai & Mok 1985: 47–48).

In contrast to the ancient emphasis on continuity and ritual, the Tang era represented a period of secular music innovation. Emperor Xuanzong was one of the innovators. He led the Pear Garden troupe as it performed music that he himself had arranged or composed. The troupe consisted of some three hundred male and several hundred female artists—talented singers, instrumentalists, and dancers—whom the emperor personally selected from the *Jiaofang* and harem. Pear Garden performers were capable of playing sixteen different instruments (Gimm & Liu 1995: 723; Liang 1985: 105).

During the latter part of Xuanzong's regime, he was able to give free rein to his passion for music, and for other entertainments, by delegating many of his administrative burdens to subordinates. He became enamored of his son's wife, Yang Yuhuan (719–756), a beautiful and musically gifted young woman, whom he brought into his harem (see the following profile). His musicians performed a piece called *Nishang yuyi qu* ('Music of the Rainbow Feather Dress') on the day of her investiture as his *guifei* ('precious consort'). That evening he put tinkling golden pendants in her hair and called her a priceless treasure. He composed a song titled "Getting My Adorned One" (Levy 1958: 344–345).

This song and others from the Tang dynasty have not survived. Only a fragment of *Nishang yuyi qu* still exists (Thrasher et al. 2001: 642). Scholars have, however, made other Tang-era music accessible for present-day performance. Working from tablatures preserved in the Dunhuang caves in China and from the scores of ancient *tōgaku* ('Tang music') in Japan, they have transcribed into modern notation simple dances and songs, as well as more-complex musical compositions (see, e.g., Cheng Yingshi 1991; Picken, Wolpert, and Nickson 1981; Wolpert, Marett, Condit, & Picken 1973).

A tenth-century writer named Yo Shi (930–1007) tried to understand how Emperor Xuanzong got the ideas for his musical compositions. Yo Shi evidently considered the process mysterious, as it may seem even today, for his 'explanations' involve dreams and a magical journey. He reports that the emperor composed a song called "Return to the Purple Clouds" after having dreamt of ten immortals descending in chariots, holding musical instruments, and singing. Dreaming of a dragon lady supposedly led him to compose the song titled "Skimming the Waves." According to Chinese legend, it was a fantastic visit to the moon that inspired his composition *Nishang yuyi qu* (Benn 2002: 153; Levy 1958: 144–145, 151, & 152).

Nishang yuyi qu was a major work, or *daqu*, comprising six movements of instrumental music, eighteen movements of lyrical songs and dances, and twelve movements of gradually accelerating music and dances. Xuanzong adapted it himself from an earlier Brahmin composition titled *Boluomen*. He transformed the original South Asian music into a refined composition, or *faqu*. This piece was so greatly admired that its title became a metaphor for exquisite music (Sun et al. 199: 30; Thrasher et al. 2001: 642).

Together with others at the palace, Xuanzong and Yang Guifei immersed themselves in the musical art. One morning, they seem to have lost track of time while practicing together. A prince was the flutist, the emperor beat the *jiegu* (an hourglass drum), Yang Guifei played *pipa* (a Chinese lute), and others performed on cymbals, reed pipe, clappers, and other instruments. When at last they ended at noon, Xuanzong joked with Yang Guifei's younger sister, who had sat through the concert, asking her to tip him for his performance. She had become hugely wealthy after Yang Guifei's arrival, and so she responded with a gratuity of three million 'cash' (the Chinese coin), which was, apparently, a jaw-dropping amount (Levy 1958: 152–153).

The affairs of state suffered as Xuanzong devoted himself increasingly to personal pleasures. Few of the men to whom he delegated authority measured up to his own leadership capabilities, and several were unscrupulous. He doted on Yang Guifei and granted plum appointments to her relatives, including the post of chief minister for her unsavory cousin Yang Guozhong (d. 756). She herself became personally involved with An Lushan (ca. 703–757), the general who rebelled and nearly destroyed the Tang dynasty (Twitchett 1978: 427–430).

Xuanzong's life of carefree extravagance came to an abrupt end in 755, when An Lushan's troops reached the capital. Under cover of darkness, the emperor fled to the west with a small entourage and a cavalry escort. They headed toward the province of Sichuan, which would potentially have offered safe haven. Along the way, however, the accompanying soldiers mutinied. They killed Chief Minister Yang and other members of the Yang clan and forced Xuanzong to order the execution of Yang Guifei. Xuanzong managed to reach safety, but he had lost the desire to govern. When his son seized power as Emperor Suzong (r. 756–762), he willingly acquiesced to the usurpation (Keay 2009: 273–279; Twitchett 1978: 409–461).

Xuanzong's 'brilliant' reign ended in multiple tragedies: He was forced to abdicate; his precious consort and her relatives were executed; An Lushan's rebellion caused terrible loss of life; Chang'an was sacked; and the rebel commander suffered assassination by his own son (*ibid.*).

The Tang dynasty survived, weakened, as did Xuanzong. A broken man, he spent the rest of his days as Retired Emperor, mourning his losses. In these final years, he seems to have felt compelled to express his sadness in music. He composed a song about a military defeat. Playing flute, he accompanied a Pear Garden singer in the "Song of Liang Prefecture," which Yang Guifei had composed. He wept when listening to the "Song of the Bell in the Misty Rain" and also at the close of a performance by a dancer who had been one of Yang Guifei's favorites (Levy 1958: 166–167).

Both Xuanzong and his son, Emperor Suzong, died of natural causes in the spring of 762. It was left to Suzong's son, Emperor Daizong (r. 762–779), to put an end in 763 to the rebellion that An Lushan had started (Keay 2009: 279; Perkins 1999: 11).

References Cited

Benn, Charles D. 2002. *China's Golden Age: Everyday Life in the Tang Dynasty.* Oxford & New York: Oxford University Press.

Cheng Yingshi. 1991. A Report on Chinese Research into the Dunhuang Music Manuscripts (translated by Coralie Rockwell). *Musica Asiatica* 6:61–72.

Embree, Ainslie Thomas, Robin Jeanne Lewis, and Richard W. Bulliet. 1988. *The Encyclopedia of Asian History, Prepared Under the Auspices of the Asia Society.* 4 vols. New York: Scribner.

Gimm, Martin, and Liu Jingshu. 1995. China. In *Die Musik in Geschichte und Gegenwart. Sachteil*, edited by F. Blume and L. Finscher. Kassel: Bärenreiter; Stuttgart: Metzler.

Keay, John. 2009. *China: A History.* New York: Basic Books.

Lai, T. C., and Robert Mok. 1985. *Jade Flute: The Story of Chinese Music.* New York: Schocken Books.

Levy, Howard S. 1958. *Harem Favorites of an Illustrious Celestial.* Taiwan: Lin Yün-p'eng.

Liang Mingyue. 1985. *Music of the Billion: An Introduction to Chinese Musical Culture.* New York: Heinrichshofen.

Perkins, Dorothy. 1999. *Encyclopedia of China: The Essential Reference to China, Its History and Culture.* New York: Facts on File.

Picken, Laurence, R. F. Wolpert, and Noel Nickson. 1981. *Music from the Tang court: transcribed from the original, unpublished, Sino-Japanese manuscripts, together with a survey of relevant historical sources (both Chinese and Japanese), and with editorial comments.* London: Music Dept., Oxford University Press.

Sun Jingchen, Luo Xiongyan, Zi Huayun, Li Jinhui, Liu Jun, and Zhang Qizhi. 1999. *Chinese Dance.* Edited by Zi Huayun. Beijing di 1 ban. ed, *Chinese Culture and Art Series.* Beijing: Culture and Art Publishing House.

Thrasher, Alan R., et al. 2001. China, People's Republic of. In *The New Grove Dictionary of Music and Musicians*, edited by S. Sadie and J. Tyrrell. New York: Grove.

Twitchett, Denis. 1978. Hsüan-tsung (reign 712–56). In *The Cambridge History of China. Vol. 3, Sui and T'ang China, 589–906. Part 1*, edited by J. K. Fairbank and D. Twitchett. Cambridge: Cambridge University Press.

Wiant, Bliss. [1965?]. *The Music of China*. Hong Kong: Chung Chi Publications.

Wolpert, Rembrandt, Allan Marett, Jonathan Condit, and Laurence Picken. 1973. 'The Waves of Kokonor': A Dance-Tune of the T'ang Dynasty. *Asian Music* 5 (1):3–9.

Further Reading

Jie, Jin. 2011. *Chinese music*. Cambridge: Cambridge University Press.

Reischauer, Edwin O., and John King Fairbank. 1960. *East Asia: The Great Tradition, A History of East Asian Civilization*. Boston: Houghton Mifflin.

Tanner, Harold Miles. 2009. *China: A History*. Indianapolis: Hackett Pub. Co.

Widdess, Richard, and R. F. Wolpert, eds. 1981. *Music and Tradition: Essays on Asian and Other Musics Presented to Laurence Picken*. Cambridge & New York: Cambridge University Press.

Yang Guifei (719–756 CE)

Yang Guifei was for eleven years imperial consort (*guifei*) to Emperor Xuanzong (present work, previous profile), who became known as the 'brilliant' emperor of the Tang Dynasty in China (r. 712–756 CE). Born Yang Yuhuan in 719 in Yongle, Puzhou, near present-day Ruicheng in Shanxi province, she was orphaned as a child. An uncle brought her up in Chengdu, Sichuan, where she grew into an unusually attractive woman. Considered the embodiment of full-figured feminine charm, she is ranked among the four exceptional beauties of imperial China (Perkins 1999: 126, 552, 581, & 595). It was doubtless her appearance that first infatuated Emperor Xuanzong, but music played a strong role in continuing the relationship. Unfortunately, her life ended in tragedy in 756.

Both Yang Guifei and Emperor Xuanzong were skilled musicians. They performed together in the Entertainment Ward orchestra at the palace, which he led while beating an hourglass drum called the *jiegu*. She played the *pipa*, a Chinese version of the lute. She was also proficient on the *bianqing*, a rack of suspended stone chimes, for which she is said to have composed music. In addition to the drum and *pipa*, the orchestra included cymbals, mouth organ, clappers—and probably other instruments as well (Benn 2002: 8; Levy 1958: 114–115).

Yang Guifei was a singer and dancer, as well as an instrumentalist (Qiao & Huo 1999: 720). She danced two well-known numbers of the time, *Huxuan wu* ("Whirling Barbarian Dance") and *Nishang yuyi qu* ("Music of the Rainbow Feather Dress"). The emperor himself composed the latter work, transforming it from earlier Brahmin music in a refined style known as *faqu*. This piece was played when Yang Guifei officially entered the harem (Levy 1958:

144). It was a major musical composition of the era, but, unfortunately, only fragments of the score have survived (Thrasher et al. 2001: 642).

In 745, when Emperor Xuanzong took Yang Guifei into his harem, she was 26 years old, and he was 60. She remained his senior consort until 756, when she was executed during the An Lushan Rebellion. Apparently, she bore the emperor no children, and yet, apart from a few tempestuous spats, the pair was intimate through the whole of this period (Levy 1958; cf. Keay 2009: 275–278 & Twitchett 1978: 427–431 & 460).

One of the spats revolved around a jade flute. Yang Guifei borrowed and played the instrument without the emperor's permission, or perhaps against his express wishes. For this infraction, he banished her from the palace. Her relatives were dismayed, because they feared that they might lose their royal indulgences. Three of Yang Guifei's sisters—all of them renowned beauties as well—had been given titles and married prominently, while several male relatives enjoyed corresponding benefits. One cousin, Yang Guozhong (né Yang Zhao), who like the three sisters became enormously wealthy, even rose to the position of chief minister in the final years of Xuanzong's reign. To deal with Yang Guifei's banishment, the worried relatives sought the advice of an imperial confidant. However, the matter was put to rest rather quickly after Yang Guifei confessed tearfully and snipped off a lock of her hair to send to the emperor (Levy 1958: 71–78 & 115–116).

The Yangs were a well-connected family, distant relatives of a high official in an earlier dynasty known as the Sui. In 736, well before her entry into the imperial harem, Yang Yuhuan married the Prince of Shou. According to the prevailing custom, the couple would have been presented to the emperor and empress at this time. She must have made quite an impression on Xuanzong, for several years later, after his favorite consort died, he set in motion an elaborate scheme to take her away from the prince: She was invested in 741 as a Taoist nun and given the religious name Taizhen, thereby dissolving her marriage ties. Then, after what may have been considered a decent interval of four years, he made her his imperial consort, a rank in the harem second only to that of the empress (Levy 1958: 84–96; cf. Twitchett 1978: 427–428).

Two aspects of this situation are striking: First, the emperor's harem contained thousands of women; for Yang Taizhen to have been brought in at the top suggests that she was indeed an exceptional person. Secondly, the Prince of Shou, to whom she had previously been married, was the emperor's own son, the eighteenth of Xuanzong's thirty male children. A few weeks before she officially entered the imperial harem, Xuanzong compensated his son by giving him another woman in exchange (Levy 1958: 93).

Yang Guifei's tragedy consisted of promoting the interests of her relatives only to have their excesses compromise her own situation. However, she herself shared in some of her relatives' unfortunate proclivities. Her relations with the powerful military general An Lushan may have proved especially damaging. She and the emperor initially favored him and even named him to be her adopted son. But a few days after his forty-eighth birthday in 751, she indulged in a demeaning prank, one which may have wounded the general's pride: She, his adoptive 'mother,' paraded her 'baby' around the palace in diapers. According to another interpretation, however, the incident fell within a pattern of imperial debauchery in which An Lushan willingly participated (Levy 1958: 116–118; Twitchett 1978: 427–428).

Both An Lushan and chief minister Yang Guozhong were hungry for power. They became bitterly antagonistic to one another, and the chief minister expressed his distrust of the general openly at court. In 755, An Lushan assembled troops and launched a full-scale rebellion. When the rebellious army penetrated the defenses of Chang'an, the Tang capital, the emperor and his entourage took flight to the west. After two days, Xuanzong's imperial guards mutinied, killing Yang Guozhong and those other members of the Yang clan whom they could capture. They demanded that Xuanzong have Yang Guifei executed as well, apparently sensing that she and her relatives had been responsible for the deterioration of dynastic authority and for An Lushan's antagonism (Keay 2009: 273–279; Perkins 1999: 11; Twitchett 1978: 453–461).

The emperor at first hesitated, but then he did agree to Yang Guifei's execution. At age 37 she walked calmly to her death at a Buddhist shrine, where the high-ranking eunuch Gao Lishi strangled her (Levy 1958: 118–121).

Emperor Xuanzong, the man who ordered Yang Guifei's death, is said to have mourned her for the rest of his life. The tale of their love and its dreadful conclusion has inspired countless stories, poems, songs, and dramas. Perhaps the most famous of these works, *The Song of Everlasting Regret* by the poet Bai Juyi (as translated by Witter Bynner in Birch & Keene 1965: 266–269), concludes with the verses:

> Earth endures, heaven endures; sometime both shall end,
>   While this unending sorrow goes on and on forever.

References Cited

Benn, Charles D. 2002. *China's Golden Age: Everyday Life in the Tang Dynasty*. Oxford & New York: Oxford University Press.

Birch, Cyril, and Donald Keene, eds. 1965. *Anthology of Chinese Literature: From Early Times to the Fourteenth Century,*

UNESCO Collection of Representative Works: Chinese Series.
New York: Grove Press.

Keay, John. 2009. *China: A History.* New York: Basic Books.

Levy, Howard S. 1958. *Harem Favorites of an Illustrious Celestial.*
Taiwan: Lin Yün-p'eng.

Perkins, Dorothy. 1999. *Encyclopedia of China: The Essential Reference
to China, Its History and Culture.* New York: Facts on File.

Qiao Weiping and Huo Lindong, ed. 1999. 中华文明史-第五卷
(Chinese Ancient Civilization). Shijiazhuang, China: Hebei
Education Publisher.

Thrasher, Alan R., et al. 2001. China, People's Republic of. In *The
New Grove Dictionary of Music and Musicians*, edited by S.
Sadie and J. Tyrrell. London: Macmillan Publishers Ltd.

Twitchett, Denis. 1978. Hsüan-tsung (reign 712–56). In *The
Cambridge History of China. Vol. 3, Sui and T'ang China, 589–
906. Part 1*, edited by J. K. Fairbank and D. Twitchett.
Cambridge: Cambridge University Press.

Further Reading

Du Wenyu, ed. 2010. 唐代宫廷史 *(Tang Royal History).* Tianjin,
China: Baihua Literature and Art Publishing House.

Edwards, J. Michele. 2001. Women in Music to ca. 1450. In
Women & Music: A History, edited by K. Pendle. Bloomington & Indianapolis: Indiana University Press. Pages
26–53.

Liang Mingyue. 1985. *Music of the Billion: An Introduction to Chinese
Musical Culture.* New York: Heinrichshofen Edition.

Peterson, Barbara Bennett, ed. 2000. *Notable Women of China: Shang
Dynasty to the Early Twentieth Century.* Armonk: M. E.
Sharpe.

Reischauer, Edwin O., and John King Fairbank. 1960. *East Asia: The Great Tradition, A History of East Asian Civilization.* Boston: Houghton Mifflin.

Fu Niang (fl. ca. 880 CE)

Late in the ninth century CE, a courtesan named Fu Niang ('Lucky Damsel') lived in the entertainment district of the ancient city of Chang'an (now Xi'an), which was the capital of the Tang dynasty (618–907). Like other courtesans of the Northern Quarter, where the entertainment district was located, she had been trained in singing and dancing. Courtesans were also commonly taught to play string instruments such as the *pipa*, a Chinese lute.

When candidates for the civil service came to the entertainment district to take a break from their studies or to celebrate having passed their examinations, music was an indispensable part of the festivities (Levy 1962 & 1964; Ping Yao 2002). Music was so important in courtesans' practice that even the names for their profession made reference to it: Two Chinese characters for courtesan or prostitute, 娼 and 妓, which are pronounced *chāng* and *jì*, respectively, are closely related to the characters that mean sing (謳) and talent (技). The resemblance suggests that musical ability had at one time been more of a distinguishing characteristic of courtesans than their provision of sexual services (Ping Yao 2002: 27–28). The historian Romain Goldren notes that "the musical profession has been linked with the courtesan since remotest antiquity" (Goldron 1968: 34). To judge from one client's description, even in the ninth century CE, music still seems to have come before sex in the entertainment quarter of Chang'an (Ping Yao 2002: 40–41).

Around the year 879, a civil-service candidate named Sun Qi often spent time with Fu Niang. Having learned a great deal about her character and life, he featured her in his *Records of the Northern*

Quarter from ca. 885. Sun Qi's report was published as an accessible English adaptation (Levy 1963) and as part of a scholarly study in French (Sun Qi & Des Rotours 1968). The latter will be followed here, except for the English translations of poems and as otherwise noted.

Fu Niang came from a village in the southwest of Shanxi province. Her home was next to that of a musician, and in her early childhood, she lived with his family, where she learned how to sew and recite songs and poetry. Before Fu Niang came of age, she became engaged to a passing stranger, who said he was going to the capital to take the civil-service examination. However, when the pair arrived in Chang'an, he abandoned his young bride in a bordello (Sun Qi & Des Rotours 1968: 138).

The head of this house of prostitution, Wang Tuan-er, may have once been a courtesan herself. At first, out of sympathy for Fu Niang's situation, Madame Wang treated her new recruit well, but after a few months, Fu Niang was forced to prepare for receiving visitors by learning songs and mastering the rules of drinking games. Like other girls in similar circumstances, she was no doubt also now given a beautiful gown to wear, for young courtesans were cherished first for their beauty and talent. Before long, a local police officer engaged her services; he took her virginity. It is also reported that two young men, the sons of government officials, spent at least 1000 pieces of gold to pay for her company (Sun Qi & Des Rotours 1968: 138–139).

Two of Fu Niang's brothers managed to find her in the Northern Quarter. They hatched a scheme to steal her back to their family, but they had little power and influence, and so she became convinced that their plan would fail. She told them: "I have already lost my chastity. I am afraid that your intervention would be useless." Madame Wang agreed to give up several hundred pieces of gold, which Fu Niang offered to her older brother. He accepted the sum and departed in tears, satisfied perhaps that the family had been appropriately compensated (*ibid.*).

The civil-service candidate Sun Qi found Fu Niang beautiful and intelligent. However, he noticed that she often became melancholy, which dampened the mood of others around her. When he asked the reason for her sadness, she indicated that she wanted desperately to escape from her situation and have a normal existence. This would only be possible if someone paid for her release and took her as a secondary wife (Sun Qi & Des Rotours 1968: 132–133).

Fu Niang spelled out her feelings in a poem:

> Though my unplanned existence grieves me daily,
> I am loathe to bare my heart to commoners[1].
> I am not trying to return to you
> Like water spilled from a pitcher,
> But wish only to know your intentions.
> (Levy 1963 (10): 121)

The phrase "water spilled from a pitcher" refers to a traditional story about a Chinese nobleman of the twelfth century BCE. This nobleman's wife divorced him, but later, after his circumstances had improved, she asked to return. He responded by pouring water onto the ground and observing that it would be as impossible for them to remarry as for her to put back the spilled water. Fu Niang's allusion was a way of indicating that she was eligible to marry Sun Qi (Levy 1963 (10): 121 n.63; Sun Qi & Des Rotours 1968: 133 n. 2).

Sun Qi got the point, but he was having none of it. He said at once that this was not an appropriate time for him to marry, be-

---

[1] Perhaps better: "to bare my heart to just anyone"; cf. Sun Qi & Des Rotours 1968: 133.

cause he had not yet passed his civil-service examination. Fu Niang pressed him further. She noted that she had not yet entered the imperial Academy of Performing Arts (*Jiaofang*) and, therefore, her release could be purchased for only a few hundred pieces of gold. When Sun Qi did not respond, she asked him to put his thoughts in writing. This he did in a poem, in which he alluded to the large and, from his point of view, insurmountable disparity in their social standing:

> Why plan ahead, young beauty?
> Don't place your faith in me,
> For I can't become your husband.
> Though the lotus in the mud is undefiled,
> I can't tansplant it in my garden.
> (Levy 1963 (10): 121)

Fu Niang read these brutal lines and wept without speaking again. Their friendly relationship had ended (*ibid.*; Sun Qi & Des Rotours 1968: 134–135).

Apart from mentioning Fu Niang's hint that she was good enough to be admitted to the *Jiaofang*, Sun Qi provides no information about her music. The *Jiaofang*, which was established early in the seventh century, had grown into a large institution employing thousands of performers. Most were recruited from among slaves or commoners, with selection based on ability and, for female dancers and musicians, beauty. In Fu Niang's time there were two divisions, which covered the gamut of music, dance, comedy-drama, and acrobatics (Liang 1985: 97 and 104–105). A courtesan who excelled in the *Jiaofang* is described in the poem "Pipa Song" by Bai Juyi (772–846). This beautiful girl mastered the *pipa* at age thirteen, before becoming famous as a singer and dancer. As she aged, her beauty faded, and she came on hard times. When the poet met her, she was eking out a lonely existence in a country hovel.

During the Tang dynasty, the popular song repertory encompassed folk music as well as settings of poetry to traditional or new melodies. The works of famous poets such as Li Bai (701–762), Bai Juyi, and Li He (790–816) entered into popular culture via this route (Gimm & Liu 1995: col. 724). It might be supposed that the Northern Quarter courtesans would concentrate in the folk arena. However, educated young men such as Sun Qi would probably also have enjoyed a more literary style.

Sun Qi's interactions with Fu Niang make it clear that she would have been able to master the subtleties of poetic song texts. The couple exchanged rather sophisticated poems in which they discussed matters of the heart, such as her desire to marry. Early on in their relationship, Sun Qi inscribed four poems on her wall, and she passed critical judgment on them by comparing them with the work of a poet who lived in the second century BCE. In general, she exhibited a level of sophistication that surprises in a young singer and prostitute. When Sun Qi was one of Fu Niang's regular visitors, she had just passed her sixteenth Chinese birthday, which means that she was only fifteen years old in Western terms (Sun Qi & Des Rotours 1968: 127–132 and 127 n.1).

Even after turning Fu Niang away as a marriage prospect, Sun Qi still had one more interaction with her. While spending a summer in Luoyang, the secondary capital of Tang China, he had begun to have second thoughts about their breakup. However, when he returned to Chang'an, he discovered that a rich patron had contracted her exclusive services. Some time later, while taking part in a springtime ritual on the shore of a pond, he heard music coming from a nearby tent. Looking in, he saw Fu Niang seated next to the head of her house, Madame Wang. They were present at a meal that Fu Niang's patron was giving for a government official. Presumably—though Sun Qi does not make this explicit—the pair was providing musical accompaniment (*ibid.*, pp. 135–137).

Sun Qi went behind the tent and arranged through one of the servants to visit Fu Niang's house the next morning. When he arrived, one of Madame Wang's younger courtesans was waiting at the door. She invited him to dismount, but he declined on a pretext. She then balled up a note from Fu Niang and tossed it up to him. It contained this poem:

> I gave you my love endlessly,
> Entrusted my self completely to you,
> Time and again,
> Revealing my heart's innermost secrets:
> The lotus in the mud has already been transplanted;
> Please don't be embittered with me for leaving you.
> (Levy 1963 (10): 122

Sun Qi rode off disappointed and never approached the house again (Levy 1963 (10): 122; Sun Qi & Des Rotours 1968: 137). This was in the year ca. 880.

Shortly thereafter, a major insurgency that had been raging in China since the 870s reached the capital and must certainly have affected Fu Niang. Sweeping through enormous swaths of territory, the rebel forces under Huang Chao (d. 884), a self-styled "heaven-storming generalissimo" (Tanner 2009: 197), had devastated cities in the north, south, and center of the country. The carnage was horrendous; as many as 120,000 civilians were slaughtered in the port city of Guangzhou alone. After capturing the secondary capital Luoyang on December 22, 880, Huang led his army victoriously into Chang'an on January 8, 881. Emperor Xizong (r. 873–888) and his entourage fled into Sichuan (Keay 2009: 289–290; Tanner 2009: 197–198).

Unfortunately, Huang could no longer control his troops, who set about destroying Chang'an. A government official and poet named Wei Zhuang (ca. 836–910) wrote an eyewitness account of their rampage. His lengthy composition paints, as the historian John Keay puts it, "a Goya-esque scene of devastation, rape, butchery and cannibalism" (p. 290). Four lines of Wei's poem draw attention to the cruel fate of 'singing-girls' like Fu Niang:

Every home now runs with bubbling fountains of blood,
Every place rings with a victim's shrieks—shrieks that cause the
very earth to quake.
Dancers and singing-girls must all undergo secret outrage;
Infants and tender maidens are torn living from their parents'
arms.
(Wei Zhuang 2000: 936).

It may be, therefore, that this melancholy young courtesan suffered even more after she knew Sun Qi than she had on account of her lowly situation before.

References Cited

Bai Juyi. 1995. Pipa Song, With a Foreword by the Poet. In *An Anthology of Chinese Poetry, Selected and Translated by Ding Zuxin*, edited by Z. Ding: Liaoning University Press.

Gimm, Martin, and Liu Jingshu. 1995. China. In *Die Musik in Geschichte und Gegenwart. Sachteil*, edited by F. Blume and L. Finscher. Kassel: Bärenreiter; Stuttgart: Metzler.

Goldron, Romain. 1968. *Ancient and Oriental Music*. Translated by S. A. Sterman. [place of publication not provided]: H.S. Stuttman Co.; distributed by Doubleday [1968].

Keay, John. 2009. *China: A History*. New York: Basic Books.

Levy, Howard S. 1962. The Gay Quarters of Chang'an. *Orient/West* 7:93–105.

———. 1963. Records of the Gay Quarters. *Orient/West* 8: (9) 121–128; (10) 115–122; (11) 103–110.

———. 1964. T'ang Women of Pleasure. *Sinologica* 8:89–113.

Liang Mingyue. 1985. *Music of the Billion. : An Introduction to Chinese Musical Culture.* New York: Heinrichshofen.

Ping Yao. 2002. The Status of Pleasure: Courtesan and Literati Connections in T'ang China (618–907). *Journal of Women's History* 14 (2):26–53.

Sun Qi (Souen K'i), and Robert Des Rotours. 1968. *Courtisanes chinoises à la fin des T'ang, entre circa 789 et le 8 Janvier 881, Pei-li tche (Anecdotes du quartier du Nord).* Translated by Robert Des Rotours, Bibliothèque de l'Institut des Hautes Études Chinoises. Paris: Presses Universitaires de France.

Tanner, Harold Miles. 2009. *China: A History.* Indianapolis: Hackett Pub. Co.

Wei Zhuang (c. 836–910). 2000. The Lament of the Lady of Qin (translated by Lionel Giles). In *Classical Chinese Literature: An Anthology of Translations. Vol. I. From Antiquity to the Tang Dynasty,* edited by J. Minford and J. S. M. Lau. New York: Columbia University Press; Hong Kong: The Chinese University Press. Pages 933–944.

Further Reading

Benn, Charles D. 2002. *China's Golden Age: Everyday Life in the Tang Dynasty.* Oxford & New York: Oxford University Press.

Thrasher, Alan R., et al. 2001. China, People's Republic of. In *The New Grove Dictionary of Music and Musicians,* edited by S. Sadie and J. Tyrrell. New York: Grove.

Musicians of Egypt

All three of the musicians profiled here were connected with the Egyptian religious establishment. During the Old Kingdom of Egypt (ca. 2700–2150), the flutist **Ipi (fl. ca. 2600 BCE)** wore the pelt of a cheetah or leopard while serving as a *sem* priest. During the New Kingdom of Egypt (ca. 1550–1070 BCE), the harpist **Raia (fl. ca. 1250 BCE)** held the position of chief of singers at the great temple of Ptah in Memphis. He performed for the Egyptian gods Ptah and Hathor. The trumpeter **Peripatjauemope (fl. ca. 1080 BCE)** worked at the prestigious temple of Amun in Thebes. Unfortunately, this musician turned to a life of crime: Peripatjauemope was arrested and convicted of tomb robbery, a capital offense in ancient Egypt.

∞

Three of Merriam's ten functions of music can be associated with these musicians:

THE FUNCTION OF ENTERTAINMENT

The flutist **Ipi** served under King Sneferu of Egypt. Ipi's titles of head flutist, director of the dancers, and master of ceremonies and festivities at the palace suggest that he entertained. He was also a *sem* priest, and the separation between ritualistic and secular music may not have been clear-cut at the time.

THE FUNCTION OF COMMUNICATION

The religious functionary **Raia** sang and played the harp to communicate with the gods, and he directed a choir of male singers, who undoubtedly performed for a similar purpose. His wife Mutemwia served as a chantress for communicating with the god Amun.

THE FUNCTION OF VALIDATION OF SOCIAL INSTITUTIONS AND RELIGIOUS RITUALS

At temples and other places of worship, Egyptian musicians and musical ensembles, including choirs, validated their religious systems by creating worshipful atmospheres and emphasizing religious precepts in their hymns. At Dahshur, the priest-musician **Ipi** played *ma't* flute and directed dancing for purposes that likely included religious validation. In Memphis, **Raia** served as the chief of singers and was himself both a singer and an instrumentalist at the great temple of Ptah. The musician **Peripatjauemope** played trumpet at the prestigious temple of Amun in Thebes.

Ipi (fl. ca. 2600 BCE)

As a musician at the court of one of the early pharaohs of ancient Egypt, Ipi played an instrument known variously as a 'longitudinal,' 'vertical,' or simply 'long' flute. He held several titles, including head flutist, director of the dancers, and master of ceremonies and festivities at the palace, and he also acted as a priest. Ipi served under King Sneferu (r. ca. 2613–2589 BCE), founder of the Fourth Dynasty of Egypt, whose name is associated with the construction of three huge tombs: a step pyramid at Meidum, the Southern or Bent Pyramid at Dahshur, and the Northern or Red Pyramid, also at Dahshur. The third of these enormous edifices is the first geometrically accurate, smooth-faced, mortuary pyramid ever built (Mieroop 2011: 57–58; Wilkinson 2010: 58–65).

Because Ipi lived so very long ago, few of his biographical details have survived. However, he is among the earliest known musicians and one of the few musicians in the Old Kingdom of Egypt about whom we have specific information (Lieven 2006: 356).

Two statues of Ipi have been recovered from his *mastaba* grave in the Dahshur necropolis (Alexanian & Seidlmayer 2002; Sourouzian 1999). Although both statues are badly damaged, one of them clearly depicts part of a long flute, which is held diagonally across Ipi's body, as if he were playing it. This instrument, called *ma't* by the ancient Egyptians, was typically made of bamboo and 50–100 cm long. It had neither a mouthpiece nor a separate air hole for exciting a tone. To make it sound, the performer excited an acoustic resonance by blowing across the sharp edge at the open upper end of the instrument. The *nāy*, an end-blown flute still in use in western Asia and northern Africa, is sounded in a similar manner. The single-piped Egyptian *ma't* was equipped with three to five finger holes at its lower extremity for use in forming a tune (Betz, Meyer, & Meyer 1995: 562–564; Hickmann 1994: 290–291; Sachs 1940: 90–91).

The *ma't* is an ancient instrument, known already in pre-dynastic Egypt. A palette dated from the thirty-first century BCE, and thought to have been used when applying makeup, is decorated with numerous wild animals and a single masked individual (or animal-headed creature), who is playing a long flute (Betz, Meyer, & Meyer 1995: 563; Sachs 1940: 90; cf. Hickmann 1994: Fig. 1). Together with the harp and double clarinet, the soft voice of the long flute remained a mainstay of Egyptian music for more than a millennium, until the era of the New Kingdom (ca. 1550–1069 BCE), when foreign musicians introduced the louder tones of the oboe within Egypt's musical ensembles (Sachs 1940: 98).

The second statue of Ipi presents him in his regalia as a *sem* priest (Alexanian & Seidlmayer 2002: 6; Sourouzian 1999: Figs. 8–11). In his left hand, he holds an *aba* scepter, which is a symbol of authority. His right hand grasps a short, smooth staff of a type that has not yet been clearly identified. On this statue, the sculptor also carved in relief the spotted pelt of a cheetah or leopard, a common element in the attire of the *sem* priests of ancient Egypt, worn draped across Ipi's right shoulder.

Sem priests were associated with funerary rituals. In his priestly role, Ipi would likely have performed the "opening of the mouth" ceremony prior to the interment of a mummy (Teeter 2011: 24–25). Ipi's musical instrument, the flute, also had a connection with funerals and otherworldly mythology. The god Osiris, Lord of the Dead, who ruled over the afterlife, was said to have invented the flute. If prehistoric Egyptian society followed a pattern observed more recently among non-literate peoples, the phallic symbolism of this instrument will have linked it early on with the giving of life and, by extension, with the concept of rebirth after death (Betz, Meyer, & Meyer 1995: 559–564; Sachs 1940: 44).

Scholars have speculated on Ipi's secular and priestly duties. Alexanian and Seidlmayer note that Ipi's musical capabilities served "for entertainment at the palace" but suggest that "probably above all, they came into action in the context of ritual" (2002: 6, my translation from the German). Sourouzian, on the other hand, was inspired to romantic fantasy by the lovely backdrop of the Dahshur monuments. They are situated at the edge of a seasonal lake, which emerges out of the desert in the autumn, as if by magic, when the water table rises. This is the setting, Sourouzian imagines, of a popular ancient story about King Sneferu (Simpson 2003: 16–18). In this story, the king, having grown bored in his palace, brings a group of beautiful women to the waters, where, dressed in pearl nets, they row him back and forth in a barque. As Sourouzian tells it, the king rejoices to see them "rowing to the rhythm of songs." She concludes: "The view of this lake from the terrace of Ipi's *mastaba* brings these young ladies, who rowed in order to divert the king, back to life again, so to speak—and, who knows, had these celebrations perhaps been organized by Ipi, the master of ceremonies at the palace?" (1999: 160, my translation from the French).

References Cited

Alexanian, A., and S. I. Seidlmayer. 2002. Die Residenznekropole von Dahschur: Erster Grabungsbericht. *Mitteilungen des Deutschen Archäologischen Instituts Abteilung Kairo* 58:1–28.

Betz, Marianne, Andreas Meyer, and Jürgen Meyer. 1995. Flöten. In *Die Musik in Geschichte und Gegenwart (Sachteil)*, edited by L. Finscher. Kassel: Bärenreiter.

Hickmann, Ellen. 1994. Alt Ägypten. In *Die Musik in Geschichte und Gegenwart (Sachteil)*, edited by L. Finscher. Kassel: Bärenreiter.

Lieven, Alexandra von. 2006. *The Social Standing of Musicians in Ancient Egypt. In Archäologische Befunde, historische Zusammenhänge, soziokulturelle Beziehungen, Vorträge des 4. Symposiums der Internationalen Studiengruppe Musikarchäologie im Kloster Michaelstein, 19.–26. September 2004*, edited by E. Hickmann, A. A. Both and R. Eichmann: Studien zur Musikarchäologie V, Musikarchäologie im Kontext.

Mieroop, Marc Van De. 2011. *A History of Ancient Egypt, Blackwell History of the Ancient World*. Chichester & Malden: Wiley-Blackwell.

Sachs, Curt. 1940. *The History of Musical Instruments*. New York: W. W. Norton & Co.

Simpson, William Kelly. 2003. *The Literature of Ancient Egypt: An Anthology of Stories, Instructions, Stelae, Autobiographies, and Poetry*. 3rd ed. New Haven: Yale University Press.

Sourouzian, Hourig. 1999. La statue du musicien Ipi jouant de la flûte et autres monuments du règne de Snofrou à Dahchour. In *L'art de l'Ancien Empire égyptien: actes du colloque organisé au Musée du Louvre par le Service culturel les 3 et 4 avril 1998*, edited by C. Ziegler and N. Palayret. Paris: Documentation française.

Teeter, Emily. 2011. *Religion and Ritual in Ancient Egypt*. New York: Cambridge University Press.

Wilkinson, Toby. 2010. *The Rise and Fall of Ancient Egypt*. London & New York: Random House & Bloomsbury.

Further Reading

Emerit, Sibylle. 2013. Music and Musicians. *UCLA Encyclopedia of Egyptology*, edited by W. Wendrich. Los Angeles:

University of California.
http://digital2.library.ucla.edu/viewItem.do?ark=21198/zz002 h77z9.

Hallo, William W., and William Kelly Simpson. 1971. *The Ancient Near East: A History*. New York: Harcourt Brace Jovanovich.

Raia (fl. ca. 1250 BCE)

During the reign of Pharaoh Ramesses II (ca. 1279–1213 BCE), Raia was chief of singers at the great temple of the creator god Ptah in Memphis, the administrative capital of ancient Egypt. He was both a singer and an instrumentalist. In a colored scene on the wall of his tiny tomb-chapel, he plays the harp and sings to statues of Ptah and the cow-headed goddess Hathor. Unfortunately, only fragments of the song have survived: "… we do not detest the mooring-post" (Martin 1991: 127).

As chief of singers, Raia exercised an important role in a cult that was centrally important to the religion of the state. Ptah was both the city god of Memphis and one of the principal gods of Egypt. This deity formed a trinity with Amun of Thebes and Re of Heliopolis. A New Kingdom text says that all the gods—of which there were many in Egypt—were forms of this trinity: "Three are all the gods: Amun, Re, and Ptah, there is none like them. Hidden is his identity as Amun. He is visible as Re. His body is Ptah" (cited by van Dijk 2001: 75–76).

Ramesses II's fourth son Khaemwaset, one of the most celebrated nobles of Ramessid Egypt, held the position of head priest in Memphis. Ramesses designated this son heir to the crown, but the younger man died in advance of his father and therefore did not ascend to the throne. During his lifetime, Khaemwaset undertook many building projects, including reconstruction of the great temple of Ptah (Gomaà 2001: 228; Rice 1999: 93–94; Mieroop 2011: 232). It is, of course, unlikely that the chief of singers would have interacted directly with a crown prince, but the eminent status of the high priest of the temple in which Raia served lends significance to his own association with the cult.

With an enclosed area of 275,000 square meters, the great temple of Ptah rivaled in size the famous, and still impressively standing, temple of Amun-Re at Karnak. Several monumental gates bounded the precinct, where stone sphinxes and colossal statues of Ptah and of Ramesses II were situated (van Dijk 2001: 74). Unfortunately, other builders scavenged materials from Khaemwaset's structure for later construction projects. All that remains of the once imposing edifice are a few fragments of stone and mud bricks scattered about in the sand (Martin 1991: 15–16).

The chief of singers Raia was married to a woman named Mutemwia. They had a daughter. In another of Raia's tomb-chapel scenes, she holds a small bird while squatting beneath her mother's chair. These relief paintings project the impression of a close-knit family, who worshipped together and mourned Raia at his funeral. Several other women appear to have been associated with the household. They may have been Raia's unmarried sisters, who would have relied on him for support (*ibid.*, p. 130).

Like her husband, Mutemwia was musical. She bore the title of chantress in the service of the god Amun (*ibid.*, p. 126). During their periods of service, chantresses attended the gods while singing hymns, playing musical instruments, jangling *sistra*, and shaking large bead necklaces known as *menit*. They chanted phrases of welcome when royal personages entered a temple. Many upper-class women served in this way, especially during Mutemwia's lifetime, in the historical period (ca. 1519–1069 BCE) known to Egyptologists as the New Kingdom (Watterson 1991: 40–41).

Geoffrey Martin discovered Raia's tomb-chapel late in the twentieth century and has described its contents. The structure is in a large cemetery known as the *Saqqara*, which bordered the ancient capital city. Limestone slabs formed the roof of the structure and probably once supported a small pyramid. Raia's tomb-chapel abuts the larger sepulcher of a contemporary builder named Paser, who may have been a friend or relative of the chief of singers. Paser's brother Tjuneroy held high official titles in the Egyptian state, including those of Royal Scribe, Overseer of All the Works of the King, Chief Lector Priest, and Master of Largesse. These connections may help to explain how Raia got permission to place his crypt in the prestigious cemetery (Martin 1991: 124–130; Rice 1999: 207; Wilkinson 2007: 247–249).

The harp depicted in the tomb-chapel is an arched instrument of the type that had been in use in Egypt for more than a millennium, since the time of the fourth dynasty (ca. 2613–2492 BCE). Raia's instrument had seven strings, but archeologists have identified other arched Egyptian harps with four to eight strings, or even as many as twelve strings. The strings were made of gut, tied securely to the resonating body below and wrapped around the top of the instrument. A series of pegs helped to maintain the appropriate tension, preventing the strings from slipping out of tune (Hickmann 1994: 284–287; Manniche 1991: 25–26).

Raia appears to be blind in the scene that shows him performing in front of divine statues. Blind musicians were common in Egypt and elsewhere in ancient times, as the profession of musician was one of the few open to these handicapped individuals. In Raia's case, however, the representation of blindness is probably only symbolic, for he appears normally sighted in two other depictions in the tomb-chapel. Artistic license may have been applied to avoid the appearance of violating a sacrosanct rule: only the select few, including purified priests and the divine pharaoh, were permitted to gaze upon the image of a deity. In real life, Raia could have positioned himself behind a screen or in an adjoining chamber, while performing for the gods (Martin 1991: 127).

The singers in Raia's choir may actually have been blind. They, or some of them, all males, took part in Raia's interment ceremony. Several are identified by name on the wall of the tomb-chapel, where in a relief painting of the ceremony, their eyes have been reduced to narrow slits. Mutemwia expresses her grief in this scene by throwing dust on her head and embracing the coffin of her deceased husband. She was later interred next to him in the same burial chamber (*ibid.*, pp. 127–128).

References Cited

Gomaà, Farouk. 2001. Khaemwaset. In *The Oxford Encyclopedia of Ancient Egypt*, edited by D. B. Redford. Oxford & New York: Oxford University Press. Vol. 2, pp. 228–229.

Hickmann, Ellen. 1994. Alt Ägypten. In *Die Musik in Geschichte und Gegenwart (Sachteil)*, edited by L. Finscher. Kassel: Bärenreiter. Vol. 1, cols. 276–296.

Manniche, Lise. 1991. *Music and Musicians in Ancient Egypt*. London: British Museum Press.

Martin, Geoffrey T. 1991. *The Hidden Tombs of Memphis: New Discoveries from the Time of Tutankhamun and Ramesses the Great*. Edited by C. Renfrew, New Aspects of Antiquity. London & New York: Thames and Hudson.

Mieroop, Marc Van De. 2011. *A History of Ancient Egypt, Blackwell History of the Ancient World*. Chichester & Malden: Wiley-Blackwell.

Rice, Michael. 1999. *Who's Who in Ancient Egypt, Who's Who Series*. London and New York: Routledge.

van Dijk, Jacobus. 2001. Ptah. In *The Oxford Encyclopedia of Ancient Egypt*, edited by D. B. Redford. Oxford & New York: Oxford University Press. Vol. 3, pp. 74–76.

Watterson, Barbara. 1991. *Women in Ancient Egypt*. New York: St. Martin's Press.

Wilkinson, Toby. 2007. *Lives of the Ancient Egyptians*. London & New York: Thames & Hudson.

Further Reading

Hallo, William W., and William Kelly Simpson. 1971. *The Ancient Near East: A History*. New York: Harcourt Brace Jovanovich.

Wilkinson, Toby. 2010. *The Rise and Fall of Ancient Egypt*. London & New York: Random House & Bloomsbury.

Peripatjauemope (fl. ca. 1080 BCE)

Peripatjauemope, known as Peripatjau, played the trumpet. This in itself was rather unusual in Ancient Egypt, where strings and woodwinds were more the norm. It was also unusual that Peripatjau worked at a temple, for Egyptian trumpeters were more often military men (H. Hickmann 1946). They sounded signals and accompanied troops while marching. Nevertheless, Peripatjau played the trumpet at the prestigious temple of Amun in Thebes. He lived around 1080 BCE, toward the end of the second Ramessid dynasty and at the close of the period that Egyptologists term the New Kingdom. He was married to a woman named Nesmut and had a son named Djehutihotep, who served as chief porter in the temple at which his father was employed (Lieven 2006: 356–357).

The earliest archeological evidence of trumpets in Egypt stems from the time of Queen Hatshepsut, some 1500 years after the beginning of the Egyptian state in ca. 3000 BCE and already half a millennium before Peripatjau took up the instrument. Earlier representations in Egyptian art show flutes, reed pipes, lyres, harps, and other melodic instruments, but not metal trumpets. The initial absence of these instruments may have been for want of a professional army, in which they would have been useful for signaling, but it is more likely that limitations in available technology delayed their introduction (E. Hickmann 1994: 281–293; H. Hickmann 1946: 47–48; Manniche 1991: 74).

The only surviving ancient Egyptian trumpets are a pair from the tomb of Pharaoh Tutankhamun (r. ca. 1336–1327 BCE). Their tubes are straight, half a meter long, and flared to a bell at one end. One of them is of silver and gold; the other, of copper or bronze with gold overlay at the ends of the tube. They have no valves or other aids to playing and no removable mouthpiece: the upper part ends in a ridge-like ring. Because the tubes have a larger diameter than those in modern trumpets, ancient musicians had to blow especially hard in order to produce a tone. Twentieth-century musicians who tried to play the relics succeeded in sounding only one or two notes, the latter separated by an octave or a twelfth (E. Hickmann 1994: 292; Manniche 1991: 74–77; Sachs 1940: 100).

The sound of the ancient trumpet was harsh and raucous, comparable to the braying of an ass, according to the Greco-Roman historian Plutarch (Sachs 1940: 100). For such an instrument to have found a place in religious observances seems in retrospect somewhat surprising, but a connection with spirituality does arise in considerations of the early history of the trumpet. It has been suggested that the instrument began as a kind of speaking tube in non-literate societies, which was later transformed for the production of musical tones. The earlier version served to distort and disguise the human voice, thereby facilitating communication with the world of the spirits (H. Hickmann 1946: 44–46; Sachs1940: 47–50).

Egyptians associated the trumpet with the god Osiris, King of the Dead, and may therefore have employed it in ceremonies designed to resurrect their departed. In an annual joyous celebration known as the Opet Festival, trumpeters and other musicians accompanied the statue of the deity Amun as it was being transported in a barque from its residence in the temple at Karnak to the temple at Luxor, and back again, a distance of a few kilometers. Scenes from an Opet Festival during Tutankhamun's reign decorate the walls of a colonnade in the Luxor temple (Manniche 1991: 70–71 & 79).

A colleague of Peripatjau's named Amenkhau also played trumpet at the temple of Amun. Amenkhau was the son of Hori, a "singer of the offering table" (Peet 1930: 146). Most likely, the temple of Amun employed a great many musicians. Hans Hickmann has deduced that a large, rich temple in the New Kingdom could employ whole groups of singers and instrumentalists, bringing them into service on specific occasions. Among such musicians were blind choristers; players of instruments having liturgical-cultic meaning, such as sistra, bells, clappers, and castanets; and trumpeters, drummers, harpists, and lutenists (Hickmann & Stauder 1970: 146–147). In addition, chantresses—temple singers from the elite classes—served on periodic rotas, entertaining the temple deities with their music (Teeter 1993: 79–86).

The temple of Amun in Thebes certainly commanded the means for employing a large assembly of musicians. Earlier in the second Ramessid dynasty, in a move aimed apparently at securing the support of the priestly class, Pharaoh Ramesses III (r. ca. 1184–1153 BCE) had donated enormous areas of agricultural land and great numbers of servants to the temples. Some eighty per cent of this wealth went to the temples in Thebes, and especially to the temple of Amun, with the result that this institution became extremely rich and the head priest, extremely powerful (Mieroop 2011: 248–249).

Peripatjau and his colleague Amenkhau are among those temple musicians whose names have been preserved from antiquity, but their posthumous fame is, unfortunately, not attributable to musical prowess. Law and order had disintegrated so dramatically during the second Ramessid dynasty that gangs of thieves began looting the tombs and mortuary temples of earlier kings and queens. Peripatjau and Amenkhau figured prominently in a group of men and women tried for such a crime. They were accused of stealing precious metals from a tomb in the Valley of the Queens (Lieven 2006: 356–357; Peet 1930; Vernus 2003: 1–49).

A written record of the criminal proceedings has been pieced together based on the texts of several papyri. During the reign of Ramesses XI (ca. 1099–1069 BCE), a high-level tribunal investigated more than thirty persons in connection with thefts of silver and gold from the Necropolis at Thebes (Peet 1930: 137). During the investigation, repeated applications of torture, an approach referred to in the twenty-first century as 'enhanced' interrogation, brought out increasingly detailed accusations and confessions from the individuals being questioned.

At the start of questioning, the herdsman Bukaaf, who headed one of the gangs of tomb-robbers, implicated several associates, including Peripatjau, Amenkhau, and—indirectly—Peripatjau's wife Nesmut. Another gang member explicitly accused Peripatjau, Amenkhau, and Nesmut, while also naming several other accomplices, including Peripatjau's son, the chief porter Djehutihotep. Nesmut had apparently been involved in a dispute over division of the loot.

For his part, Peripatjau accused, among others, his temple colleague Amenkhau of complicity in the crime. After several beatings, Peripatjau even surrendered the name of his own son Djehutihotep, confirming the earlier accusation.

Amenkhau vehemently denied the charges against him. He admitted to knowing about the robbery and claimed to have rebuked Peripatjau for taking part in it. Amenkhau proved able to withstand torture and stick to his story. After a second interrogation five days later, he was released, despite having been accused by two gang members, a chain of events that has led a recent scholar to speculate that Amenkhau may have bribed his way to freedom (Lieven 2006: 357).

For his confessed thievery, Peripatjau most likely suffered far worse than the beatings he received during his interrogation. He and the ringleader Bukaaf appear on a list of convicted thieves, and it is known that his wife was imprisoned. His ultimate fate remains undocumented, but ancient Egyptians considered tomb-robbery a heinous crime, for which the penalty was death by impalement (Peet 1930: 27).

References Cited

Hickmann, Ellen. 1994. Alt Ägypten. In *Die Musik in Geschichte und Gegenwart (Sachteil)*, edited by L. Finscher. Kassel: Bärenreiter.

Hickmann, Hans. 1946. *La trompette dans l'Égypte ancienne, Supplément aux Annales du Service des Antiquités de l'Égypte*. Le Caire: Imprimerie de l'Institut Français d'Archéologie Orientale.

Hickmann, Hans, and Wilhelm Stauder. 1970. *Orientalische Musik. Mit Beiträgen von Hans Hickmann und Wilhelm Stauder*. In *Handbuch der Orientalistik. Erste Abt: Der Nahe und der Mittlere Osten. Ergänzungsband IV*. Edited by B. Spuler. Leiden: E. J. Brill.

Lieven, Alexandra von. 2006. The Social Standing of Musicians in Ancient Egypt. In *Archäologische Befunde, historische Zusammenhänge, soziokulturelle Beziehungen, Vorträge des 4. Symposiums der Internationalen Studiengruppe Musikarchäologie im Kloster Michaelstein, 19.–26. September 2004*, edited by E. Hickmann, A. A. Both and R. Eichmann: Studien zur Musikarchäologie V, Musikarchäologie im Kontext.

Manniche, Lise. 1991. *Music and Musicians in Ancient Egypt*. London: British Museum Press.

Mieroop, Marc Van De. 2011. *A History of Ancient Egypt, Blackwell History of the Ancient World*. Chichester & Malden: Wiley-Blackwell.

Peet, T. Eric. 1930. *The Great Tomb-Robberies of the Twentieth Egyptian Dynasty*. Oxford: Clarendon Press.

Sachs, Curt. 1940. *The History of Musical Instruments*. New York: W. W. Norton & Co.

Teeter, Emily. 1993. Female Musicians in Pharaonic Egypt. In *Rediscovering the Muses: Women's Musical Traditions*, edited by K. Marshall. Boston: Northeastern University Press.

Vernus, Pascal. 2003. *Affairs and Scandals in Ancient Egypt*. Ithaca & London: Cornell University Press.

Further Reading

Hallo, William W., and William Kelly Simpson. 1971. *The Ancient Near East: A History*. New York: Harcourt Brace Jovanovich.

Hickmann, Hans. 1954. *Le métier de musicien au temps des pharaons*. 2. ed., rev. Le Caire: Éditions des Cahiers d'histoire égyptienne.

———. 1957. Hufu-'anh und andere ägyptische Musiker. In *Die Musik in Geschichte und Gegenwart: Allgemeine Enzyklopädie der Musik*, edited by F. Blume. Kassel - Basel - London: Bärenreiter-Verlag.

Sarkissian, Margaret, and Edward H. Tarr. 2001. Trumpet. In *The New Grove Dictionary of Music and Musicians*, edited by S. Sadie and J. Tyrrell. New York: Grove.

Wilkinson, Toby. 2010. *The Rise and Fall of Ancient Egypt*. London & New York: Random House & Bloomsbury.

Musicians of Europe

In the twelfth century CE, the troubadours of Occitania in southern France introduced a vital form of poetry and music, the *art de trobar*. Its influence spread first to the north of France and then on to Germany and Austria. The Occitanian troubadour **Marcabru (fl. ca. 1130–1150 CE)** created songs that project abundant wit and biting satire. The Austrian *Minnesänger* **Walther von der Vogelweide (ca. 1170–1230 CE)** composed *Minnelieder* (songs that deal with courtly love) and didactic pieces called *Sangsprüche* ('song-sayings').[1]

∞

---

[1] Some readers may wonder why the troubadours' famous contemporary, Hildegard of Bingen (1098–1179 CE), has not been profiled here. On the nine-hundredth anniversary of her birth, an international conference of scholars, held in Bingen, concluded that significant, commonly accepted aspects of her involvement with music were "historically untenable" (see Annette Kreutziger-Herr. Feb. 1999. Hildegard of Bingen Conference. *Early Music* 27 (1):156–157). Kreutziger-Herr characterizes Hildegard's image, with respect to music, as "extremely overdrawn." In view of these critical observations by specialized scholars, I felt under-qualified to prepare an unassailable profile of this remarkable woman. For a biography in print, see Fiona Maddocks. 2001. *Hildegard of Bingen: The Woman of Her Age*. New York: Doubleday. For an online biography, see Ian D. Bent and Marianne Pfau. 2001/2010. Hildegard of Bingen. *Grove Music Online*, https://doi.org/10.1093/gmo/9781561592630.article.13016.

Three of Merriam's ten functions of music can be associated with these musicians:

THE FUNCTION OF EMOTIONAL EXPRESSION

The songs *A la fontana del vergier* by the troubadour **Marcabru** and *Under der linden* by the *Minnesänger* **Walther von der Vogelweide** are musical expressions of the sadness and joy, respectively, of love. Marcabru's heroine weeps inconsolably for her absent lover, who is away on a crusade. Walther's heroine thrills to the memory of her secret love tryst in a meadow, observed only by a nightingale, "which will not say a word."

THE FUNCTION OF ENFORCING CONFORMITY TO SOCIAL NORMS

Marcabru excoriates his contemporaries for indulging in philandering and adultery, which violated the outward social norms of his medieval society. The texts of his songs follow hardline orthodox moral principles in confronting such behavior.

THE FUNCTION OF VALIDATION OF SOCIAL INSTITUTIONS AND RELIGIOUS RITUALS

Both **Marcabru** and **Walther von der Vogelweide** composed crusading songs in favor of Church-related religious warfare. Walther's *Palästinalied* condones Christian claims to the Holy Land. Marcabru's *Pax in nomine Domini!* contains repeated references to a *lavador* ('washing place'), at which the souls of crusaders would supposedly be cleansed.

Marcabru (fl. ca. 1130–1150 CE)

The medieval troubadour Marcabru performed his compositions at the courts of nobles in his home territory in southern France as well as in northern Spain. He was untitled and of possibly humble origins, but aspects of his texts suggest that he was well educated (Gaunt, Harvey, & Paterson 2000: 5; Paterson 1993: 112). A thirteenth-century miniature shows him standing with his arms folded and without a musical instrument, a hint that he may have sung *a cappella* or perhaps accompanied by an instrumentalist. (Stevens, Butterfield, & Theodore 2001: Fig. 2; Egan 1984: Plate 18). Noting the performance demands of Marcabru's surviving songs, a recent scholar suggests that this troubadour had "a singing voice of suppleness and range" (Pollina 2003).

Troubadours are perhaps best known for courtly love songs, but in fact this stereotype fails to do justice to their creations. They composed vocal music in many genres and thematic categories, including the love-themed *canso*, the moralizing or didactic *sirventes*, the argumentative *tenso*, the erotically charged *pastorela*, the funereal *planh*, the crusading song, and more (Aubrey 1996: xix–xx; Egan 1984: 113–114; Stevens, Butterfield, & Karp 2001: 800–801). Using the spoken *langue d'oc* or Occitan language of their region and developing melodies that lift their texts "immensely far above the level of everyday communication" (van der Werf 1995: 148), they "produced the earliest surviving repertory of [European] vernacular songs" (Fassler 2014: 141).

In his active years between ca. 1130 and ca. 1150 CE, Marcabru helped to establish several important troubadour genres. His subtle and gripping songs anticipate a later style of composition known as *trobar clus* (Chaytor 1912: 34–35 & 43; Haynes 2001: 807;

Lindsay 1976: 53). He peppered his lyrics with learned allusions and obscenities, and he hurled invective against philandering and adultery, contrasting their debilitating effects with the ennobling benefits of pure love, or *fin' amor*. Marcabru's moral stance and innovative style had a profound influence on later troubadours (Gaunt & Kay 1999: 287), six of whom mention their innovative forerunner by name (Haynes 2001: 807).

Two *vidas* (brief biographies) of Marcabru appear in a pair of thirteenth-century song collections, which are known to scholars as *chansonniers A* and *K* (Egan 1984: 67–68; present text follows Gaunt, Harvey, & Paterson 2000 [abbr. GHP] for all English translations). The two *vidas* present complementary views of his life.

According to the *vida* in *A* (GHP: 37), a certain Sir Aldric del Vilar (about whom very little is known) raised Marcabru, who had been abandoned at Sir Aldric's gate. Afterwards, the future musician is said to have stayed with another troubadour named Cercamon (fl. 1137–1149; see Gaunt & Kay 1999: 281–282). He began to compose under the name *Pan-Perdut* ('lost bread'), before adopting the name *Marcabrun* ('brown mark'). He became famous and widely known, but listeners feared his vituperative tongue. The *vida* concludes: "at the end the castellans of Guyenne whom he had criticized so much put him to death."

According to the *vida* in *K* (GHP: 38), Marcabru came from Gascony, and his mother was a poor woman named Marcabruna. This *vida* cites a stanza from one of Marcabru's songs (labeled PC293.18):

> Marcabru, the son of Lady Bruna, was begotten under such a moon that he knows how love wreaks havoc, —Listen!—for he never loved any woman, nor was he loved by another.

The *vida* characterizes Marcabru's "*vers* and *sirventes*" (two types of troubadour songs) as "miserable," which, however, may be an oblique reference to their subject matter and tone, rather than their quality (GHP: 38 n.9). The biographical note concludes with the comment that Marcabru "spoke ill of women and of love."

As the *vidas* clearly suggest, Marcabru seems to have been born without independent means. Indeed, he and Cercamon may have had to earn their livings by their art, working as the first 'professional' troubadours (Lindsay 1976: 52). However, Gaunt, Harvey, and Paterson caution against such conclusions and suggest instead that the courts employed Marcabru as a clerk (GHP: 5).

The account of Marcabru's murder has not been historically confirmed, and the dates of his birth and death are unknown. A 1970s study speculates that his birthdate was ca. 1110. Jack Lindsay, the author of the study, notes that around 1157–1158, another troubadour "refers to [Marcabru] in the past tense and suggests that he has fallen into neglect," which would indicate that Marcabru died prior to the mid-1150s (p. 52).

Both *vidas* are recognizably based on Marcabru's song texts. Margarita Egan, who studied many troubadour *vidas*, suggests that, in some cases, scribes simply made mini-biographies out of information inferred from the lyrics that they were copying (1984: xxv). In the absence of independent historical sources, present-day scholars also look to Marcabru's songs for information about his life (GHP: 1–5).

Forty-four of Marcabru's song texts have survived to the present, including four that are complete with their melodies, but fewer than 20 of these are datable. These show him moving from Poitou in southwestern France early in the 1130s, where William X (1099–1137), duke of Aquitaine, gave him support; to Castile in northern Spain some five to ten years later, where Alfonso VII

(1105–1157), king of Castile-Leon and self-proclaimed Spanish emperor, was, for a short time, his patron.

Alfonso was a leader of the Spanish *Reconquista*, in which Christians fought to recover for their faith the Iberian territory that Muslims had taken over nearly 400 years earlier. Marcabru's crusading songs, PC293.22 and PC293.35, were likely composed in support of Alfonso's military campaigns (Fauriel & Adler 1966: 445–448; O'Callaghan 2003: 46–47), which closely resembled those of crusaders to the Holy Land, who were active in this same era (Koenigsberger 1987: 192). The better known of Marcabru's crusading songs, PC293.35, begins "*Pax in nomine Domini!* (Peace in the name of the Lord!)." It contains repeated references to a *lavador* ('washing place'), at which the souls of crusaders would supposedly be cleansed.

Back in Gascony after 1137, Marcabru may have found employment with Peire de Gabaret, viscount of Béarn (d. 1153). The wording of the song PC293.15, which starts with "*Cortesamen vuoill comensar un vers* (I wish to begin a *vers* in a courtly way)," suggests that Marcabru remained in Europe during the Second Crusade (1147–1149). Marcabru dedicates this song to one of the crusaders: his fellow troubadour "Jaufre Rudel *outremar* ('across the sea')."

Marcabru's speech characteristics support the idea that he came from Gascony, where he seems to have spent a large part of his career (Aubrey 2004: 1034). The palace of his first known patron, William X, was at Poitiers in Poitou, which borders on Gascony. Only after April 1137, when William X died while on pilgrimage to Santiago de Compostela, did Marcabru leave southern France and solicit the patronage of Alfonso VII (GHP: 3. Cf. songs PC293.22 and PC293.23 in this source). Evidently, he returned to north of the Pyrenees when the relationship with this patron broke down.

Already in the thirteenth century, Marcabru had acquired a reputation for misogyny, as indicated by the comment at the end of the *vida* in *K* (cf. Wilhelm 1970: 63–65). Although his song texts can be used to justify such a reputation, misogyny is nevertheless a doubly misleading attribute for this troubadour. In the first place, he criticizes the philandering and adultery of men as clearly as he attacks the immoral behavior of women, and so the term misanthropy might be more appropriate than misogyny. However, Gaunt, Harvey, and Paterson use neither epithet in their characterization of Marcabru, emphasizing instead the moral dimension of his verses:

> Our own impression of Marcabru is of a poet with more learning than he has generally been credited with […], in contact with some of the most important secular political figures of his day and familiar with the atmosphere and intrigues of their courts, whose songs are often vehicles for *a hard-line, clerical, orthodox morality* (GHP: 4, emphasis added).

Secondly, in two situations in which Marcabru abandons impersonal moralizing in order to present more realistic characters and narratives, his depictions of women are far more positive than the depictions of men in these or any other of his songs. The female protagonists in his two *pastorelas* (PC293.30 and PC293.1) display more intelligence or wit and greater emotional maturity than their male counterparts. Both these songs revolve around the situation in which an upper-class man tries to seduce a pretty girl in the countryside.

Pastorela PC293.30 starts: "*L'autrer jost' una sebissa / trobei toeta mestissa, / de joi e de sen masissa* (The other day, beside a hedge, I found a common little wench brimming with joy and wisdom)."

Through the course of fourteen stanzas, the "common little wench" proves more than a match for the wiles of her aristocratic would-be seducer. He starts by calling her a "lovely thing" and his "sweet, dear pretty one." He attempts to praise this "courtly peasant woman" by suggesting that her father must have been a knight, seemingly unaware that his remark is insensitive and insulting to her mother—although, of course, it also points to the subject of noble/peasant intercourse, which is his aim. She parries by contrasting the solidity of her background and life with those of her shallow admirer. Even though he displays the airs of a knight, she suggests, he is basically no nobler than a peasant:

> 'My lord, I can see all my lineage and family going
> back and returning to the sickle and plough, sir,'
> thus said the peasant woman to me, 'whereas a
> man may act like a knight who should do the
> same six days a week.'

He presses his suit by recasting the earlier allusion to nobility and beauty, and then he graphically blurts out his purpose:

> 'My pretty one,' said I, 'a noble fairy fashioned
> you when you were born: there is in you a pure
> and rarified beauty, and it would be easily dou-
> bled with just one union, me on top and you un-
> derneath.'

She recognizes that he would pay for the privilege, but she refuses "to exchange [her] maidenhood for the title of whore." Citing the norms of "Christian people," she suggests that he pursue his adventure with women of his own class. She sends him packing, while he sputters a final arrogant insult: "Wench, never have I seen *in the likes of you* a more perfidious woman in all of Christendom" (emphasis added).

The personages in the second *pastorela*, PC293.1, react to the absence of a man who is away on a crusade, and in contrast to Marcabru's crusading songs, it does not present a favorable view of religious warfare. This song begins "*A la fontana del vergier* (By the spring in the orchard)." The narrator, an aristocrat, comes across a beautiful young noblewoman, "the daughter of the lord of a castle," standing alone in the countryside. He hopes that the joys of springtime will help him to win her favor, but she remains true to her absent lover and easily deflects his advances. The text makes it clear that her lover is a crusader. Specific allusions date the piece at around 1147, during the Second Crusade (GHP: 40–41), and the song comments indirectly on the societal disruption that this campaign caused within Europe.

The Cistercian abbot Bernard of Clairvaux (1090–1153) was the moral force behind the Second Crusade (Koenigsberger 1987: 192). In a report sent to the pope, the abbot vaunts his success in getting European men to join the crusaders (cited in Faurriel & Adler 1966: 424):

> The cities and castles are deserted to such an extent that there is scarcely a man left for seven women: everywhere we see nothing but widows whose husbands are yet alive.

Marcabru's heroine would seem to represent one of those women, and she is none too happy about it. "Cursed be King Louis," the young noblewoman says, "who orders the call to arms and the preaching which are the cause of this grief entering my heart!" She weeps and sighs for her absent lover, while the stranger urges her to stop, so as not to spoil her "looks and complexion." God has made the trees come into leaf, he adds, and can give her joy. She offers a bitter response:

> 'Sir', she said, 'I do believe that God will have
> mercy on me forever in the next world, as He will
> on many other sinners; but here He is taking
> away from me the one person who gave me joy
> […], but he thinks little of me, for he has gone so
> far away from me.'

Faurriel observes dryly that this song "does not indicate a very lively enthusiasm for the second crusade in the countries of the Provençal tongue" (Faurriel & Adler 1966: 425).

Melodies have survived for "*L'autrer jost' una sebissa*" and "*Pax in nomine Domini!*" Also preserved are the words and melodies for two of Marcabru's songs on the quality of love: the *canso* PC293.13, which begins "*Bel m'es quant son li frug madur* (I like it when the fruits are ripe)," and the *sirventes* PC293.18, which begins "*Dire vos vouilh ses doptanssa / d'aqest vers la comenssanssa* (Without hesitation, I want to recite to you the beginning of this *vers*)."

Hendrick van der Werf and Gerald Bond have released transcriptions of Marcabru's songs (1984: 224*–227*). A glance at the scores reveals characteristics in common with other troubadour melodies (Stevens, Butterfield, and Karp 2001: 810; van der Werf 1995): pitch ranges of around one octave, conjunct motion (small pitch changes), arch-shaped phrases, strophic structures (the melody does not vary from stanza to stanza), descending patterns to the final notes, and moderate occurrence of melisma (the sounding of several notes on a single syllable).

The four texts have different verse patterns and rhyme schemes, and the melodic structures are similarly varied. Two are through-composed, in the sense that the melody varies for each of the verses in the stanza. The *sirventes* has a three-syllable refrain. This song is essentially through-composed, apart from considerable similarity in the first and third verses, whereas the *pastorela* has a more-regular repetition pattern. All of Marcabru's melodies incorporate a major triad above their initial pitch and end on a minor third below the initial (Aubrey 1996: 207; 2004: 1035).

As of 2016, performances of all these pieces were available on the Internet. According to Margot Fassler, *"L'autrer jost' una sebissa"* is "one of the most popular troubadour songs recorded today" (2014: 130). The feminist impact of this piece, together with its alternating regularity and a lively melody that hints of traditional dance (Pollina 2003), may help to explain its popularity.

Marcabru was preeminent among the first generation of poet-composers following Duke William IX of Acquitaine (1071–1127), whose songs of courtly love had launched the troubadour movement (Wilhelm 1970:21–59). In contrast to William IX, Marcabru was an untitled commoner, and he excoriated the immorality of the upper classes from this vantage point. His uncompromising exposure of their faults would have made for heavy reading (and listening), were it not for an ample command of poetic wit. The engaging moral tone of *"L'autrer jost' una sebissa"* was never to be matched by Marcabru's successors; as James Wilhelm comments, "after his passing, [morality] was never again quite so funny" (1970: p. 86).

References Cited

Aubrey, Elizabeth. 1996. *The Music of the Troubadours*. Bloomington: Indiana University Press.

———. 2004. Marcabru. In *Die Musik in Geschichte und Gegenwart. Allgemeine Enzyklopädie der Musik begründet von Friedrich Blume. Personenteil in zwölf Bänden*, edited by L. Finscher. Kassel - Basel - London - New York - Prag / Stuttgart - Weimar: Bärenreiter-Verlag / Metzler.

Chaytor, H. J. 1912. *The Troubadours*. Cambridge: The University Press.

Egan, Margarita. 1984. *The Vidas of the Troubadours*, Garland
        Library of Medieval Literature. New York & London:
        Garland Publishing.

Fassler, Margot Elsbeth. 2014. *Music in the Medieval West, Western
        Music in Context: A Norton History*. New York & London:
        W. W. Norton & Company.

Fauriel, C. C., and G. J. Adler. 1966. *History of Provençal Poetry*. New
        York: Haskell House. Original edition, New York: Derby
        & Jackson, 1860.

Gaunt, Simon, Ruth Harvey, and Linda M. Paterson. 2000.
        Marcabru: A Critical Edition. Cambridge & Rochester: D. S.
        Brewer.

Gaunt, Simon, and Sarah Kay. 1999. *The Troubadours: An
        Introduction*. Cambridge; New York: Cambridge University
        Press.

Haynes, Stephen. 2001. Marcabru. In *The New Grove Dictionary of
        Music and Musicians*, edited by S. Sadie and J. Tyrrell. New
        York: Grove.

Koenigsberger, H. G. 1987. *Medieval Europe, 400–1500, History of
        Europe*. London & New York: Longman.

Lindsay, Jack. 1976. *The Troubadours & Their World of the Twelfth and
        Thirteenth Centuries*. London: Frederick Muller Ltd.

O'Callaghan, Joseph F. 2003. *Reconquest and Crusade in Medieval
        Spain, The Middle Ages Series*. Philadelphia: University of
        Pennsylvania Press.

Pollina, Vincent. 2003. Marcabru the Musician. *Tenso* 18 (1–2):39–
        49.

Stevens, John, Ardis Butterfield, and Theodore Karp. 2001.
        Troubadours, Trouvères. In *The New Grove Dictionary of
        Music and Musicians*, edited by S. Sadie and J. Tyrrell. New
        York: Grove.

van der Werf, Hendrik. 1995. Music. In *A Handbook of the Troubadours, Publications of the UCLA Center for Medieval and Renaissance Studies*, edited by F. R. P. Akehurst and J. M. Davis. Berkeley: University of California Press.

van der Werf, Hendrik, and Gerald A. Bond. 1984. *The Extant Troubadour Melodies: Transcriptions and Essays for Performers and Scholars*. Rochester: H. van der Werf.

Wilhelm, James J. 1970. *Seven Troubadours: The Creators of Modern Verse*. University Park & London: Pennsylvania State University Press.

Further Reading

Colish, Marcia L. 1997. *Medieval Foundations of the Western Intellectual Tradition, 400–1400*. New Haven: Yale Univesity Press.

Goldin, Frederick. 1973. *Lyrics of the Troubadours and Trouvères: An Anthology and a History*. Garden City: Anchor Books.

Kennedy, Hugh. 1996. *Muslim Spain and Portugal: A Political History of al-Andalus*. London & New York: Longman.

Léglu, Catherine. 1999. Moral and Satirical Poetry. In *The Troubadours: An Introduction*, edited by S. Gaunt and S. Kay. Cambridge & New York: Cambridge University Press.

Nichols, Stephen G. 1999. The Early Troubadours: Guilhem IX to Bernart de Ventadorn. In *The Troubadours: An Introduction*, edited by S. Gaunt and S. Kay. Cambridge & New York: Cambridge University Press.

O'Callaghan, Joseph F. 1975. *A History of Medieval Spain*. Ithaca: Cornell University Press.

Paterson, Linda M. 1993. *The World of the Troubadours: Medieval Occitan Society, c. 1100–c. 1300*. Cambridge: Cambridge University Press.

Räkel, Hans-Herbert, and Elisabeth Aubrey. 1998. Troubadours, Trouvères. In *Die Musik in Geschichte und Gegenwart*.

Allgemeine Enzyklopädie der Musik begründet von Friedrich Blume. Sachteil in neun Bänden, edited by L. Finscher. Kassel - Basel - London - New York - Prag / Stuttgart - Weimar: Bärenreiter-Verlag / Metzler.

Reilly, Bernard F. 1998. *The Kingdom of Léon-Castilla under King Alfonso VII, 1126–1157, The Middle Ages Series*. Philadelphia: University of Pennsylvania Press.

Walther von der Vogelweide (ca. 1170– 1230 CE)

During the European Middle Ages, Walther von der Vogelweide became famous in Austria and southern Germany for *Minnelieder*, songs that deal with courtly love, or *Minne*, and for didactic pieces called *Sangsprüche* ('song-sayings'), which comment on social, political, moral, and other issues. Walther wrote in Middle High German, the vernacular of the times. He traveled to the courts of his noble patrons, for whom he composed and sang. Many of Walther's lyrics and several of his melodies have survived through the ages. His contemporaries held him in high regard, and present-day scholars consider him to have been one of the most significant medieval German poet-composers (Brunner 2007; Firges 2007; Klaper 2001; Scholz 2005).

Walther came into the world around 1170 CE. He was probably born in South Tirol, but his birthplace and parentage remain a subject of controversy (Scholz 2005: 5–9). His image as a thinker appears as miniatures in the thirteenth-century *Codex Manesse* and other medieval manuscripts. The basis for these paintings is a written self-portrait at the start of a poem, in which Walther laments the impossibility of living an ethical life, while adhering to the secular values of society (W1996: **2** I; translated in Goldin 1973: 102–103):

> I sat down on a rock,
> crossed one leg over the other leg,
> set my elbow on top,
> nestled my chin and one
> cheek in my hand.
> Then I thought very hard

about how a man should live in the world.

Walther lived until around 1230 CE and was interred, according to a fourteenth-century source, in the courtyard of the Würzburg Cathedral in Germany (Klaper 2001: 62). There is no record of a wife or family.

In addition to a longer poem called a *Leich*, Walther composed at least 500 stanzas of lyrical poetry, of which two-thirds falls under the heading of *Minnelieder*, and slightly more than a quarter, under the heading of *Sangsprüche*. The slight balance, or 7%, is religious in nature (Scholz 2005: 18). Walther's poetry is virtually the only source of information about his life. The single surviving bit of independent written evidence is the record of a payment by the bishop of Passau, who gave Walther five schillings on November 12, 1203, so that he could purchase a fur coat (Klaper 2001: 62; Scholz 2005: 11–12). Scholars have found Walther's *Sangsprüche* especially helpful in piecing together his biography, for many of these poems comment on political and military events, which can be correlated with information in other historical sources. Some 80 of Walther's *Minnelieder* and 100 of his *Sangsprüche* have survived (Thomas 1968: 107).

In the 1190s, Walther was at the Babenberg court in Vienna, where he interacted with the established minnesinger Reinmar von Hagenau (fl. 1185–1205; d. ca. 1205). Reinmar may have been Walther's teacher. Several of Walther's songs express the sentiments of unattainable courtly love that are typical of Reinmar's work. However, the pair became rivals, and in a literary dispute, which was carried out in an exchange of poems, Walther carved out an artistic path of his own. Nevertheless, when Reinmar died, Walther mourned the beautiful poetry and lovely melodies that the senior poet had composed (Firges 2007: 18 & 125–129; Goldin 1973: 96–101).

In 1198, Walther's patron in Vienna, the Babenberg duke Frederick I, died while on a crusade to the Holy Land. Frederick was succeeded by his younger brother, Leopold VI. At this point, the musical artist was forced to leave Vienna and begin the life of an itinerant musician. He had to seek patronage in order to put a roof over his head and food on the table. Because of the unsettled political climate, this task proved challenging.

Following the death of the Hohenstaufen emperors Frederick Barbarossa in 1190 and Henry VI in 1197, a protracted struggle for power had erupted, pitting heads of the Hohenstaufen and Guelph dynasties against one another. At stake was leadership in Germany and in the Holy Roman Empire. The initial German contenders in the struggle were Barbarossa's youngest son, Philipp of Swabia, and, on the Guelph side, the future Emperor Otto IV (r. 1209–1215). Involvement of the Roman papacy, with its own political and territorial interests, further complicated a complex situation. Armed conflict subsided only after the election of the Hohenstaufen scion Frederick II as German king in 1215 and as Holy Roman emperor in 1220 (Detwiler 1999: 35–45).

Walther's wanderings took him first to the court of King Philipp of Swabia, who was then attempting to become emperor. Walther's association with Philipp lasted until 1201, or perhaps somewhat later (Scholz 2005: 14). The poet later criticized his former patron for lack of generosity (Firges 2007: 51–52).

Philipp was murdered in 1208, opening the path for his arch rival from the Guelph family to accede to the imperial throne. Adapting to a changed political landscape, Walther sought patronage from the newly installed ruler, Otto IV. Walther is known to have attended Otto's court day in Frankfurt-am-Main in 1212, and the emperor is thought to have patronized the poet until the following year, 1213 (Firges 2007: 75–82; Scholz 2005: 14).

Other nobles with whom Walther interacted, and from whom he may have received support, include Landgrave Hermann of Thuringia (in 1201), Hermann's son-in-law Margrave Dietrich of Meissen (in 1212–1213), Duke Bernhard II of Carinthia (in, perhaps, 1215 or 1216), Count Diether II of Katzenellenbogen (after 1220), and, for an unknown period, Duke Ludwig I of Bavaria (Brunner 2007: 447; Scholz 2005: 14).

Walther had hoped to stay on in Vienna after Leopold VI took charge of the Babenberg court in 1198. Losing the Viennese position cost Walther a great deal of his self-confidence. As he writes in one of the *Sangsprüche* (W1996: **9** IV; Firges 2007: 37–38—my translation from the German), his "proud crane step" vanished into the earth together with Duke Frederick I's remains: "Then I crept around like a peacock," he writes, "with my head hanging down to my knee." Philipp of Swabia's acceptance of him restored the self-confidence, but this relationship, like those that followed, ended all too soon, forcing Walther to move continually from patron to patron.

Throughout this period, Walther tried repeatedly, it would seem, to return to the Viennese court. There is evidence to suggest that he visited Vienna in 1201 and 1203: for Duke Leopold's knighting ceremony on the former occasion and for the duke's wedding on the latter (Scholz 2005: 14). Walther promised praise if the duke would become his patron and expressed anger when this did not happen. "In Austria I learned singing and writing," he notes in one of his *Sangsprüche* (W1996: **12** IV; Firges 2007: 61—my translation from the German), implying that Austria therefore had a responsibility to support him. If Leopold would only grant him protection, he writes, his anger would be assuaged. Sadly for Walther, a Viennese position never materialized (Firges 2007: 56–65).

As Walther aged, the itinerant life became harder for him to bear. In 1219 or thereabouts, when he was approximately fifty years old, he asked the king and future emperor Frederick II to grant him a home in which he could "warm himself at his own fire." Walther was overjoyed when the king granted this request. "I have my fief," he exclaims in one of the *Sangsprüche* (W1996: **11** X), "I shout it to the entire world: I have my fief!" (Firges 2007: 84–87; my translation from the German).

Walther's *Minnelieder* have attracted attention through the ages. One of his accomplishments was to shift the focus away from noble wives, who were unattainable as love objects, to women who could be his own companions and lovers. A charming example is the so-called "dream song" (W1996: **51** I–V), in which the narrator imagines flirting in a meadow with a pretty country girl, to whom he gives a garland of flowers. Awakening at daybreak, he realizes that he has been dreaming, but he is so taken by the memory of his fantasy that he searches at all the summer dances for her equal in reality: "Ladies, by your good grace, / push back your hats. / O if underneath a garland I saw her face" (Goldin 1973: 120–123).

Walther's "dream song" has been related to the earlier *pastorelas* of Provençal troubadours such as Marcabru (Firges 2007: 138–139; present work, previous Profile). Walther moves still farther from the traditional *Minnelied* in *Under der linden* ('Under the Linden Tree') by presenting a love tryst in a meadow from the woman's perspective (W1996: **16** I–IV). The nightingale was already singing, the narrator relates, when her lover greeted her like a lady and kissed her "a thousand times, at least, / *tandaradei*, / look now, how my mouth is red." She would be ashamed if anyone learned of what they had done, she adds, but the only witness had been "one little bird, / *tandaradei*, / which will not say a word" (Goldin

1973: 124–127). Here the refrain, *tandaradei*, may represent the nightingale's song.

Walther composed both texts and melodies for his songs. The melodies should not be thought of as musical 'settings,' but rather as integral parts of the poetic compositions. Such compositions are said to correspond to different *Töne* (singular *Ton*), a terminology that characterizes the verse form together with the melody in medieval German literature (Brunner 2001). Ewald Jammers (1963) has noted that, as a result of generic differences, *Minnelieder* melodies tend to differ from those associated with *Sangsprüche*. He points out that *Sangsprüche* were directed to understanding. They convey "awareness, teachings, admonitions, folklore, and political challenges: thus, the music only has to support declamation," and an open, recitative form of melody is appropriate (p. 80; my translation from the German). The *Lieder*, however, "try to grip the listeners, to build and edify" (p. 93; my translation from the German). Here emotional content becomes important, and the melody takes on more of a closed form, as in an aria (p. 94).

The earliest known transcribable examples of Walther's melodies are in a fourteenth-century artifact known as the Münster fragment. It contains the complete melody for his *Palästinalied* ('Palestine Song') and portions of the melodies for two of his *Sangsprüche*: the *Konig-Friedrichs-Ton* ('King Frederick's *Ton*') and the *2. Philippston* ('Second Phillip's *Ton*'). Despite the incomplete nature of the transmission, the surviving portions of these three melodies provide useful information about Walther's music. Earlier musical representations are in staffless neumes, which cannot be transcribed into modern notation. More recent examples from the fifteenth and sixteenth centuries are even farther removed from Walther's lifetime and will not be considered here (Klaper 2001; W1996: XLII–XLV).

The range of the *Palästina* melody (W1996: **7** [p. 24]) extends over a single octave, from C_4 to C_5. It begins and ends on the same note, D_4, and the final cadence echoes that at the close of the first and second pair of verses (the so-called *Stollen*). The form thereby encapsulates the melody closely. Melismatic elements are moderate: two to four notes underlie the singing of several individual syllables.

Since the melodic portions of the *Konig-Friedrichs-Ton* (W1996: **11** [p. 48]) and the *2. Philippston* (W1996: **8** [p. 30]) have not survived in their entirety, only a limited amount of musicological information can be extracted from them. The partial melodies range from D_4 to A_5 in the first instance and from C_4 to C_5 in the second. Both tunes start and end on the same note—A_4 and F_4, respectively—but in the latter case, only the introductory portion has been preserved. Jammers, in his analysis, relates the *Konig-Friedrichs-Ton* explicitly to the recitative form (pp. 84–85).

The *Palästinalied* is a hymn in support of the crusades, the series of European attempts in the Middle Ages to conquer and maintain control of the Holy Land. Walther's text seeks to justify Christian claims to the region (W1996: **7**; translated in Thomas 1968: 122–124):

> Strife is heard on every hand:
> ours the only just demand,
> He will have us rule the land.

Crusaders mounted five overseas religiomilitary campaigns during Walther's lifetime. At least three of his benefactors, Duke Frederick I of Austria, King Philipp of Swabia, and Emperor Frederick II of the Holy Roman Empire, were active crusaders (Koenigsberger 1987: 193–197 & 251–257).

Thoughts of the Holy Land would recur to Walther in his old age. In his last known poem *Elegy* (W1996: **97**; translated in Goldin 1973: 134–139), composed late in the 1220s, he laments changes for the worse in society:

> Alas, how miserable are the young today,
>   whose spirits soared in times gone by.
> They know only sorrow—how can they live that way?
> Wherever I turn on this earth no one is content,
>   dancing, laughing, singing have passed on into care.

Crusading seems a brighter alternative:

> If I could make that beloved voyage across the sea,
>   I would sing "Joy!" and never more "Alas,"
>   never more alas.

As it would have been ludicrous, however, for the aged poet-composer to undertake an overseas military campaign, Walther's fantasy is meant to encourage others—the knights and, especially, the emperor, who had overshot the deadline on his crusader's oath—to do their duty, as he saw it (Firges 2007: 148–149).

Walther thrived professionally during his difficult life as an itinerant poet-composer and performer, depicting human emotions and foibles in ways that have led subsequent generations to marvel. He set the highest of literary standards in his *Minnelieder* and commented meaningfully on significant political and social issues in his *Sangsprüche*. Walther was a man of his times, not above the prejudices of his age but not more intolerant than his contemporaries.

References Cited

Brunner, Horst. 1997. Minnesang. In *Die Musik in Geschichte und Gegenwart. Allgemeine Enzyklopädie der Musik begründet von Friedrich Blume. Sachteil in neun Bänden*, edited by L.

Finscher. Kassel - Basel - London - New York - Prag / Stuttgart - Weimar: Bärenreiter-Verlag / Metzler.

————. 2001. Ton. In *The New Grove Dictionary of Music and Musicians*, edited by S. Sadie and J. Tyrrell. New York: Grove.

Detwiler, Donald S. 1999. *Germany: A Short History*. 3rd ed. Carbondale & Edwardsville: Southern Illinois University Press.

Firges, Jean. 2007. *Walther von der Vogelweide : Dichter der Stauferzeit, Exemplarische Reihe Literatur und Philosophie*. Annweiler am Trifels: Sonnenberg.

Goldin, Frederick. 1973. *German and Italian Lyrics of the Middle Ages: An Anthology and a History*. 1st ed. Garden City: Anchor Press/Doubleday.

Jammers, Ewald. 1963. *Ausgewählte Melodien des Minnesangs: Einführung, Erläuterung und Übertragung*. Tübingen: M. Niemeyer.

Klaper, Michael. 2001. Walther von der Vogelweide. In *The New Grove Dictionary of Music and Musicians*, edited by S. Sadie and J. Tyrrell. London: Macmillan Publishers Ltd.

Koenigsberger, H. G. 1987. *Medieval Europe, 400–1500, History of Europe*. London & New York: Longman.

Manesse family, Zürich. Ca. 1300–1340. *Große Heidelberger Liederhandschrift (Codex Manesse)*. Digitized version is at http://digi.ub.uni-heidelberg.de/diglit/cpg848.

Scholz, Manfred Günter. 2005. *Walther von der Vogelweide*. 2., korrigierte und bibliographische ergänzte Aufl. ed, *Sammlung Metzler*. Stuttgart: Verlag J. B. Metzler.

Thomas, J. W. 1968. *Medieval German Lyric Verse in English Translation, University of North Carolina Studies in the Germanic Languages and Literatures, No. 60*. Chapel Hill: University of North Carolina Press.

Walther von der Vogelweide. 1996. *Leich, Lieder, Sangsprüche.*
        Edited by C. Cormeau. 14., völlig neubearbeitete Auflage
        der Ausgabe Karl Lachmanns mit Beiträgen von Thomas
        Bein und Horst Brunner. Berlin & New York: Walter de
        Gruyter. [Abbreviated 'W1996' in the present text.]

Further Reading

Brunner, Horst. 2007. Walther von der Vogelweide. In *Die Musik
        in Geschichte und Gegenwart. Allgemeine Enzyklopädie der Musik
        begründet von Friedrich Blume. Personenteil in zwölf Bänden,*
        edited by L. Finscher. Kassel - Basel - London - New
        York - Prag / Stuttgart - Weimar: Bärenreiter-Verlag /
        Metzler.

Colish, Marcia L. 1997. *Medieval Foundations of the Western Intellectual
        Tradition, 400–1400.* New Haven: Yale Univesity Press.

Fulbrook, Mary. 2004. *A Concise History of Germany.* 2nd ed,
        Cambridge Concise Histories. Cambridge & New York:
        Cambridge University Press.

Kippenberg, Burkhard, and Lorenz Welker. 2001. Reinmar
        [Reimar] (der Alte) von Hagenau. In *The New Grove
        Dictionary of Music and Musicians,* edited by S. Sadie and J.
        Tyrrell. London: Macmillan Publishers Ltd.

Kippenberg, Burkhard. 2001. Minnesang. In *The New Grove
        Dictionary of Music and Musicians,* edited by S. Sadie and J.
        Tyrrell. New York: Grove.

———. 2001. Spruch. In *The New Grove Dictionary of Music and
        Musicians,* edited by S. Sadie and J. Tyrrell. London:
        Macmillan Publishers Ltd.

Leger, Louis, and William E. Lingelbach. 1928. *Austria-Hungary.*
        Memorial ed, *The History of Nations, vol. XVII.* New York:
        P. F. Collier & Son Company.

Rettelbach, Johannes. 1998. Ton. In *Die Musik in Geschichte und Gegenwart. Allgemeine Enzyklopädie der Musik begründet von Friedrich Blume. Sachteil in neun Bänden,* edited by L. Finscher. Kassel - Basel - London - New York - Prag / Stuttgart - Weimar: Bärenreiter-Verlag / Metzler.

Richey, Margaret Fitzgerald. 1969. *Essays on Mediæval German Poetry.* 2nd ed. New York: Barnes & Noble.

Walther von der Vogelweide. 2006. Gedichte: *Mittelhochdeutscher Text und Übertragung, ausgewählt, übersetzt und mit einem Kommentar versehen von Peter Wapnewski.* 26th unchanged ed. Frankfurt am Main: Fischer Taschenbuch Verlag.

Musicians of Greece

During the fifth and fourth centuries BCE, the Classical Period in ancient Greece, performance music grew increasingly more complex. The poet-composer **Pindar (ca. 520–440 BCE)** filled commissions for a large number of victory odes, or *epinikia*, which were sung at the victory celebrations of Olympic athletes. A lyre or *aulos* (reed pipes) provided instrumental accompaniment. The reed-piper **Pronomos (ca. 470–390 BCE)** became a star performer in Athens, where he attracted attention by moving about on stage and using his face to register emotion. He made technical improvements to the *aulos*. The concert-lyre, or *cithara*, player **Stratonicus (ca. 410–360 BCE)**, traveled widely to participate in music competitions, from which he often departed with large cash prizes. He was an exponent of 'New Music,' which brought harmonic modulation, physical mimesis, and playing-to-the-crowd into Greek theater and music competitions.

∞

Five of Merriam's ten functions of music can be associated with these musicians:

THE FUNCTION OF AESTHETIC ENJOYMENT

The performance innovations of **Pronomos** and **Stratonicus** respresented new styles of musical expression, which furthered, and responded to, shifts in the aesthetic appreciation of music by concert-going listeners.

THE FUNCTION OF ENTERTAINMENT

Pronomos played during theatrical productions in Athens, and **Stratonicus** entertained audiences at music competitions in diverse regions of Hellenic influence.

THE FUNCTION OF SYMBOLIC REPRESENTATION

Some Greek songs represented human emotions and activities symbolically. **Pronomos** altered his facial expression as a way of helping audiences to recognize musical representations of emotion.

THE FUNCTION OF ENFORCING CONFORMITY TO SOCIAL NORMS

The *epinikia* created by the poet-composer **Pindar** celebrate victories of outstanding athletes. Because athletics was a pastime of the aristocracy, to which Pindar belonged, his *epinikia* had the effect of encouraging conformity to the traditional social norms of his class.

THE FUNCTION OF CONTRIBUTION TO THE INTEGRATION OF SOCIETY

During fifty-two active years, **Pindar** composed more than forty-five victory odes. Commmissioning such a composition from the famous poet, as many others had done, would have made the individual sponsor of athletics feel connected with other patrons, who lived widely dispersed around the Hellenic world.

Pindar (ca. 520–440 BCE)

The Greek poet-composer Pindar, who was active in the first half of the fifth century BCE, perfected the most specialized of musical genres. He wrote victory odes, or *epinikia*, and set them to music and dance, for the purpose of honoring athletes and others who had won crowns during the series of public festivals that constituted an Olympiad.

Pindar created many kinds of hymns and songs. A few centuries after his death in ca. 440 BCE, conservators at the famous library in Alexandria collated his writings:

> These scholars divided the large corpus into seventeen books (actually papyrus rolls) containing hymns to various gods (one roll); paeans, hymns addressed mainly to Apollo (one); dithyrambs, hymns addressed mainly to Dionysos (two); *prosodia*, hymns for approaching a god's shrine (two); *parthenia*, hymns sung by maidens (three); *hyporchemata*, dancing songs (two); *enkomia*, lighter songs of praise for men at banquets (one); *threnoi*, songs of lament (one); and *epinikia*, victory songs (four). (Race 1997: 279)

Since most of these works have vanished, the texts of the victory odes form the primary basis for Pindar's posthumous reputation. They provide tantalizing hints about the music and dance that must have contributed to their appeal.

Pindar was born ca. 520 BCE near Thebes in the Boeotian village of Cynoscephalae. A verse in one of his victory odes puts him within the Aigeidai clan of ancient Thebes and Sparta (*Pythian* 5.72–81). Like many other aspects of Pindar's life, the names of his close relatives are uncertain. His mother may have been called

Cleodice or Cledice, and his wife may have been called Megakleia. There is stronger evidence about a son, whose name was Daïphantus. Pindar composed a song for him to be performed at the Daphnephoria, a Theban religious festival. Citing a tradition of naming children for their grandparents, commentators have presumed that Pindar's father may also have had the name Daïphantus (Lefkowitz 2012: 61–69 & 146–147).

Myrtis of Anthedon, a female poet of the sixth century, is said to have been Pindar's teacher. After an initial exposure to the arts in Thebes, Pindar went on to study music, poetry, and choreography in Athens. Skopelinos, who may have been Pindar's uncle, taught him *aulos* (Greek musical pipes) and may have referred him to Lasus of Hermione for music instruction. He apprenticed in choral direction under Apollodoros or Agathokles (Lefkowitz 2012: 61–69; Schmidt 2005: 268–269). A brief ancient biography, the so-called *Ambrosian Vita*, reports that Pindar made a favorable impression by directing the dithyrambic choruses in his mentor's absence (Drachmann 1969: 1–3; translated in Lefkowitz 2012: 145–147).

Pindar lived for 80 years, during which his society changed profoundly and the region endured many wars small and large (Dillon & Garland 2013: 370–442; Murray 1993: 137–301). He avoided openly taking sides during conflicts among the Hellenic city-states, but he made clear his support for the homeland in its battles against foreign powers. Socially, he remained conservative, an aristocrat who consistently upheld the values of his class. Even as Athenian democracy strengthened through his lifetime, and aristocratic influence waned, Pindar managed successfully to practice his art.

The most serious conflicts took place as Greece struggled to deflect the expansionist aims of the Persian Empire. During the Persian War of 480–479, Pindar's home city of Thebes surrendered "earth and water" to the invaders and fought alongside them against Athens and Sparta. By praising Greek victories, Pindar emphasized his pan-Hellenic loyalties (cf. *Pythian* 1.75–78, *Isthmian* 5.46–50, *Isthmian* 8.6–11). He infuriated Thebans by describing Athens as "shining and violet-crowned and celebrated in song, / bulwark of Hellas" (frag. 76). His reputation in Greece emerged unscathed (Bowra 1964: 115–116).

In 498, Pindar composed his first *epinikion* in honor of a young sprinter from Thessaly, who won the 400-yard dash at Delphi (*Pythian* 10). A half-century later, in 446, he produced the last of his *epinikia*, an ode that praises a wrestling champion from the island of Aegina (*Pythian* 8). The texts of forty-five of Pindar's victory odes have survived to the present day in their entirety, while several others exist only in fragmentary form (Pindar & Race 1997: I 9–10). The numbers work out to approximately one Pindaric *epinikion* per year, on average.

Oswyn Murray has asserted that Greek society was "the first to exhibit the cult of the sportsman" (p. 202). While sharing enthusiastically in the tendency of his society to honor athletes, Pindar, like two other poet-composers of the pre-classical years, also exploited this 'cult' as a way of earning money. The poet Simonides (ca. 556–468) is thought to have established the profession of choral composer working for hire, and he is credited with developing the victory-ode genre. Simonides's nephew Bacchylides flourished as a composer of victory odes in the first half of the fifth century. He competed with Pindar for commissions (p. 205).

Olympiads took place over a four-year period, during which contests were held in four different places: Olympia, Delphi, Nemea, and the Isthmus. The Olympian contests and the Pythian contests (those held at Delphi) occurred only once in four years, whereas the Nemean and Isthmian contests repeated biennially.

Their schedules were staggered in such a way that one or two of these Pan-Hellenic festivals took place every year.

Victors had undoubtedly been rejoicing in their successes in the Olympiads already from the time of their inception early in the eighth century. Pindar imagines a victory celebration following the first of the Olympian games:

> [...] Then the lovely light
> of the moon's beautiful face
> lit up the evening,
>
> and all the sanctuary rang with *singing amid festive joy*
> in the fashion of victory celebration
> (*Olympian* 10, 73–77, emphasis added).

Kathryn Morgan has suggested that in the course of time the athletes' spontaneity mutated into formality, so that "instead of unrehearsed dancing and singing [...], a professional poet was hired to create the song and a chorus was hired to dance and sing it" (1993: 10).

The texts of Pindar's *epinikia* reveal that a lyre and/or an *aulos* accompanied a group of singers and dancers during their performance. To celebrate a victory in chariot-racing by Theron of Akragas in 476, for example, Pindar mixes "in due measure the varied strains of the lyre, the sound of pipes, and the setting of words" (*Olympian* 3.8). For the celebration of a similar victory by Hieron of Syracuse in 470, the stringed instrument initiates the proceedings:

> Golden Lyre, rightful possession of Apollo
> and the violet-haired Muses, to you the footstep listens
> as it begins the splendid celebration,
> and the singers heed your signals,
> whenever with your vibrations you strike up

the chorus-leading preludes
(*Pythian* 1.1–4).

Subsequent verses in this famous passage emphasize the potency of music: It quenches "the warring thunderbolt," calms the eagle on Zeus's scepter, and causes the war god Ares to slumber (*Pythian* 1.5–12).

Like many Greek choral works, most of Pindar's *epinikia* are written in a triadic metrical structure: The first of three stanzas in a triad is called a *strophē* (meaning 'turn'). The second is named *antistrophē* (meaning 'counterturn'), and the third is called an *epōidē* (meaning 'after-song'). This triadic sequence is repeated through the course of the poem. The labels 'turn,' 'counterturn,' and 'after-song' have been taken to indicate how dancers should move (Anderson 1997: 94–95).

The victory odes may have been set to traditional melodies (Anderson 1997: 106). In *Nemean* 4.44–45, Pindar speaks to his instrument, mentioning a mode, or 'harmony,' which came into usage during the colonization of Asia Minor: "Quickly now, sweet lyre, weave out this song too / in Lydian harmony …" He labels a section of music in *Pythian* 2 as "the Kastor song in Aeolic strains" (69). "Kastor song" is a reference to a traditional melody, the *Kastoreion*, used to celebrate victories in horse or chariot races. Pindar refers to it as well in *Isthmian* 1.16 and *Olympian* 1.100–102. "Aeolic" might refer either to the meter or to a musical mode (Anderson 1997: 96–97; Pindar & Race 1997: I57 n.3). Noting that the inventive sixth-century poet-composer Lasus of Hermione composed in the Aeolic mode, a recent study suggests that he inspired his pupil Pindar to musical innovation (Prauscello 2012).

Because Pindar sometimes makes use of the first-person singular pronoun, it would seem that he himself, or his proxy, took part in the performances. His patrons—wealthy aristocrats, princes, and tyrants who paid for the forty-five victory odes—were scattered around the Hellenic world: twelve in mainland Greece, eleven on the island of Aegina, seventeen in Sicily or southern Italy, three in Cyrene on the Libyan coast, and one on each of the islands of Rhodes and Tenedos (Race 1997: 283). If Pindar visited all these places in person, he was well-traveled indeed. He may have resided for as long as two years at the courts of wealthy Sicilian tyrants (Schmidt 2005: 270–271), who hosted other mainland Greek intellectuals as well, including Aeschylus (Landels 1999: 170). In some of Pindar's *epinikia* (e.g., *Pythian* 2.67–8), however, Pindar refers to dispatching an ode to his patron (Landels 1999: 6).

Although Pindar did not conceal the fact that he charged fees for his victory odes, two aspects of the practice seem to have troubled him. First, for an aristocrat, such as he was, to work as a professional musician was to break with Greek tradition. Secondly, to take money for praising a client could easily have been seen as compromising the sincerity of his poetic expression (Anderson 1997: 101; Bowra 1964: 355–357).

Pindar reveals his unease as a taker of fees in the first antistrophe of *Isthmian* 2, in which he refers to "soft voiced songs with their faces silvered over being sold / from the hand of honey-voiced Terpsichore" (7–8). Here Pindar is presenting his songs as prostitutes and the Muse Terpsichore as a madam (Pindar & Race 1997: II147 n.2). The phrase "silvered over" may have recalled to his listeners the practice of applying white lead to lighten the skin (cf. Bowra 1964: 356). In any case, the image could scarcely have been less flattering. Nevertheless, as Morgan notes, "the body of the ode moves towards a more balanced appreciation of the place of money in society: when used properly in pursuit of poetic glory, money is not necessarily to be despised" (1993: 14). Bowra asserts that Pindar was saved from saying anything against his own convictions by "his conception of his own calling, by his secure social position, even by the respect which was paid to poets in his time" (1964: 357).

All the ancient commentators regarded Pindar's *epinikia* as songs to be performed by a chorus (Carey 1991: 192). Some two millennia later, this view was challenged by certain scholars who argued that it was more likely for these complex texts to have been sung by a soloist (see Heath & Lefkowitz 1991). A lively debate has proved unable to resolve this issue (see Heath & Lefkowitz 1991 and Carey 1991; cf. Morgan 1993). Pindar's translator took note of the controversy in 1997 and attempted, it would seem, to achieve a compromise:

> The evidence for choral or solo performance is not conclusive either way, but given the fact that other Pindaric genres such as paeans, dithyrambs, partheneia, and hyporchemata were performed by choruses and that the formal features of the epinikia are similar to those of tragic choruses, it seems probable that at least some of the epinikia were performed by a choir that sang in unison and danced to the accompaniment of lyres or *auloi* or both combined (Pindar & Race 1997: 115).

More recently, an entry in *The New Grove* has adopted the traditional view of the *epinikion* as "choral lyric" (Anderson & Mathieson 2001).

The epinikean was a short-lived genre. The three major Greek composers of victory odes had no worthy successors, and the demand for such works appears to have faded rapidly with the deaths of Pindar and his younger contemporary, Bacchylides (Race 1997: 279; Schmidt 2005: 272). Despite the apparent narrowness in subject matter, Pindar's *epinikia* continued for many centuries to fascinate scholars and poets. He can be seen as a spokesman for his society, rather than as someone who was simply expressing personal attitudes and feelings. There is little doubt, however, that it was his poetics that provided the greatest attraction.

Pindar's verse is complex, difficult, and intriguing. He made frequent use of the *priamel*, a poetic device in which alternatives are listed as foils to the true subject. In praising the Olympian games, for example, he first extols water, gold, and the sun:

> Best is water, while gold, like fire blazing
> In the night, shines preeminent amid lordly wealth.
> But if you wish to sing of athletic games, my heart,
> Look no further than the sun
> For another star shining more warmly by day
> through the empty sky,
> Nor let us proclaim a contest greater than Olympia
> (*Olympian* 1.1–11).

Pindar sprinkled his texts with words from several ancient dialects, as well as with neologisms of his own creation. He interpolated hymns and mythical narratives into his poems. Distorted word order makes understanding of the *epinikia* difficult. He used meters that are so complicated that some writers mistakenly considered him to have been an exponent of free verse (Nisetich 1984: 438; Race 1997: 280).

Pindar mastered a style of composition known as *poikilia*. In his poems, he piled metaphors on top of images and analogies and avoided repetition of individual formulations (Race 1997: 280; Schmidt 2005: 259). The Roman poet Horace (65–8 BCE.) compared him to a flooding river:

> Like a rain-fed river running down
> from the mountains and bursting its banks—
> seething immeasurable, deep-mouthed,
> Pindar races along in spate,

> Winning the laurel of Apollo as he rolls
> new words down the bold current
> of his dithyrambs, rushing along in rhythms
> that know no law ...
> (Odes 4.2.5–12)

Pindar bound his complexities with precision. A recent scholar calls him "the most careful architect that poetry has ever had" (Schmidt 2005: 259). In later antiquity, he was classed as "one of the greatest of Hellenic poets" (Burnett 2008: 10). His admirers have included ancient Greek, Hellenistic, and Roman poets; numerous French and English writers of the Early Modern period and beyond; and German and English Romantics of the nineteenth century. Detractors have included Dryden, Tennyson, and in the twentieth century, Ezra Pound (Burnett 2008: 10–13; Pindar & Race 1997: I31–33; Robbins 2007: 270–271). Few individuals in history have had such an extended legacy.

References Cited

Anderson, Warren D. 1997. *Music and Musicians in Ancient Greece*. Ithaca: Cornell University Press.

Anderson, Warren, and Thomas J. Mathieson. 2001. Pindar. In *The New Grove Dictionary of Music and Musicians*, edited by S. Sadie and J. Tyrrell. New York: Grove.

Bowra, C. M. 1964. *Pindar*. Oxford: Clarendon Press.

Burnett, Anne Pippin. 2008. *Pindar, Ancients in Action*. London: Bristol Classical Press.

Carey, Christopher. 1991. The Victory Ode in Performance: The Case for the Chorus. *Classical Philology* 86 (3):192–200.

Dillon, Matthew, and Lynda Garland. 2013. *The Ancient Greeks: History and Culture from Archaic Times to the Death of Alexander*. London & New York: Routledge.

Drachmann, A. B. 1969. *Scholia vetera in Pindari carmina*. Editio Stereotypa ed. 3 vols. Amsterdam: Adolf M. Hakkert.

Heath, Malcolm, and Mary Lefkowitz. 1991. Epinicean Performance. *Classical Philology* 86 (3):173–191.

Horace and David Alexander West. 2000. *The Complete Odes and Epodes*. Translated by D. A. West. Oxford & New York: Oxford University Press.

Landels, John G. 1999. *Music in Ancient Greece and Rome*. London and New York: Routledge.

Lefkowitz, Mary R. 2012. *The Lives of the Greek Poets*. 2nd ed. Baltimore: Johns Hopkins University Press.

Morgan, Kathryn A. 1993. Pindar the Professional and the Rhetoric of the ΚΩΜΟΣ. *Classical Philology* 88 (1):1–15.

Murray, Oswyn. 1993. *Early Greece*. 2nd ed. Cambridge: Harvard University Press.

Nisetich, Frank J. 1984. Pindar. In *Great Foreign Language Writers*, edited by J. Vinson and D. L. Kirkpatrick. New York: St. Martin's Press.

Pindar and William H. Race. 1997. *Pindar, edited and translated by William H. Race*. 2 vols. Cambridge: Harvard University Press.

Prauscello, Lucia. 2012. Epinician Sounds: Pindar and Musical Innovation. In *Reading the Victory Ode*, edited by P. Agócs, C. Carey and R. Rawles. Cambridge & New York: Cambridge University Press.

Race, William H. 1997. Pindar (circa 518 B.C.–circa 438 B.C.). In *Ancient Greek Authors*, edited by W. W. Briggs. Detroit, Washington, & London: Gale Research.

Robbins, Emmet. 2007. Pindarus (Pindar, the Greek Writer of Choral Lyrics). In *Brill's New Pauly*, edited by H. Cancik and H. Schneider. Leiden & Boston: Brill.

Schmidt, Michael. 2005. *The First Poets: Lives of the Ancient Greek Poets*. 1st American ed. New York: Alfred A. Knopf.

Further Reading

West, M. L. 1992. *Ancient Greek Music*. Oxford: Clarendon Press.

Pronomos (ca. 470–390 BCE)

Classical Greek audiences thrilled to the way the musician Prono-mos moved about on stage and used his face to register emotion. Aristophanes mentions Pronomos in the play *The Ecclesiazusae* from ca. 390 BCE. Thebes, Pronomos's native city in the province of Boeotia, erected a statue in his honor. He became a star enter-tainer in Athens at a time when virtuosity and professionalism were challenging traditional attitudes to music (Anderson & Mathieson 2001; Kemp 1966; West 1992: 366–367; Wilson 2007 & 2010).

Pronomos played the *aulos*, a versatile wind instrument of the times (Bélis 2001). Aulos-players performed in cultic rites and ac-companied theatrical choruses. The aulos marked time for oars-men on triremes. Slave girls entertained revelers with this instru-ment. During the sixth century BCE, solo aulos and aulos-accompanied voice were performance categories at music compe-titions. Through the course of the fifth century, the aulos became increasingly common in professional entertainment on stage.

The hollow pipes of the aulos had either single or double reeds to excite the sound and finger holes to vary the pitch. Although single-piped auloi were not uncommon, a doubled version served more often in concerts. The performer controlled one pipe with the right hand and the other with the left, while blowing simulta-neously through the reeds of both, which were inserted into the mouth.

The best reeds originated from Lake Copais in Boeotia, where the instrument had traditionally been used by cultic groups. Here, in the province in which Pronomos's family was rooted, aulos-playing developed into something of a national art. Boeotia was one of two Greek regions, the other being Argolis, that were known in classical times for the excellence of their aulos virtuosi (Bélis 2001; Kemp 1966: 221; Wilson 2010: 188–191).

Pronomos was born around 470 BCE and died some 80 years later (Wilson 2007). Curiously, a painting from ca. 400 BCE depicts him as young and beardless and with abundant curly hair, even though he was then about 70 years old. The apparent contradiction has been attributed to a stylistic convention that dictated youthful idealizations (Wilson 2010: 187). As a mature man, Pronomos may not have been clean-shaven, for in Aristophanes's *The Ecclesiazusae*, the protagonist Praxagora refers to "the beard of Pronomos" while ridiculing an effeminate city leader (cf. Wilson 2010: 197, 200–201).

The painting appears on a relic, a mixing bowl known as the Pronomos *krater*, at the National Archeological Museum in Naples, Italy. It shows the musician slouching on a *klismos* chair, while playing or, more likely, warming-up on a double aulos. He wears an elaborate robe and has a garland in his hair. A satyr play appears to be in preparation, and Pronomos is the central figure in the production. His foot rests on a *kroupeza*, a type of clapper used to mark time for the chorus (Landels 1999: 22)

In performance, Pronomos would certainly have been standing, and he may have worn a strap known as a *phorbeia* to support his cheek muscles and lips. Like a beard, however, the brace would have restricted the facial expressiveness for which he was famous. M. L. West contends that Pronomos was able to maintain facial composure even while blowing strongly (1992: 106). With respect to the comment in Aristophanes's script, Peter Wilson points out that the playwright may have been joking—referring to a beard on someone who was actually clean-shaven (2010: 200–201).

Although the details of Pronomos's appearance are contested, there is agreement that he moved about expressively on stage. He was not unique in this aspect of performance; indeed he was part of a growing trend, but he was apparently one of its best practitioners, for his name was associated with the fashion. Aristotle later described such mimesis as vulgar: for an aulos-player to twist and twirl on stage or bump into the chorus leader so as to illustrate the text amounted to catering to an unrefined audience (*Politics*, Book 8, part II; *Poetics*, part XXVI).

Pronomos's most historically significant contribution in music involves a technical advancement. Greek tunes traditionally conformed to one or another of an accepted set of musical 'modes,' referring to the arrangement of tones in a musical scale. Because only a limited number of tones can be sounded by covering or uncovering finger holes on a wind instrument, the performer was effectively limited to playing in a single mode on any given aulos. Pronomos invented a way to circumvent this limitation. His invention probably involved augmenting the openings with additional holes that could be covered or uncovered with the help of rotatable sleeves (Landels 1999: 35–38). By today's standards, this would seem a rather crude way to control tonality, but in the context of the times, it supported a tendency to modulation that enabled Greek musicians to expand on traditional forms. A contemporary of Pronomos, Diodorus of Thebes, is credited with a related invention (West 1992: 87).

Pronomos was also a composer of music and probably of words as well. He created a choral hymn (a *prosodion*) for the Chalkidians to use in their processions to Delos. His songs and those of the older Sakadas of Argos were performed in celebration of the rebuilding in 369 BCE of the walls of Messene (Gevaert 1875–1881: II478).

Three generations of Pronomos's family were musically active in Athens, the cultural center of the Greek world. Pronomos's son Oeniades, who like his father was a professional aulos-player, accompanied winning choruses at the Thargelia of 384/383 and 354/353 BCE. In the following century, another descendent, who was also named Pronomos, directed a victorious boys chorus at the Dionysia of 271/270 BCE (Wilson 2010: 196–197).

References Cited

Anderson, Warren, and Thomas J. Mathieson. 2001. Pronomus. In *The New Grove Dictionary of Music and Musicians*, edited by S. Sadie and J. Tyrrell. New York: Grove.

Bélis, Annie. 2001. Aulos. In *The New Grove Dictionary of Music and Musicians*, edited by S. Sadie and J. Tyrrell. New York: Grove.

Gevaert, François Auguste. 1875–1881. *Histoire et théorie de la musique de l'antiquité* 2 vols. Gand: Typ. C. Annoot-Braeckman.

Kemp, J. A. 1966. Professional Musicians in Ancient Greece. *Greece & Rome* 13 (2):213–222.

Landels, John G. 1999. *Music in Ancient Greece and Rome*. London and New York: Routledge.

West, M. L. 1992. *Ancient Greek Music*. Oxford: Clarendon Press.

Wilson, Peter. 2007. Pronomos and Potamon: Two Pipers and Two Epigrams. *The Journal of Hellenic Studies* 127:141–149.

———. 2010. The Man and the Music (and the Choregos?). In *The Pronomos Vase and Its Context*, edited by O. Taplin and R. Wyles. Oxford & New York: Oxford University Press.

Further Reading

Chaniotis, Angelos. 2009. A Few Things Hellenistic Audiences Appreciated in Musical Performances. In *La Musa dimenticata: Aspetti dell'esperianza musicale greca in età ellenistica*, edited by M. C. Martinelli, F. Pelosi and C. Pernigotti. Pisa: Edizioni della Normale.

Edmonds, J. M. 1927. *Lyra Graeca*. 3 vols. London: William Heinemann.

Michaelides, Solon. 1978. *The Music of Ancient Greece: An Encyclopaedia*. London: Faber and Faber Limited.

Pickard-Cambridge, Arthur Wallace. 1968. *The Dramatic Festivals of Athens by the late Sir Arthur Pickard-Cambridge*. Revised by John Gould and D. M. Lewis. 2nd ed. London: Oxford at the Clarendon Press.

Pöhlmann, Egert, Olympia Psychopedis-Frangou, and Rudolf Maria Brandl. 1995. Griechenland. In *Die Musik in Geschichte und Gegenwart*, edited by L. Finscher. Kassel: Bärenreiter

Wilson, Peter. 2002. The Musicians Among the Actors. In *Greek and Roman Actors: Aspects of an Ancient Profession*, edited by P. E. Easterling and E. Hall. Cambridge: Cambridge University Press.

Stratonicus (ca. 410–360 BCE)

The Greek musician Stratonicus performed solo on the *cithara*, a concert version of the lyre, in the years between approximately 410 and 360 BCE. He was an outstanding citharist and an early example of a successful itinerant professional. Because Stratonicus was clever with words, he formulated a large number of witticisms, which were collected and published by Athenaeus of Naucratus (Athenaeus 8:347f–8:352d).

Stratonicus is said to have introduced *polychordiā* (multiplicity of notes) into solo *cithara*-playing. He most likely played on one of the newer instruments that were fitted with as many as eleven strings. He is also remembered as a music theoretician, who developed a visual representation of the musical scales, and as a teacher (Athenaeus 8: 352c; West 1992: 367–368; Wilson 2004: 290).

Scholars have placed Stratonicus within a movement known as "The New Music," which originated in Athens late in the fifth century BCE. The New Music brought harmonic modulation, physical mimesis, and playing-to-the-crowd into Greek theater and music competitions. Stratonicus's professional success in performing *cithara* music without song was provocative within an ideological environment in which melody and rhythm were deemed subordinate to *logos* (or text). He was a star entertainer who bragged of making money in his trade, in contrast to the refined upper-class amateurs, whose compositions and performances had dominated high musical culture in the past (Csapo 2004s; West 1992: 356–372; Wilson 2004: 303–306).

Perhaps the most striking departure associated with The New Music was the practice of modulating seamlessly between different musical modes within a given piece. This practice—also referred to as "bending"—became possible when technological developments expanded the range of just six or seven notes that had been available earlier on concert instruments (West 1992: 183, 194–196, 229–230, 356–357). Modulation is a subtle concept that called for both theoretical underpinning and practical training. Stratonicus was able to provide both. He became "a successful teacher with many students," according to the fourth-century comic poet Philetaerus (Gilula 2000: 424).

Stratonicus's income depended upon doing well in musical competitions, for which he had to travel long distances from his home base in Athens. His witticisms focus on this aspect of his career, which took him to venues on the Greek mainland and beyond: to Macedonia, Thrace, Asia Minor, the Black Sea, Rhodes, and Cyprus. Stratonicus seems to have interacted with many strata of society, including common folk, fellow musicians, and royalty. The interpretation of the published witticisms demands circumspection, however, because Athenaeus collected his information from earlier sources long after Stratonicus died. Nevertheless, they present an intriguing picture of the musician: sharp-tongued and arrogant, he expresses his disdain for the backwater places he visits, his disgust when audiences fail to respond, and his scorn for less-able competitors (Athenaeus 8:347f–8:352d; Gilula 2000).

The witticisms make it clear that Stratonicus took little pleasure in moving about in the world. He asserts that he followed an itinerant lifestyle simply because it was a way for him to earn money:

> When someone asked why he traveled all over Greece, rather than settling down in one city, [Stratonicus] told him that the Muses had awarded him all the Greeks as his source of support, and that he was allowed to extract pay from them as a

consequence of their lack of musical talent (8:350e).

He seems never to have come across a place he liked. One rapid-fire burst of one-liners puts down Aenus, Pontus, Rhodes, Heracleia, Byzantium (this, "the armpit of Greece"), Leucas—and Heracleia for a second time:

> He used to look both ways when he went out through the gates of Heracleia; when someone asked why he did this, he said that he was ashamed to be seen, because it was like leaving a whorehouse (8:852d).

He frets about the quality of available drinking water (8:352a) and pillories bathhouses for their cold water and dirty soap, and for charging extra to serve travelers (8:351b, 8:351e, & 8:352a).

In the witticisms, Stratonicus uses puns, satire, and poetic citations to criticize competitors and unresponsive listeners. A comment about a Rhodian crowd expresses his annoyance at audience apathy:

> He put on a show in Rhodes, and when no one applauded, he said on his way out of the theater: "Why do I think I'm going to get money out of you, when you won't do something that's yours for free?" (8:350b).

After winning a music contest, he vaunts his victory in a trophy inscription:

> When [Stratonicus] defeated the other competitors in Sicyon, he dedicated the trophy in the sanctuary of Asclepius with the inscription: "Stra-

tonicus, from the spoils of bad *cithara*-players"
(8:351f).

Applying literary wit, he adapts a verse from the *Iliad* to put down a fellow musician:

> Once when [Stratonicus] was invited to listen to a citharode, he said after the performance (*Il.* 16.250):
>> The father granted him one request, but refused the other.
>
> When someone asked "What do you mean?", he said: "He granted him the ability to play the *cithara* badly, but refused him the ability to sing well" (8:350d).

Stratonicus attacks one individual after another: a bad piper at a sacrifice would do better to remain silent (8:349c), a citharode sings like an ox (8:349c–d), an untalented citharode shows off a pupil to his own disadvantage (8:349f), a piper 'plays' a woman on his pipe (8:350f), a musician has an unmusical name (8:351b), a lyre student displays incompetence (8:351b), a former gardener should have stuck to his trade (8:351d), a piper makes music that sounds like burping (8:351e), a composition could have been composed by a crab (8:351f), and a poet takes false pride in a student (8:352b); and Stratonicus sends a harp player packing with a rude pun (8:352b).

Stratonicus's verbal aggression against fellow performers would appear to have been his way of making publicity. It is an approach that has survived in the entertainment industry.

Two anecdotes *about* Stratonicus report the musician's demise while visiting Cyprus. According to both, his tongue proved too sharp when dealing with royalty. The first of the anecdotes says that Stratonicus was drowned for insulting Queen Biothea

(8:349e); the second, that "the Cyprian king Nicocles forced him to drink poison, because he poked fun at the king's sons" (8:352d).

References Cited

Athenaeus. 2008. *The Learned Banqueters.* Translated by S. D. Olson, *Loeb Classical Library.* Cambridge: Harvard University Press.

Csapo, Eric. 2004. The Politics of the New Music. In *Music and the Muses: The Culture of 'Mousikē' in the Classical Athenian City,* edited by P. Murray and P. Wilson. Oxford & New York: Oxford University Press.

Gilula, Dwora. 2000. Stratonicus, the Witty Harpist. In *Athenaeus and His World: Reading Greek Culture in the Roman Empire,* edited by D. Braund and J. Wilkins. Exeter: University of Exeter Press.West, M. L. 1992. *Ancient Greek Music.* Oxford: Clarendon Press.

West, M. L. 1992. *Ancient Greek Music.* Oxford: Clarendon Press.

Wilson, Peter. 2004. Athenian Strings. In *Music and the Muses: The Culture of 'Mousikē' in the Classical Athenian City,* edited by P. Murray and P. Wilson. Oxford & New York: Oxford University Press.

Further Reading

Barker, Andrew. 2000. Athenaeus on Music. In *Athenaeus and His World: Reading Greek Culture in the Roman Empire,* edited by D. Braund and J. Wilkins. Exeter: University of Exeter Press.

Musicians of India

Muslim incursions that led to the founding of the Delhi Sultanate in 1206 CE brought Persian and Arabic elements into the 'Hindustani' music of northern India, but had only a smaller effect on the 'Carnatic' music of the South. The Hindu composer **Jayadeva (12th century CE)** created a musical setting of the *Gītagovinda*, a legend in which Krishna, an incarnation of Lord Vishnu, has a love affair with a cowherdess. This work, which has influenced Rajput paintings and inspired dance performances, is still part of the Carnatic tradition. The poet-composer **Amīr K̲h̲usrau Delhavī (1253–1325 CE)**, who was the son of a Turkic immigrant father and an Indian mother, served under the sultans in Delhi. He is credited with making the *ghazal* love song, the *tarana* singing style, and Sufi *qauls* part of Hindustani music.

∞

Four of Merriam's ten functions of music can be associated with these musicians:

THE FUNCTION OF AESTHETIC ENJOYMENT
Amīr Khusrau Delhavī enriched the stylistic repertory in Delhi by blending Persian and Arabic elements with the local musical tradition.

THE FUNCTION OF ENTERTAINMENT

Amīr Khusrau Delhavī performed music that contributed to the festive mood at the *majlis* held in the Sultan of Delhi's palace.

THE FUNCTION OF SYMBOLIC REPRESENTATION

Conservative imams in Delhi considered the music composed and sung by **Amīr Khusrau Delhavī** to be symbolic of culturally defined evil.

THE FUNCTION OF VALIDATION OF SOCIAL INSTITUTIONS AND RELIGIOUS RITUAL

The dramatic lyrical work known as the *Gītagovinda*, which **Jayadeva** created, validates Hinduism by expressing metaphorically the power of an individual to elicit a divine response. **Amīr Khusrau Delhavī** bridged the world of the secular court with that of mystical Islam. By composing and performing religious songs known as *qauls*, he helped to validate Sufism on the Indian subcontinent.

Jayadeva (12th century CE)

A charming Hindu legend tells of the dance of Krishna, the eighth *avatāra* (or incarnation) of Lord Vishnu, with a group of *gopīs* (milkmaids or cowherdesses). Krishna was raised by Nanda, a cowherd, and his wife Yasoda, and so it was to be expected that in his adolescence, he would be attracted to *gopīs*. In the legend, Krishna walks one night into the forest at Vrindavan, where he was living, while playing a flute. Finding the music irresistible, the *gopīs* follow him to the bank of the Jumna River. Here they gather in a circle and perform the *rāsa-līlā*, or 'dance of divine love.' In a popular rendering of this story, Krishna magically creates copies of himself, so that every *gopī* has Krishna as her partner (Miller 1977: 25).

The legend seems to suggest the attraction and extent of divine love, which reaches beyond individuals to the greater multitude. A complementary view emerges in a dramatic lyrical work known as the *Gītagovinda*, which was composed in the twelfth century CE by the eastern Indian poet-composer named Jayadeva. The *Gītagovinda* describes in eight cantos and twenty-four songs the power of an individual to attract a divine response.

The story in the *Gītagovinda* encompasses two nights and the intervening day, during which an unabashedly sexual relationship develops between Krishna and Rādhā, his favorite among the *gopīs*. After an initial encounter, Krishna appears to abandon Rādhā. While he is making love to others, Rādhā's jealousy keeps her apart, and yet her longing for Krishna intensifies. Made aware of her condition, Krishna now finds her irresistibly attractive. He sings in the tenth canto (Miller 1977: 112):

> You are my ornament, my life,
> My jewel in the sea of existence.

> Be yielding to me forever,
> My heart fervently pleads!
> Rādhā, cherished love,
> Abandon your baseless pride!
> Love's fire burns my heart—
> Bring wine in your lotus mouth!

Surrender intermingles with triumph, when at the end Rādhā once again abandons herself to her divine lover.

Indians have revered the *Gītagovinda* for many centuries. It became popular first in eastern India, where it was composed, but soon it was being performed as well in other regions of the subcontinent. As early as the thirteenth century, it had reached Gujarat, in western India, where a temple inscription from that period quotes from the composition. In 1499, Mahārāja Pratāparudradeva ordered dancers in the Jagannātha Temple of Puri to perform the Jayadeva's songs nightly, a practice that reportedly continued until at least the late 1900s. Even after some 800 years, the songs of the *Gītagovinda* were still being sung in religious and other settings, notably in Bengal and Orissa, but also in the southern state of Kerala, in Nepal to the north, and in places in-between. The *Gītagovinda* also influenced Rajput paintings and has inspired dance performance (Donaldson1995: 45–47; Mandal 2006; Miller 1977: ix–xi; Ramakrishna 2010: 141; Siegel & Jayadeva 1978: 229).

Jayadeva composed his masterpiece in Sanskrit, adopting different meters for the songs and the intervening classical *kāvya* verses. The songs have eight stanzas with a repeating refrain, a form known as *aṣṭapadī* (meaning 'eight stanzas'), and they follow a musical meter that resembles the meters of medieval Indian vernacular poetry. In early manuscripts, the *rāgas* (melodic frameworks) and *tālas* (time measures) were specified for the various songs. In the absence of notation, these *rāgas* and *tālas* have changed in the intervening years. Singers now decide for themselves which musical basis they should use (Miller 1977: 7–14; Panigrahi 1995; Singh & Sharma 1995: 106).

The ability to compose on a religious theme in classical and vernacular meters in the language of Sanskrit presupposes an appreciable level of education and knowledge. Jayadeva refers to himself in the *Gītagovinda* as a *kavi* (a master poet or bard), a profession that was normally filled at the time by Brahmins, members of the small upper class of Hindu intellectuals and priests. Siegel has described the difficult learning path of aspiring *kavis*, who had to immerse themselves in classical Hindu texts, the Epics, ancient poetry, and the various *śāstras* (scriptural commentaries), and also to acquire proficiency in the arts and sciences—lexicography, grammar, poetics, erotics, vernacular languages, etc.—on their way of mastering the rhetorical complexities and the literary and aesthetic conventions of Sanskrit *kāvya* (Siegel & Jayadeva 1978: 206–208).

Aspiring *kavis* would visit courts and attend literary meetings for the purpose of perfecting their craft and impressing potential patrons. At an assembly of scholars and *kavis*, a young poet might be asked to extemporize on any conventional subject. One of the poems attributed to Jayadeva may be a response to such a challenge, that of incorporating within a single verse about Shiva the Sanskrit words for earth, water, fire, air, and ether (Siegel & Jayadeva: 203). This practice of poetical *Wanderschaft* for aspiring *kavis* might help to explain a long-held belief among scholars that Jayadeva served as a court poet at the court of Raja Lakṣmaṇasena of Bengal (see, for example, Chatterji 1973: 3–8).

Much of our knowledge of Jayadeva comes from legends formed after his lifetime. However, the text of the *Gītagovinda* does provide some specific biographical detail. The tenth verse in the third canto identifies the poet's place of birth as "Kindubilva village" (Miller 1977: 84). In the twelfth canto, Jayadeva vaunts his own musical and poetic talents, together with his religious credentials (p. 125):

> His musical skill, his meditation on Vishnu,
> His vision of reality in the erotic mood,
> His graceful play in these poems,
> All show that master-poet Jayadeva's soul
> Is in perfect tune with Krishna—
> Let blissful men of wisdom purify the world
> By singing his Gītagovinda.

In the verse following this one, Jayadeva provides the names of his father and mother, Bhojadeva and Rāmadevī. He urges that his poem be recited by "devotees like sage Parāśara." Legends describe Jayadeva's parents as Brahmin immigrants from Kanauj and Parāśara as a friend who accompanied him on pilgrimages (Siegel and Jayadeva 1978: 42 & 285 n.193).

Although scholars of Bengal, Orissa, and Bihar have claimed Jayadeva for their regions, several recent publications favor Orissa (Donaldson 1995; Ghosh & Mahābharātī 2011: 467–468; Miller 2005). They place the village of Jayadeva's birth, now known as Kenduli Sassan, on the Prachi River and close to the city of Puri. (The term Sassan identifies the Brahmin section of this village.) Apparently acknowledging such a conclusion, in 2009 the Indian Post Office issued commemorative stamps in Orissa in honor of Jayadeva and his *Gītagovinda* (see the Orissan news section in the online edition of *The Hindu*, July 28, 2009).

Legendary accounts associate Jayadeva with the temple of Jagannātha in Puri, an impressive edifice that dates from the era in which the poet lived. Formerly a tribal god, Jagannātha later became identified with Vishnu. Near the start of the twelfth century, Anantavarman Chodaganga of Kalinga had conquered Orissa, and it is supposed that he built the temple as a way to appease vanquished Orissan tribesmen. Like the rulers of the Ganga Dynasty, which Anantavarman founded, Jayadeva became a devotee of Vishnu (Kulke and Rothermund 2010: 101, 129, & 131; Miller 1977: 5).

The legends relate that Jayadeva abandoned scholarship to become a wandering ascetic, but again took up a worldly existence after a Brahmin from Puri convinced Jayadeva to marry his daughter. The Brahmin had dedicated the girl as a dancer at the Jagannātha Temple. He claimed nevertheless that it was the wish of the Lord Jagannātha that the marriage take place. This life-changing experience purportedly led Jayadeva to create the *Gītagovinda*: He composed, while his wife danced (Donaldson 1995: 42).

Other legends that were collected and published in the seventeenth century describe truly miraculous occurrences, such as Vishnu's reattachment of Jayadeva's severed hands and resurrection of Jayadeva's deceased wife. Through these stories, the poet acquired saintly status in the *Vaiṣṇavan* branch of the Hindu religion (Siegel & Jayadeva 1978: 213–227).

Jayadeva praised his own skill as a musician, which raises the possibility that he may have performed his own songs. According to a recent account, Jayadeva and his wife traveled to the south, where he sang and she danced a version of the *Gītagovinda* (Ghosh & Mahābhāratī 2011: 468). In general, songs consist of lyric and melody, and a suitable combination of the two is normally the basis of musical appeal. Be that as it may, the persistent popularity of Jayadeva's songs must rest primarily on the lyrics, since the melodic structures have varied through the centuries. Perhaps the musical quality of his poetry embodies the true greatness of Jayadeva as a composer.

References Cited

Chatterji, Suniti Kumar. 1973. *Jayadeva*. New Delhi: Sahitya Akademi.

Donaldson, Thomas E. 1995. Gopinatha and Jayadeva. In *Jayadeva and Gītagovinda in the Traditions of Orissa*, edited by D. Pathy, B. Panda and B. K. Rath. New Delhi: Harman Pub. House

Ghosh, Nikhil, and Saṅgit Mahābhārātī. 2011. *The Oxford Encyclopaedia of the Music of India*. 3 vols. New Delhi & New York: Oxford University Press.

Kulke, Hermann, and Dietmar Rothermund. 2010. *A History of India*. 5th ed. London & New York: Routledge.

Mandal, Paresh Chandra. 2006. Jayadeva. In *Banglapedia: The National Encyclopedia of Bangladesh*, ed Sirajul Islam. http://www.banglapedia.org (accessed Jan. 24, 2013).

Miller, Barbara Stoler. 1977. *Love Song of the Dark Lord: Jayadeva's Gītagovinda*. New York: Columbia University Press.

———. 2005. Jayadeva. In *Encyclopedia of Religion*, edited by L. Jones. Detroit: Macmillan Reference USA.

Panigrahi, Nila Mādhava. 1995. Music. In *Jayadeva and Gītagovinda in the Traditions of Orissa*, edited by D. Pathy, B. Panda and B. K. Rath. New Delhi: Harman Pub. House.

Ramakrishna, Lalita. 2010. *Sampradāya Saṅgīta: Indian Classical Musical Tradition*. 2nd ed, Kalpatharu Research Academy Publications. Delhi: B. R. Rhythms.

Siegel, Lee, and Jayadeva. 1978. *Sacred and Profane Dimensions of Love in Indian Traditions, as Exemplified in the Gītagovinda of Jayadeva*. Delhi, London, & New York: Oxford University Press.

Singh, Jaideva, and Prem Lata Sharma. 1995. *Indian Music*. 1st ed, *Sangeet-Paridarshini Series*. Calcutta: Sangeet Research Academy; Sole distributor, Vishwavidyalaya Prakashan.

Further Reading

Chakravarti, Monmohan. 1906. Sanskrit Literature in Bengal During the Sena Rule. *Journal and Proceedings of the Asiatic Society of Bengal* 2 (5):157–176.

Holroyde, Peggy. 1972. *The Music of India*. New York - Washington: Praeger Publishers.

Pathy, Dinanath, Bhagaban Panda, and B. K. Rath, eds. 1995. *Jayadeva and Gītagovinda in the Traditions of Orissa*. New Delhi: Harman Pub. House.

Qureshi, Regula, et al. 2001. India. In *The New Grove Dictionary of Music and Musicians*, edited by S. Sadie and J. Tyrrell. New York: Grove.

Raghavan, V., ed. 1979. *Composers*. New Delhi: Publications Division, Ministry of Information and Broadcasting, Govt. of India.

Tagore, Sourindro Mohun. 1982. *Six Principal Ragas: With a Brief View of Hindu Music*. Delhi. New Delhi: Neeraj Pub. House; Distributed by D.K. Publishers' Distributors. Original edition, 1877.

Amīr Khusrau Delhavī (1253–1325 CE)

The poet-composer Amīr Khusrau Delhavī (1253–1325 CE) introduced Persian and Arabic elements into Indian music. His contributions include songs based on the *ghazal*, a form of Persian love poetry; *tarana*, a style of singing in which melodies are rendered in strings of Arabic and Persian syllables; and *qauls*, lyrics sung by Indian Sufis during religious services.

Born of a Turkic immigrant father and an Indian mother, Amīr Khusrau embodied the syncretism of Persian and South Asian cultures. His father, Sayf al-Dīn Maḥmūd, who may once have been a slave, became an officer in the army of Sultan Īltutmish (r. 1211–1236). His mother was the daughter of 'Imād al-Mulk, a wealthy Indian Muslim noble (Hardy 1960: 444; Raghavan 1979: 67).

Sayf al-Dīn Maḥmūd died when his son was just eight years old. The orphan moved into the luxurious household of his maternal grandfather, where he received personal instruction in theology, the Qu'ran, Persian, Arabic, logic, calligraphy, and poetry. He learned to appreciate music and began himself to write poems (Raghavan 1979: 67).

'Imād al-Mulk was astonishingly rich and almost incredibly long-lived. He is said to have served eighty years at court and survived until the age of one hundred thirteen (Sharma 2005: 15–17). In his personal service, he reportedly had "two hundred Turkish and two thousand Hindu slaves and servants and a thousand troopers" (Mirza 1962: 31). Leading scholars, poets, and musicians attended his *majlis* (festive gatherings), offering inspiration to the aspiring young poet-composer.

The tragedy of death and the contrasting experience of extreme luxury and high culture during childhood prefigured Amīr Khusrau's adult existence. He rose to the very top of his profession. He became wealthy and universally respected. Along the way, however, he suffered the brutality of warfare and had to survive dangerous court intrigues. At the Sultanate in Delhi, several of Amīr Khusrau's sovereigns were ruthlessly murdered by their successors (Kulke & Rothermund 2010: 117–123).

Despite the recurring violence, Amīr Khusrau managed to compose and publish a great number of works in poetry and prose. His first *divan*, a collection of poems written during adolescence, appeared when he was just twenty years old. From age twenty-four until his death at age seventy-two, he was a courtier. Initially patronized by princes and nobles, he later became the sultan's chief poet. He published four additional *divans*; a group of five romances known as the *Khamsa*; the *Ghazali y yāt*, or lyrical poems; several substantial prose pieces; and a number of historical poems that depict contemporary events (Hardy 1960: 444).

Early on in his career, Amīr Khusrau served as *nadīm* (boon companion) to 'Ala' al-Dīn Kishlū Khān, a nephew of Sultan Ghiyāth al-Dīn Balban (r. 1266–1287). After two years, he fell out of favor with this patron, apparently as a result of having accepted a gift from the emperor's younger son, Nāsir al-Dīn Bughrā Khān. Prince Bughrā Khān now became the Amīr Khusrau's second benefactor. With him, the poet traveled to the Punjab for a short time and then on to Bengal to quell a rebellion (Hardy 1960: 444; Sharma 2005: 20).

After Amīr Khusrau returned to Delhi, in 1280 he accepted the patronage of Muḥammad Kā'ān Malik, eldest son of Sultan Balban (Hardy 1960: 444). This prince has been described as a "warm, generous, and charming" patron of the arts, who was "fond of poetry and gathered the best poets around him" (Sharma 2005:

21). His court at Multan (now part of Pakistan) was notable as a cultural center.

Tragedy struck in 1284. Mongol invaders killed the prince and took the young poet-composer captive. It was a horrid, unforgettable experience for Amīr Khusrau. Brutally force-marched over a considerable distance, he eventually managed to slip away, when his mounted captor paused to quench his thirst, and that of his horse, at the side of a river (Mirza 1962: 60–62).

Amīr Khusrau returned to Delhi. He spent some time with his mother before taking service at Avadh in what is now Uttar Pradesh with the new governor, the freedman Malik 'Alī Sardjāndār Ḥātam Khān. In 1289, while Amīr Khusrau was visiting Delhi, Sultan Mu'izzuddīn Kayqubād (r. 1287–1290) commissioned a narrative poem about the sultan's reunion with his father Bughrā Khān, who had been the poet's second patron (Hardy 1960: 444; Sharma 2005: 23).

Sultan Kayqubād was overthrown in 1290, and when the first ruler in the Khaljī succession, Djalāl al-Dīn Khaljī (r. 1290–1296), took power, he called Amīr Khusrau into the court. Amīr Khusrau had now progressed from serving provincial officials to become the chief poet of the sultanate, a position that he held until his death in 1325. Djalāl al-Dīn Khaljī was a zealous supporter of the arts. He awarded Amīr Khusrau, officially named the keeper of the Qur'an, a stipend of 1200 *tankas*, plus horses, clothing, and slaves (Hardy 1960: 444; Raghavan1979: 67; Sharma 2005: 23 & 26).

Djalāl al-Dīn's nephew 'Alā' al-Dīn al-Dīn Khaljī succeeded to the throne upon the death of his uncle in 1296. He reigned until 1316. This sultan oversaw an exceptional cultural renaissance in Delhi, the greatest in the city until the Mughals took power some two centuries later. His reign marked Amīr Khusrau's most prolific period, when the poet-composer was in his forties and fifties and at the peak of his creative abilities. This was the time also in which Amīr Khusrau became personally involved in the religious movement known as Sufism (Hardy 1960: 444; Sharma 2005: 24–26).

Amīr Khusrau managed to retain favor with the subsequent three sultans, all of whom were murdered by their successors. Ḳutb al-Dīn Mubarak Shāh (r. 1316–1320) seized power in a bloody coup in which he killed his own brother. He in turn was killed by his male lover, Khusro Khan, who survived in office for only a few months before dying at the instigation of Ghiyāth al-Dīn Tughluq (r. 1320–1325), a reputedly pious and orthodox Muslim, who founded the Tughluq dynasty (Kulke & Rothermund 2010: 123).

According to an anecdote recorded a few years later, Ghiyāth al-Dīn died when his son Muḥammad Shah Tughluq arranged to crush him to death in a collapsible wooden building (Ibn Battuta et al. 1971: 654–655). This Tughluq ruled from 1325 to 1351. Amīr Khusrau was still alive for only a few months at the start of his reign (Hardy 1960: 444; Sharma 2005: 33–34).

In addition to linking West- and South-Asian literary and musical traditions, Amīr Khusrau bridged the world of the court with that of mystical Islam. He became a disciple of Shaikh Niẓāmuddīn Auliya (1238–1325), leader of the *Chishtiya* order in Delhi, whom Indian Sufis revere as a saint. Services held at Auliya's *khanqah* (hospice) in Delhi attracted Sufis as well as representatives of other Indian religious orders, with whom the Shaikh would debate. Here, Amīr Khusrau experienced the practice of *samā'*, in which music and dancing lift believers into a state of mystical ecstasy. The *khanqah* broadened his musical horizon, and he took to composing religious lyrics. His *qauls* were sung at the Sufi gatherings, as were settings of his Persian and Arabic love lyrics known as *ghazals*. Both types of song were also performed at the festive *majlis* in the palace, and both have become staples of Indian classical music (Katz 2001; Sharma 2005: 27–32; Trivedi 2010: 70–73).

Conservative clerics in Delhi, "the raging orthodoxy," as Shabab Sarmadee has termed them (1975: 246), strongly disapproved of musical entertainment. Despite their attitude, however, music thrived during the Sultanate, albeit in varying degrees, depending on the proclivity of the sultan in power (Trivedi 2010: 66–75). Initially resistant to musical entertainment, Muꞌizzuddīn Kayqubād, for example, soon became a devotee, and melodies came to be "heard in every lane of the city," according to a fourteenth-century description (cited in Trivedi 2010: 66). Later rulers continued to patronize the art, though toward the end of Amīr K̲h̲usrau's life, Sultan G̲h̲iyāt̲h̲ al-Dīn Tug̲h̲luḳ did not, apparently, favor cultural gatherings at his palace (Trivedi 2010: 71).

Amīr K̲h̲usrau exerted an immense influence on northern Indian music. The scholar Madhu Trivedi cites observations by the historiographer Ziyā'uddīn Baranī (1285–1357), who was personally acquainted with the poet-composer:

> Amīr Khusrau was a master of the Persian language and a prolific poet and prose writer. He also had command over every lyrical genre. For these attributes Baranī called him the king of poets [...] of all time. Baranī further mentioned his great expertise in the art of singing and melody-making [...] and noted that every musical form was strengthened and imparted an elegance by his creative genius. (p. 70)

Trivedi argues that Amīr K̲h̲usrau played a central role in the "synthesis" of Indian and Persian art music that took place from around this time (pp. 66–67). Praised by many, this admixture of foreign elements has been deplored by some traditionalists (Mirza

1962: 238–239), who regret a loss in "the purity of pristine Indian music, i.e. Hindu music." (F. N. Delvoye in Sarmadee et al. 2004: xxii–xxiii).

Amīr K͟husrau addresses the subject of music in the second section or *Risāla II* of a prose work titled *Ras'il'ul I'jāz* (Sarmadee et al. 2004: 1–49). *Risāla II* from the years 1283–1285 describes courtly and other secular musical practices in Delhi. In a portion of the text that reveals personal engagement, Amīr K͟husrau offers special praise for a group of local musicians, who were preparing for a contest with visiting foreigners:

> Any *chang*-player, learning his first grip
> over the instrument,
> Does every time come to learn from us
> the latest subtleties of the art (p. 18).

He vaunts his knowledge of many musical instruments:

> Of course, we know, as one should, what is right and what is wrong about any of the instruments of music; the *chang*: as it remains downcast over the pallor of its body; the *nāy*: whose belly sounds when blown into; the *miskak*: which cries with breathing; the *nawālak*: when tightness of breath chokes its throat; and *duff*: which is struck when heat brings about its pounding—yes, I do know how to correct their flaws. I do know how to feel the pulse of *rabāb* and breathe the vein of *barbat* so as to make them wholesome and worthy in accordance with the scientific laws (*ibid.*).

The *chang* (a harp), the *nāy* (bamboo flute or reed pipe), and the *duff* (frame drum) were the principal instruments played at the palace of the Delhi sultan. The *miskak* and the *nawālak* are evidently types of wind instruments, while the plucked *barbaṭ* and the plucked or bowed *rabāb* fall under the rubric of strings. Referring, it would seem, to his own singing, Amīr Khusrau writes: "This voice of ours—soaring high in resonant sonority—surpasses Venus, comes down to break in minute subtleties even when scratched" (p. 19).

In 1325, while Amīr Khusrau was with the sultan on a military campaign in the east, Shaikh Nizāmuddīn Auliya died. On returning to Delhi, where Amīr Khusrau heard the sad news, it is said that his heart broke. He declared that he would soon join his master and, in fact, he did pass away a few months later. His grave is near that of the saint in Delhi. Both tombs have become sites of pilgrimage for Indian Sufis (Kaul 1985: 124–126; Raghavan 1979: 68; Sharma 2005: 35).

References Cited

Hardy, P. 1960. Amīr Khusrau Dihlawī. In *The Encyclopaedia of Islam*, edited by H. A. R. Gibb et al. Leiden: E. J. Brill.

Ibn Battuta, C. Defremery, B. R. Sanguinetti, and H. A. R. Gibb. 1971. "The City of Dihlī and its Sultans" in Vol. III of *The Travels of Ibn Battuta, A.D. 1325–1354. Works Issued by the Hakluyt Society* (2nd ser., no. 141): 619–656.

Katz, Jonathan. 2001. Khusrau, Amir. In *The New Grove Dictionary of Music and Musicians*, edited by S. Sadie and J. Tyrrell. New York: Grove.

Kaul, Hari Krishen. 1985. *Historic Delhi: An Anthology*. Delhi, Bombay, Calcutta, & Madras: Oxford University Press.

Kulke, Hermann, and Dietmar Rothermund. 2010. *A History of India*. 5th ed. London & New York: Routledge.

Mirza, Mohammad Wahid 1962. *The Life and Works of Amir Khusrau*, Panjab University Oriental Publications. Lahore: Panjab University Press.

Raghavan, V., ed. 1979. *Composers*. New Delhi: Publications Division, Ministry of Information and Broadcasting, Govt. of India.

Sarmadee, Shahab. 1975. Ameer Khusrau's Own Writings on Music. In *Life, Times & Works of Amīr Khusrau Delhavi*, edited by Z. Ansari. New Delhi: National Amīr Khusrau Society.

Sarmadee, Shahab, Prem Lata Sharma, and Françoise 'Nalini' Delvoye. 2004. *Amīr Khusrau's Prose Writings on Music in Ras'il'ul Ijāz Better Known as Ijāz-i Khusrawī, Translated by Shahab Sarmadee*. 1st ed. Kolkata: ITC Sangeet Research Academy (Amit Mukerjee, Executive Director).

Sharma, Sunil. 2005. *Amir Khusraw: The Poet of Sufis and Sultans*. Oxford: Oneworld.

Trivedi, Madhu. 2010. Music Patronage in the Indo-Persian Context: A Historical Overview. In *Hindustani Music: Thirteenth to Twentieth Centuries*, edited by J. Bor, F. N. Delvoye, J. Harvey and E. t. Nijenhuis. New Delhi: Manobar Publishers & Distributors.

Further Reading

Ansari, Zoe. 1975. *Life, Times & Works of Amīr Khusrau Delhavi*. New Delhi: National Amīr Khusrau Society.

Bor, Joep, Françoise 'Nalini' Delvoye, Jane Harvey, and Emmie te Nijenhuis. 2010. *Hindustani Music: Thirteenth to Twentieth Centuries*. New Delhi: Manohar Publishers & Distributors.

Fatimi, S. Qudratullah. 1975. *Amir Khusrau's Contribution to the Indus-Muslim Music*. 1st ed. Islamabad: Publication Cell, Pakistan National Council of the Arts.

Holroyde, Peggy. 1972. *The Music of India*. New York - Washington: Praeger Publishers.

Qureshi, Regula, et al. 2001. India. In *The New Grove Dictionary of Music and Musicians*, edited by S. Sadie and J. Tyrrell. New York: Grove.

Ramakrishna, Lalita. 2010. *Sampradāya Sangīta: Indian Classical Musical Tradition*. 2nd ed, Kalpatharu Research Academy Publications. Delhi: B. R. Rhythms.

Schimmel, A. 1985. Amīr Kosrow Delhavī. In *Encyclopaedia Iranica*, edited by E. Yarshater. London, Boston, Melbourne, and Henley: Routledge & Kegan Paul.

Singh, Jaideva, and Prem Lata Sharma. 1995. *Indian Music*. 1st ed, *Sangeet-Paridarshini Series*. Calcutta: Sangeet Research Academy; Sole distributor, Vishwavidyalaya Prakashan.

Musicians of Japan

Against a background of strong continental-Asian and Buddhist musical influences, a new style of poetry and song known as *imayō* gained popularity during the Heian period in Japan (794–1185 CE). Late in this period, professional singer **Otomae (1085–1169 CE)** gained reknown and respect for her *imayō* repertory. Retired emperor Go-Shirakawa, a devotee of the *imayō* genre, brought Otomae into his court as his music teacher.

A terrible civil conflict, the Gempei War (1180–1185 CE), put an end to the Heian period and ushered in the Kamakura shogunate. The blind singer and lutenist **Akashi no Kakuichi (ca. 1300–1371 CE)** created a monumental musical chronicle of the Gempei War. His *Heike monogatari* (*The Tale of the Heike*) became a sort of national epic for Japan and has inspired hundreds of efforts by other writers and artists.

∞

Five of Merriam's ten functions of music can be associated with these musicians:

THE FUNCTION OF AESTHETIC ENJOYMENT
By promoting *imayō* and teaching this genre to Retired Emperor Go-Shirakawa, **Otomae** broadened the form and content of popular Japanese music.

THE FUNCTION OF ENTERTAINMENT

As a professional entertainer, **Otomae** performed *imayō* publicly for many years, before she was summoned into the palace.

THE FUNCTION OF SYMBOLIC REPRESENTATION

Akashi no Kakuichi created a multifaceted symbol of the Japanese warrior community in his *Heike monogatari*.

THE FUNCTION OF ENFORCING CONFORMITY TO SOCIAL NORMS

In the *Heike monogatari*, **Akashi no Kakuichi** describes brave warriors, who joyfully sacrifice their all—their very lives—out of loyalty to their masters. This depiction of accepted military behavior provided a compelling model for Japanese soldiers to emulate.

THE FUNCTION OF CONTRIBUTION TO THE CONTINUITY AND STABILITY OF CULTURE

Otomae was already an elderly woman, when she taught the *imayō* style to Retired Emperor Go-Shirakawa. As a result of her instruction, he was moved subsequently to preserve many *imayō* in a work titled *Songs to Make the Dust on the Rafters Dance*.

Akashi no Kakuichi's *The Tale of the Heike* guided Japanese cultural attitudes for hundreds of years. Even as recently as the turn of the twenty-first century, when *Heike* performances had virtually disappeared in Japan, the tradition was still discernible in print, film, television, manga, anime, and other media.

Otomae (1085–1169 CE)

In 1169 CE, when the professional singer Otomae died in *Heian-kyō* (later renamed Kyōto), Japan, retired emperor Go-Shirakawa mourned her passing twice daily for fifty days. He sponsored a special memorial service on the first anniversary of her death, during which he personally sang *imayō*—a type of popular song of the era—and dedicated a prayer to her. Thereafter, he held annual memorial services on her behalf (Kim 1994: 20–21).

Ten years previously, Go-Shirakawa had brought Otomae into his court. Quite early in his life, he had developed an unquenchable passion for *imayō*, and he now wished to learn as much as he could about the genre. His intention was for Otomae to serve as his singing teacher. She was well qualified for this task. She came from a clan known as *kugutsu*, which was closely associated with *imayō*, and had become a leading practitioner of the art.

Imayō were composed and performed for the most part by women of marginal status. These musicians created songs that depict wide-ranging aspects of life in medieval Japan. The relaxed poetic form, in comparison with traditional *waka* poetry, and the mode of presentation by female singers served to increase the appeal of the genre. Religious motifs are common, but *imayō* lyrics point also to "the infirmities, squalor, and cacophony of secular life" (Kim 1994: xiv). *Imayō* were generally sung to the beat of a small drum or by tapping a closed fan against the palm of the hand. Sadly, no information about melody and meter has survived (*ibid.*, p. 4).

Otomae, born around 1085 CE, was some forty years older than Go-Shirakawa. She was in her early seventies, when she took him on as her pupil. At first, she had resisted his call, feeling herself too old and the situation inappropriate, because of the social distance that separated them. The *kugutsu* from which she originated had been puppeteers, and the women were reputed to have engaged in prostitution. According to an account written by Ōe no Masafusa (1041–1111), while *kugutsu* men were manipulating their puppets and exhibiting tricks of magic:

> The women [would] put on "sad-face" makeup, do the "bent-at-the-hip" walk, and smile the "toothache-smile"; donning vermilion and wearing white powder, they [would] sing songs and provide licentious pleasures and thus seek to charm. Their parents and husbands do not [admonish them] (cited by Kawashima 2001, p. 297).

Little is known of Otomae's early life, but Go-Shirakawa's memoire mentions that she had two daughters (Kawashima 2001: 87). During the Heian period (794–1185), other groups of professional Japanese women also proffered musical entertainment together with sexual services. The *asobi* rowed out from ports of call to ply their trade on pilgrims and other travelers along the Yodo River, which connects Kyōto with Osaka Bay. *Shirabyōshi* dancers achieved popularity somewhat later than *asobi* and *kugutsu*. They dressed in male attire and wore swords as they performed, perhaps seeking thereby to enhance their erotic appeal in the emerging era of warrior-dominated society (Goodwin 2007: 11–40).

Minamoto Kiyotsune, a visiting government official, discovered Otomae at her birthplace at Aohaka in Mino Province, when she was twelve or thirteen years old. He brought her back to the capital together with her teacher and adoptive mother, an *imayō* singer named Mei (Kim 1994: 15 & 165–166 n.76). Otomae had an impressive *imayō* lineage. It extended through four generations of virtuosae: Mei, who was the disciple of Shisan, who in turn was taught by Nabiki, who had been trained by Miyahime (Ruch 1990: 528).

In the capital *Heian-kyō*, Mei and her lover Kiyotsune continued to guide Otomae's development. Striving for excellence, *kugutsu* singers underwent strenuous training, practicing long hours and splashing their faces or even plucking their eyelashes to stay awake (Kim 1994: 15). When Otomae in her youth complained of having to sing constantly, Kiyotsune urged her to think soberly of the future:

> When you are young, you can be like this, but when you grow old and there is no one to pay attention to you, since [songs] are things that never disappear from the world, there may be some upper-class nobles who favor songs who, when they have doubts about the way a song is sung may come calling on you, saying "Such-and-such person might know." Only if [you] know the art of song can [you] have such things happen [to you after you grow old] (cited by Kawashima 2001, p. 50).

Kiyotsune no longer found Mei attractive after she had grown old, but he continued to care for and support her because of her exceptional singing skills (*ibid.*, p. 49).

Several *imayō* allude to the difficult situation of aging courtesans, for example:

> As my mirror clouds,
> so my body has grown gaunt;
> as my body grew gaunt,
> so men become distant.
> (Kim 1994: 135)

Fortunately for Otomae, she appears to have taken heed of Kiyotsune's counsel. She became a famous singer and as a result was able to enjoy a productive and comfortable old age in Go-Shirakawa's court.

As a song-mistress, Otomae imposed on the retired emperor much of the pedagogical rigor that she herself had faced in her youth. She made him relearn his entire *imayō* repertory in the Mino tradition (Kim 1994: 15). He proved an able and dedicated student. Toward the end of her life, when she had fallen ill, he sat at her bedside and sang an *imayō* related to the healing Buddha, Yakushi Nyorai:

> In the time of the Imitation Dharma,
> the vows of Yakushi are trustworthy!
> Hear his sacred name once only,
> they say, and escape even a million ills.
> (Kim 1994: 20)

She appreciated the *imayō* more than sutras. He repeated the song once or twice, and she wept for joy (Kawashima 2001: 83; Ruch 1990: 529).

After Otomae's death, Go-Shirakawa completed a work titled *Ryōjin hishō* (*Songs to make the dust on the rafters dance*). The original text consisted of two parts: *Kashishū*, a collection of *imayō* lyrics; and *Kudenshū*, providing information on origins, scores, notations, and performance instructions, together with anecdotes. Each part is thought to have comprised ten books. Unfortunately, only a fraction of the total has survived, including, however, some 566 songs and Go-Shirakawa's memoir. Despite the losses, the work remains the largest extant collection of medieval *imayō*. Go-Shirakawa's memoir is the only known source of information about Otomae. The curious title *Ryōjin hishō* refers to a Chinese legend about two singers who performed so wondrously that the reverberating sound caused dust on the rafters to dance for three days after the singing ended (Kim 1994: xiv).

References Cited

Goodwin, Janet R. 2007. *Selling Songs and Smiles: The Sex Trade in Heian and Kamakura Japan.* Honolulu: University of Hawai'i Press.

Kawashima, Terry. 2001. *Writing Margins: The Textual Construction of Gender in Heian and Kamakura Japan*, Harvard East Asian Monographs. Cambridge: Harvard University Asia Center (distributed by Harvard University Press).

Kim, Yung-Hee. 1994. *Songs to Make the Dust Dance: the Ryōjin hishō of Twelfth-Century Japan.* Berkeley: University of California Press.

Ruch, Barbara. 1990. "The Other Side of Culture in Medieval Japan." In *Medieval Japan*, edited by K. Yamamura: Cambridge University Press. *Cambridge Histories Online.* Cambridge University Press. 07 December 2011 DOI:10.1017/CHOL9780521223546.013

Further Reading

Edwards, J. Michele. 2001. Women in Music to ca. 1450. In *Women & Music: A History*, edited by K. Pendle. Bloomington & Indianapolis: Indiana University Press. Pages 26–53.

Morton, W. Scott, and J. Kenneth Olenik. 2005. *Japan: Its History and Culture.* 4th ed. New York: McGraw-Hill.

Shigeo Kishibe, David W. Hughes, Hugh de Ferranti, W. Adriaansz, Robin Thompson, Charles Rowe, Donald P. Berger, W.P. Malm, David Waterhouse, Allan Marett, Richard Emmert, Fumio Koizumi, Kazuyuki Tanimoto, Masakata Kanazawa, Linda Fujie, and Elizabeth Falconer.

2001. Japan. In *The New Grove Dictionary of Music and Musicians*, edited by S. Sadie and J. Tyrrell. New York: Grove.

Akashi no Kakuichi (ca. 1300–1371 CE)

Akashi no Kakuichi, a blind fourteenth-century Japanese musician, created a remarkable musical narrative based on the events and personalities in the Gempei War of 1180–1185 CE. This conflict had pitted against one another the two most powerful warrior clans in Japan: the Taira (or Heike) against the Minamoto (or Genji). By 1185, the Taira had been utterly vanquished, leaving the Genji, under the ruthless Minamoto no Yoritomo, in firm control (Morton & Olenik 2005: 52–67). His ascendancy brought the culturally refined Heian Period of Japanese history to an end. It ushered in many centuries of military rule.

Because Kakuichi was blind, he developed his composition orally. Toward the end of his days, he dictated the libretto to a disciple named Teiichi. Kakuichi's *Heike monogatari* (*The Tale of the Heike*) is a mammoth oratorio-like work, in which some 1000 characters—many of them historically verified—are represented within some 182 cantatas, each of which lasts thirty to forty minutes in performance. It would be difficult to overstate the cultural significance of this composition. The work has maintained its relevance for hundreds of years and inspired hundreds of efforts by other writers and artists. It has become "the central national myth of Japanese society" (Ruch 1990: 44).

The Tale of the Heike brims with dashing battle scenes and descriptions of brave warriors, men who joyfully sacrifice their all—their very lives—out of loyalty to their masters. Its mood of warlike bravado is softened by portrayals of suffering women—the dancer Gio at the beginning, the widow Kenreimon'in at the close of the chronicle—who retreat into religious isolation in the hope of attaining salvation.

The Tale of the Heike follows the rise and fall of Kiyomori, head of the Taira, and of his clan, as foreshadowed in the famous opening passage:

> The sound of Gion Shōja bells echoes the impermanence of all things; the color of the *śāla* flowers reveals the truth that the prosperous must decline. The proud do not endure, they are like a dream on a spring night; the mighty fall at last, they are as dust before the wind (McCullough 1988: 23).

It is the grand sweep of Kakuichi's narrative and its Buddhistic themes of impermanence and karmic retribution that lift the work into the realm of great literature.

Kakuichi was already an adult, perhaps in his early thirties, when some unknown agency struck him blind. He had been living as a monk at the Buddhist monastery of Shoshazan in the mountains near Akashi to the west of Kyōto. The sight loss was tragic in the extreme, but Kakuichi's situation at least gave him the opportunity to learn a remunerative trade. The monastery was a center for both liturgical and secular music, where he could learn to play the *biwa* (lute) and absorb an early narrative of the Gempei War (Ruch 1990: 40–41).

In ca. 1330, Kakuichi moved to Kyōto, becoming one of Japan's many *biwa hōshi*: blind lutenists and singers, who earned their livings by reciting war stories and chanting sutras. These men existed on the margins of medieval Japanese society. They performed for alms and found shelter in Buddhist shrines and temples. With their shaven heads and religious attire, the *biwa hōshi* resembled priests (*hōshi*), even if most of them—unlike Kakuichi— had received no formal religious training; they were simply impoverished laymen. Images from the era show these sad figures as they trod the streets of the city, while enduring the taunts of youngsters and dogs. The *biwa hōshi* might be guided by a child, who bore the *biwa* for his elder (de Ferranti 2009: 19–67; Fritsch 1996: 58–70; Matisoff 1978: 15–28).

The Gempei War had impacted all levels of Japanese society and proved a popular subject for *biwa hōshi* narration. The first *Tale of the Heike* of record, though the text has not survived, was written ca. 1220 by a former court official named Yukinaga, who had become a monk at the Enryakuji monastery on Mount Hiei. By the start of the fourteenth century, a number of different *Heike* narratives were in circulation. At Shoshazan, Kakuichi learned a version now known as the Kamakura-*bon Heike*, which had probably been created at this monastery when he was still a child (Fritsch 1996: 69; McCullough 1988: 7; Ruch 1990: 41).

Kakuichi moved to Kyōto with the intention of performing the Kamakura-*bon Heike*. In the city, he made connection with a *biwa hōshi* named Joichi, who also had spent time at Shoshazan. Joichi was the most famous performer of the Yashiro-*bon Heike*, and he had even created yet another version, the Chikuhakuen-*bon Heike*. Kakuichi apprenticed himself to Joichi, with whom he shared musical talent and an innovative spirit. As a sign of the important bond that developed between these men, Joichi and Kakuichi— and one or two others—took the character *ichi* (first) as part of their names (McCullough 1988: 7; Ruch 1990: 41).

Kakuichi acquired a reputation in Kyōto for his creative interpretations of the *Heike*. In 1340, a court noble named Nakahara no Moromori wrote in a diary that Kakuichi had performed a "different" version of the narrative. The comment may have referred both to the text and to Kakuichi's style of presentation, which, as Helen Craig McCullough speculates, "seems to have been more complex, colorful, and melodic than anything previously attempted" (p. 8). The diary entry reveals that Kakuichi had access to an upper-class audience and that this audience respected *Heike* narration as a performance art. Between 1340 and 1362, Nakahara no Moromori is said to have attended many of Kakuichi's recitals, which were held typically at shrines and temples throughout the city. Kakuichi and a colleague are reported also to have given a private joint performance as a way of distracting a sick man named Musashi no kami Kō no Moronau from his pain (Ruch 1990: 42).

Kakuichi's circumstances did not conform with those of an itinerant mendicant. He acquired students and disciples. He was the driving force behind the establishment of a school of performance known as *Ichikata-ryū*, which remained viable long after its main rival, *Yasaka-ryū*, had expired. He established, or perhaps only strengthened, a guild of blind singers known as the *tōdō-za*, which continued to serve blind professionals until as recently as 1871, when the Meiji government withdrew its protection and support. The *tōdō-za* divided musicians hierarchically into ranks. From 1363, Kakuichi belonged to the highest division, known as *kengyō* (de Ferranti 2009: 56–57; Fritsch 1996: 70–78; McCullough 1988: 9; Ruch 1990: 42).

The development of a superior repertory of melodies and their combination into dramatically effective patterns were likely to have been key elements of Kakuichi's success as a performer. In the absence of more direct information on this subject, McCullough argues that later, seventeenth-century descriptions probably reflect Kakuichi's musical practice to a considerable degree. According to these descriptions, the *biwa* was silent during the vocal part of the performance, which included portions of both declamation and singing. There were as many as thirty-three types of sung melodies, of which eight or nine were especially important: The *sanjū* served for passages of elegant beauty; the *origoe*, for pathos and tragedy; the *hiroi*, for fighting and valor; etc. During intervals between vocal sections, simple *biwa* music set or heightened the mood and established the pitch for the start of the next song (McCullough 1988: 10).

Kakuichi's *Heike* remained dominant in the *biwa hōshi* performance tradition for a century after his death. It is estimated that 500–600 *biwa hōshi* were active in Kyōto in 1462. Few of these would perform all of the *Heike*, but they might intersperse individual cantos with other material. Following the destructive Onin War of 1467–1477, *biwa hōshi* numbers declined, while newer art forms, such as *nō* theater, *kyōgen* comedy, *otogizōshi* prose stories, and *kōwaka mai* ballad drama, grew in popularity—in part by dramatizing episodes from Kakuichi's *Heike*. He inspired the seventeenth-century creators of *kabuki* dance dramas and *ningyō jōruri* puppet plays, as well as novelists in the more-recent Meiji, Taishō, and Showa periods. Even though *Heike* singers had virtually disappeared in Japan by the close of the twentieth century, the tradition was still discernible in print, film, television, manga, anime, other media (de Ferranti 2009; 13; McCullough 1988: 9; Ruch 1990: 43). As McCullough sums up the influence of Kakuichi's libretto, "[W]e can probably say that no single Japanese literary work has influenced so many writers in so many genres for so long a time as the *Heike*" (p. 9).

References Cited

de Ferranti, Hugh. 2009. *The Last Biwa Singer: A Blind Musician in History, Imagination, and Performance*, Cornell East Asia Series. Ithaca: East Asia Program, Cornell University.

Fritsch, Ingrid. 1996. *Japans Blinde Sänger: im Schutz der Gottheit Myōon-Benzaiten*. München: Iudicium Verlag.

Matisoff, Susan. 1978. *The Legend of Semimaru, Blind Musician of Japan*. New York: Columbia University Press.

McCullough, Helen Craig. 1988. *The Tale of the Heike*. Stanford: Stanford University Press.

Morton, W. Scott, and J. Kenneth Olenik. 2005. *Japan: Its History and Culture*. 4th ed. New York: McGraw-Hill.

Ruch, Barbara. 1990. Akashi no Kakuichi. *The Journal of the Association of Teachers of Japanese* 24 (1):35–47.

Further Reading

Frédéric, Louis. 2002. *Japan Encyclopedia*. Translated by K. Roth, *Harvard University Press Reference Library*. Cambridge: Belknap Press of Harvard University Press.

Goldron, Romain. 1968. *Ancient and Oriental Music*. Translated by S. A. Sterman. [place of publication not provided]: H. S. Stuttman Co.; distributed by Doubleday [1968].

Groemer, Gerald, and Chikuzan Takahashi. 1999. *The Spirit of Tsugaru: Blind Musicians, Tsugaru-jamisen, and the Folk Music of Northern Japan, with the Autobiography of Takahashi Chikuzan, Detroit Monographs in Musicology/Studies in Music*. Warren: Harmonie Park Press.

Guignard, Silvain. 1994. Biwa. In *Die Musik in Geschichte und Gegenwart (Sachteil)*, edited by L. Finscher. Kassel: Bärenreiter.

Kōdansha. 1993. *Japan: An Illustrated Encyclopedia*. Tokyo and New York: Kodansha Ltd. (distributed by Kodansha America).

Shigeo Kishibe, David W. Hughes, Hugh de Ferranti, W. Adriaansz, Robin Thompson, Charles Rowe, Donald P. Berger, W.P. Malm, David Waterhouse, Allan Marett, Richard Emmert, Fumio Koizumi, Kazuyuki Tanimoto, Masakata Kanazawa, Linda Fujie, and Elizabeth Falconer. 2001. Japan. In *The New Grove Dictionary of Music and Musicians*, edited by S. Sadie and J. Tyrrell. New York: Grove.

Tyler, Royall. 2012. *The Tale of the Heike*. New York: Viking.

Musicians of Mali

Descriptions of music in the West African empire of Mali (ca. 1230–1670 CE) begin with the *djelis* (called 'griots' in many non-native accounts), who served the kings as musicians, praise-singers, advisers, go-betweens—and in many other capacities, as well. **Balla Fasséké Kouyaté (fl. ca. 1230 CE)** was the personal *djeli* of Sundiata, a thirteenth-century monarch who founded the Mali Empire. Kouyaté played a type of xylophone known as *bala* or *balafon*, which, according to oral tradition, was taken from a defeated rival king. Just over a century later, **Dugha (fl. ca. 1352 CE)** served a king named Mansā Sulaymān (r. ca. 1341–1360). Dugha had four wives and about 100 concubines, and he probably owned slaves. He may have been a direct descendent of Balla Fasséké, and he probably played on the same *bala* that Sundiata's *djeli* had acquired from the rival king.

∞

Four of Merriam's ten functions of music can be associated with these musicians:

THE FUNCTION OF ENTERTAINMENT

Dugha supplied the music during ceremonial events at the court of Mansā Sulaymān. His entertaining performances may have been inspired by traditional animistic rituals.

THE FUNCTION OF SYMBOLIC REPRESENTATION
Following Muslim services on Friday afternoons, **Dugha** led outdoor musical extravaganzas, which were richly symbolic of Mande values in the kingdom of Mali.

THE FUNCTION OF VALIDATION OF SOCIAL INSTITUTIONS AND RELIGIOUS RITUALS
Balla Fasséké Kouyaté lauded the thirteenth-century king Sundiata with song. His praise-singing served to validate Sundiata's rule. In the next century, **Dugha** staged and performed elaborate entertainments for Mansā Sulaymān. **Dugha** played the *bala* while intoning praises of Sulaymān's campaigns and deeds. Dugha's wives and concubines sang along with him, and a group of slave boys beat on their drums, resulting in an impressive display of pomp and circumstance in validation of the state.

THE FUNCTION OF CONTRIBUTION TO THE CONTINUITY AND STABILITY OF CULTURE
The *bala* on which **Dugha** performed at the fourteenth-century court of Mansa Sulayman is thought to have been the very same musical instrument that **Balla Fasséké Kouyaté** had acquired in the thirteenth century, during Sundiata's successful campaign to seize power. Hundreds of years later, in 2000, the original *bala*, now at a closely guarded site in Guinea, was still being revered as a relic. This remarkable record of continuity associates a musical instrument with the ongoing role of *djelis* in West African culture.

Balla Fasséké Kouyaté (fl. ca. 1230 CE)

Balla Fasséké Kouyaté sang, played a type of xylophone, and composed music for a king. However, he was not a court musician of the sort encountered elsewhere in the world. He was the personal *djeli* of Sogolon Diata, called Sundiata, the thirteenth-century West African monarch who created the Mali Empire (Levitzion 1973: 113–114).

Djelis (often called 'griots' in non-native accounts) are a caste of African musicians and oral historians (Charry 2000: 90–91; Hale 1998: 20). In the past, they served nobles and kings, and they exercised a leading role in court ceremonies. *Djelis* interpreted, entertained, exhorted, served as ambassadors, and acclaimed (Levtzion 1973: 113). However, their status in an occupational caste subjected them to taboos, including restrictions on marriage and burial (Charry 2000: 90; Hale 1998: 83 & 111–112). Through the centuries, *djelis* have been looked down upon by 'free' individuals, but they have also been feared because of their sharp tongues (Hale 1998: 67–71; Levitzion 1973: 114).

Sundiata's father, Maghan Kon Fatta, was a chief, or *mansā*, in the Keita clan of the Malinke people, who controlled a fertile swath of land near the upper reaches of the Niger River. Shortly before Maghan died, he literally gave Balla Fasséké to Sundiata as a present (Niane 1994: 17). *Djeli* was a hereditary profession; Balla's father was Maghan's *djeli*. Balla Fasséké was a few years older than Sundiata, and he acted as guardian, companion, servant, and teacher to his young master (Niane 1994: *passim*).

In the 1220s, when Sundiata was a child, king Sumanguru of Sosso raided and subjugated the lands of the Malinke. Sundiata was not killed, however, and after he had grown into manhood, he recruited his clansmen and their allies into an army of liberation. A decisive battle unfolded in 1235 at Kirina near modern Bamako on the Niger River. Sumanguru's forces were routed, and all of his recent conquests, including much of former Ghana, came under Sundiata's control. Sundiata was hailed as the *mansā* over all of the empire that he had created (Asante 2015: 112–116; Shillington 1995: 94–96).

During the quarter century of Sundiata's rule, Mali grew and prospered. Sundiata had set the course for further expansion, which peaked early in the 1300s. From the imperial capital at Niani, near one of the main goldfields at Bure, the *mansā* of Mali now ruled all the land between the northern fringes of the forest in the southwest and the Sahel in the north and between the Atlantic Ocean in the west to beyond the bend of the upper Niger in the east. Based on trade in gold, salt, and kola nuts, the economy had grown strong, and Mali attracted the attention and envy of lands in the Near East and Europe (Shillington 1995: 94–101).

Unsurprisingly, Mansā Sundiata came to be revered as a hero. He was glorified in a patriotic epic that was passed down orally through many generations of *djelis* until it was first written down around the turn of the twentieth century (cf. Bulman 1997). It is largely thanks to the Sundiata epic that we have knowledge not only of the founder of the empire, but also of his *djeli* Balla Fasséké Kouyaté. Different versions of the history vary in detail, but the rendering of Balla's life and actions is sufficiently consistent from version to version to justify reporting on them in this biographical sketch.

The epic provides an early example of Balla's song-writing. This occurs at the climax of an episode in which Sundiata, whose childhood handicap has made him slow to stand and walk, succeeds in pulling himself into a standing position with the aid of an iron rod obtained by his *djeli*. Sundiata's exertions cause the rod to distort into the shape of a bow. Balla celebrates his young master's arousal by composing "Hymn to the Bow":

> Take your bow, Simbon,
> Take your bow and let us go.
> Take your bow, Sogolon Diata
> (Niane 1994: 21).

Here Simbon, a Mande word for 'hunter's whistle,' acts as a metonym to suggest that the prince will become a great hunter. In another version of the epic, Balla celebrates this event by composing a different hymn, "Niama," which prophetically praises Sundiata for shielding his people against their enemies (Camara 1984: 135).

An episode that unfolds while Balla is carrying out an embassy to the kingdom of Sosso reveals his proficiency as an instrumentalist. The king of Sosso, a vicious monarch called Sumanguru Kanté, or Soumaoro, has a secret room that contains a collection of hideous war trophies. It also houses a musical instrument known as a *bala* (or *balafon*), a xylophone made of wooden bars positioned above resonator gourds. Balla breaks into the room and starts to play on the *bala*. When the infuriated monarch discovers him, the *djeli* is able to save his life by improvising a praise song:

> There he is, Soumaoro Kanté.
> All hail, you who sit on the skins of kings.
> All hail, Simbon of the deadly arrow.
> I salute you, you who wear clothes of human skin
> (Niane 1994: 40).

Sumanguru is flattered by this song and decides to keep Balla as his personal *djeli*. In some versions of the epic, the king makes it difficult for Balla to escape by cutting his Achilles tendons (Charry 2000: 143).

The Sundiata epic reaches its climax in the terrible battle at Kirina, where Sundiata achieved ultimate victory over Sumanguru. During the buildup of troops, while Sumanguru's attention is absorbed by the exigencies of war, Balla manages to escape and rejoin Sundiata. At this point, he takes on a many-faceted public role (Niane 1994: 56–78; Camara 1984: 198–217). He directs demonstrations of valor by the assembled kings. He exhorts the troops to victory. He recounts history, including Malinke genealogy, and he praises Sundiata. He rides into battle with his master, while soldiers sing "Hymn to the Bow."

After the battle, Balla interprets the westward movement of a whirlwind to urge Sundiata back toward his homeland. During an imperial assembly at Sibi, when allied kings swear allegiance to Sundiata, Balla transmits their words to the soldiers and onlookers. The crowd sings "Hymn to the Bow," and in one version of the epic, this is when Balla composes "Niama":

Niama, Niama, Niama,
You, you serve as a shelter for all,
All come to seek refuge under you.
And as for you Niama, nothing serves you for shelter,
God alone protects you
(Niane 1994: 75).

When Sundiata addresses his subjects for the first time as the imperial *mansā*, he speaks softly to Balla, who shouts the words to the crowd. Sundiata appoints Balla to be the first *djeli* of the Mali Empire.

One of the currently extant clans of West African *djelis*, the Kouyatés, traces its lineage directly to Balla Fasséké Kouyaté. The Kouyatés were still performing "Niama" as recently as in the 1960s (Niane 1994: 95 n.75).

Following Sumanguru's defeat, his *bala* is thought to have been passed on to Balla and his descendants. The description of how Sundiata's *djeli* acquired Sumanguru's *bala* may have been dramatized for the epic, but placing its origin in Sosso, a kingdom of blacksmiths, is considered appropriate, for they would have had the technology necessary to create such an instrument. As of the year 2000, Balla Fasséké Kouyaté's musical instrument still existed as a closely guarded relic in a remote village in Guinea (Charry 2000: 133–145).

References Cited

Asante, Molefi Kete. 2015. *The History of Africa: The Quest for Eternal Harmony*. 2nd ed. New York: Routledge.

Bulman, Stephen P. D. 1997. A Checklist of Published Versions of the Sunjata Epic. *History in Africa* 24:71–94.

Camara, Laye. 1984. *The Guardian of the Word = Kouma Lafôlô Kouma*. Translated by J. Kirkup. 1st American ed, The Vintage Library of Contemporary World Literature. New York: Aventura.

Charry, Eric. 2000. *Mande Music: Traditional and Modern Music of the Maninka and Mandinka of Western Africa*. Chicago: University of Chicago Press.

Hale, Thomas A. 1998. *Griots and Griottes: Masters of Words and Music*. Bloomington: Indiana University Press.

Levtzion, Nehemia. 1973. *Ancient Ghana and Mali, Studies in African History*. London: Methuen.

Niane, Djibril Tamsir. 1994. *Sundiata: An Epic of Old Mali*. Translated by G. D. Pickett. Harlow: Longman.

Shillington, Kevin. 1995. *History of Africa*. Rev. ed. New York: St. Martin's Press.

Further Reading

Charry, Eric. 2001. Griot. In *The New Grove Dictionary of Music and Musicians*, edited by S. Sadie and J. Tyrrell. New York.

Curtin, Philip D. 1995. Africa North of the Forest in the Early Islamic Age. In *African History: From Earliest Times to Independence*, edited by P. D. Curtin, S. Feierman, L. Thompson and J. Vansina. London & New York: Longman.

Davidson, Basil. 1974. *Africa in History: Themes and Outlines*. New rev. ed. New York: Macmillan.

Kubik, Gerhard. 2001. Africa. In *The New Grove Dictionary of Music and Musicians*, edited by S. Sadie and J. Tyrrell. New York: Grove.2.7.2. Dugha (fl. ca. 1352 CE).

Dugha (fl. ca. 1352 CE)

We first catch sight of Dugha when he is performing as a musician during an outdoor assembly in the capital Niani of the West African kingdom of Mali. On one of the Muslim festival days of 1352 or 1353 CE, following afternoon prayers, King Mansā Sulaymān, who reigned between ca. 1341 and ca. 1360, is holding court on a raised platform. He is surrounded by men-at-arms with fancy weapons, four military officers (*amirs*) holding silver accoutrements, another group of military commanders (*farariyya*), a Muslim judge (*qadi*), and a preacher.

Dugha has made an impressive entrance. Accompanying him are his four wives and about 100 concubines. The women are splendidly attired, and they wear head bands and pendants of silver and gold. Accompanying them, or perhaps arriving separately, are some 30 slave boys dressed in red robes and white caps. The boys have drums suspended from their necks.

Dugha sits down on a chair and begins to play on "an instrument made of reeds [more likely, wooden bars—LMH] with tiny calabashes below it" (Ibn Battuta, Hamdun, & King 2005: 52). This is the West African xylophone known as a *bala*, which was revered since ancient times by the *djelis* of Mali (Hale 1998: 109; present work: previous profile). While Dugha plays, he sings praises of the king. As he celebrates the monarch's campaigns and deeds, the wives and concubines sing along with him, and the slave boys beat on their drums.

Next on show is Dugha's retinue of male acrobats, who perform turns and juggle with swords. Dugha also engages in skillful swordplay.

At the end of the performance the king rewards Dugha with a purse of 200 *mithqals* (approximately 1.6 lbs!) of gold dust. The *farariyya* twang their bows in appreciation, and on the next day, they also present gifts to the musician.

This description of Dugha's recital is taken from a colorful eyewitness account by a remarkable fourteenth-century Moroccan traveler named Abū ʿAbd Allāh ibn Baṭṭūṭa (Dunn 2005; Euben 2006; Ibn Battuta, Defremery, Sanguinetti, Gibb, & Beckingham 1994; Ibn Battuta, Hamdun, & King 2005), who spent about eight months of the years 1352–1353 in the Malian capital. Soon after ibn Baṭṭūṭa arrived in Mali, he met Dugha, who acted as the traveler's dragoman or interpreter. However, even though ibn Baṭṭūṭa invariably refers to Dugha as an interpreter, it soon becomes clear from the narrative that this imperial official was much more than just a mediator between languages.

Mali was nominally a Muslim country when ibn Baṭṭūṭa arrived, but Islam had not yet completely spread to the majority of the people in the countryside, who still adhered to their traditional Mande beliefs. One scholar has suggested that Dugha's performance following afternoon Muslim prayers, as well as other actions that ibn Baṭṭūṭa may not have correctly interpreted, may have been designed to accommodate traditional religious celebrations, "since it was these rituals which had strengthened and upheld the legitimacy of the kingship" (Levitzion 1973: 193). Under the circumstances, the kings were obliged to seek a middle ground: "they were neither real Muslims nor complete pagans" (*ibid.* p. 190). This view would make Dugha the most visible manifestation of pagan culture in the Muslim capital of Mali.

In addition to performing in accordance with local traditions as musician, praise-singer, and swordplayer, Dugha also undertook an impressive number of other duties. It was he who officially welcomed ibn Baṭṭūṭa to the capital by presenting him with a bull. During imperial audiences, Dugha transmitted the words of the king to his subjects and the petitions of the subjects to the king.

He expertly advised ibn Baṭṭūṭa, helping him to obtain from the king both housing and money for expenses. And when Sulaymān's chief wife Qāsā was accused of conspiring to overthrow her husband, Dugha acted as state prosecutor.

Mansā Sulaymān had come into office around the year 1341, and he ruled for approximately 20 years. His brother Mansā Mūsā (r. 1312–1337) was the king who brought Mali into the world's limelight, as a result of his glittering pilgrimage to Mecca in 1324–1325. An entourage of many thousands of people had accompanied Mūsā. In Cairo he distributed so much of Mali's gold that the value of the precious metal is said to have plummeted. Mansās Sulaymān and Mūsā were both grandsons of Abū Bakr (Levitzion 1973: 71), a brother of the founding king Sundiata Keita (present work: previous profile). Scions of different dynastic branches in Mali squabbled with one another during much of the imperial history (Levitzion 1973: 63–72). It has been suggested that the trial of Queen Qāsā, in which Dugha participated, revolved around a rebellious prince who had been embittered by her husband's murder of Mansā Maghā (r. 1337–1341). Mansā Maghā was the prince's father. This rebel managed to seize power in 1360 and rule (ignominiously) for fourteen years as Mansā Diata (*ibid.*, pp. 67–68).

Mansā Sulaymān's palace had attached to it a cupola with wooden arches in which the king often would sit. It could be entered directly from the inside of the palace. On certain days this cupola served as the audience chamber in which the king received petitions from his subjects. Dugha played a vital role on such occasions, and his exalted bearing and appearance conformed to the extensive pomp and circumstance that were the order of the day.

The king's audiences were announced by the hanging of an Egyptian scarf from the grillwork in one of the arches. Bugles and drums sounded, while 300 armed slaves came into the courtyard. A pair of horses and a pair of rams were led in to ward off the "evil eye," and then the king took his place in the cupola, surrounded by a retinue of advisers and officials.

On these occasions, Dugha positioned himself at the door of the audience chamber. He would be dressed in robes of embroidered brocade and wore a fringed turban. A sword in a gold scabbard girded his waist, and he held in his hands two small spears, one of gold and one of silver, with points of iron. His feet were clothed in light boots and spurs.

During an audience, spoken intercourse with the king would take place via Dugha and another official, the pair acting in tandem as a double intermediary. If someone wished to communicate with the king, he spoke to Dugha, who relayed the message to the other official, standing inside the cupola, who in turn passed the message on to the king.

Music was also performed during the audiences. It was common for military commanders to be in attendance, and each would be accompanied by subordinates who carried spears, bows, drums, and bugles made of elephant tusks. They played on *balas*, producing "a wonderful sound," in the words of ibn Baṭṭūṭa (Ibn Battuta, Hamdun, & King 2005: 47–48). Evidently Dugha did not participate in this music-making; his virtuosity would presumably have been reserved for solo recitals as described above.

Eric Charry presents genealogical evidence to suggest that Dugha was a direct descendant of Balla Fasséké Kouyaté, the personal *djeli* of Sogolon Diata, or Sundiata Keita, the founder of the Mali Empire (2000: 145). Charry's source—a *djeli* named Jemori Kouyate who specialized in oral history—traced the movement of Balla Fasséké Kouyaté's *bala* from generation to generation. If Jemori's evidence can be trusted, Dugha probably made music on the very same instrument that his ancestor is said to have acquired from the tyrant Sumamoro of Sosso (present work: previous profile).

Even though ibn Baṭṭūṭa never refers to Dugha as a *djeli* (a Mande term that became Europeanized as 'griot'), it seems reasonable to place him in this category, as does the scholar Ross E. Dunn (2005: 301). Ibn Baṭṭūṭa refers in his narrative to a group of *djelis*, but these individuals performed without music as oral historians and exhorters (Ibn Battuta, Hamdun, & King 2005: 53–54; Ibn Battuta et al. 1994: 962). For different *djelis* to have different specialties in the fourteenth century would be consistent with more recent practice, for, as Charry has noted, few, if any, modern *djelis* are trained to perform expertly in all three of their principal roles as oral historians, singers, and instrumentalists (2000: 90–91).

References Cited

Charry, Eric. 2000. *Mande Music: Traditional and Modern Music of the Maninka and Mandinka of Western Africa*. Chicago: University of Chicago Press.

Dunn, Ross E. 2005. *The Adventures of Ibn Battuta, A Muslim Traveler of the Fourteenth Century*. Rev. ed. Berkeley & Los Angeles: University of California Press.

Euben, Roxanne Leslie. 2006. *Journeys to the Other Shore: Muslim and Western Travelers in Search of Knowledge, Princeton Studies in Muslim Politics*. Princeton: Princeton University Press.

Hale, Thomas A. 1998. *Griots and Griottes: Masters of Words and Music*. Bloomington: Indiana University Press.

Ibn Battuta, C. Defremery, B. R. Sanguinetti, H. A. R. Gibb, and C. F. Beckingham. 1994. *The Country of the Blacks. Vol. IV of The Travels of Ibn Battuta, A.D. 1325–1354*. Works Issued by the Hakluyt Society (2nd ser., no. 178): 946–978.

Ibn Battuta, Said Hamdun, and Noël King. 2005. *Ibn Battuta in Black Africa; With a New Foreword by Ross E. Dunn*. Expanded ed. Princeton: Markus Wiener.

Levtzion, Nehemia. 1973. *Ancient Ghana and Mali, Studies in African History*. London: Methuen.

Further Reading

Asante, Molefi Kete. 2015. *The History of Africa: The Quest for Eternal Harmony*. 2nd ed. New York: Routledge.

Charry, Eric. 2001. Griot. In *The New Grove Dictionary of Music and Musicians*, edited by S. Sadie and J. Tyrrell. New York.

Curtin, Philip D. 1995. Africa North of the Forest in the Early Islamic Age. In *African History: From Earliest Times to Independence*, edited by P. D. Curtin, S. Feierman, L. Thompson and J. Vansina. London & New York: Longman.

Davidson, Basil. 1974. *Africa in History: Themes and Outlines*. New rev. ed. New York: Macmillan.

Kubik, Gerhard. 2001. Africa. In *The New Grove Dictionary of Music and Musicians*, edited by S. Sadie and J. Tyrrell. New York: Grove.

Shillington, Kevin. 1995. *History of Africa*. Rev. ed. New York: St. Martin's Press.

Musicians of Rome

The imperial cities of the Roman Empire acted as magnets for foreign musicians, while local artists appropriated exotic musical forms. Toward the middle of the first century BCE, a Sardinian named **Tigellius (fl. ca. 50 BCE)** immigrated to Rome, where he sang and played the *tibia*, or reed-pipes, for three of the most famous individuals in Western history: Julius Caesar, Cleopatra, and Octavian, the founding ruler of the Roman Empire, who took the name Augustus.

Nero (37–68 CE) was both a Roman emperor (r. 54–68 CE) and a serious musician. He sang and performed publicly on the *cithara*, a concert version of the lyre. He toured Greece for more than a year, while competing professionally in the Greek festivals, and he established a new festival of music and athletics in Rome, which he modeled on the Greek agonistic contests.

Bishop Ambrose (339–397 CE) introduced Eastern religious musical practices to his Roman Catholic congregation in Milan. When Ambrose's church came under siege by elements of the Roman army, inspirational music played a part in strengthening the resolve of the worshippers. The practice of hymn-singing spread to other Catholic dioceses and became a staple element in Catholic services.

∞

Five of Merriam's ten functions of music can be associated with these musicians:

THE FUNCTION OF ENTERTAINMENT

The Sardinian piper **Tigellius** played and sang as entertainment for the supreme Roman leaders. During his bizarre musical career, **Emperor Nero** 'entertained' numerous audiences by singing and accompanying himself on *cithara*.

THE FUNCTION OF SYMBOLIC REPRESENTATION

Emperor Nero made clear to his audiences the symbolism in the music he performed: he appeared elaborately costumed and acted out various scenes before the public, most infamously when singing of a woman giving birth. The hymns of **Bishop Ambrose** express symbolically the communal spirit of Roman Catholic worshipers.

THE FUNCTION OF VALIDATION OF SOCIAL INSTITUTIONS AND RELIGIOUS RITUALS

Emperor Nero underwent strenuous musical training and launched a career as a concert musician, based on the ill-conceived notion that this would validate his rule. He was badly mistaken, and his excursion into the arts would be laughable were it not overshadowed by his record of detestable cruelty. In the Christianized Roman Empire, **Bishop Ambrose** sought to valildate the Catholic Church by introducing hymns that communicate religious dogma.

THE FUNCTION OF CONTRIBUTION TO THE CONTINUITY AND STABILITY OF CULTURE

The practice of hymn-singing, which **Bishop Ambrose** brought to the Milanese basilica, spread to other Catholic dioceses and became a lasting element in Catholic services. Several of Ambrose's own hymns have survived to the present day.

THE FUNCTION OF CONTRIBUTION TO THE INTEGRATION OF SOCIETY

The course of a doctrinal conflict between **Bishop Ambrose** and Emperor Valentinian II provides clear evidence that music can aid in societal integration. Ambrose had refused both to debate an Arian bishop and to allow Arian worship in a Milanese basilica. When the emperor dispatched troops, the bishop responded by retreating with his followers into a sanctuary, where he led his congregation in round-the-clock vigils of religious music and prayer. This musical expression of faith stiffened the resistance of Ambrose's followers and helped to unite them under his religious leadership.

Tigellius (fl. ca. 50 BCE)

The piper Tigellius performed in Rome from 54 BCE for three of the most famous individuals in Western history: Julius Caesar, Cleopatra, and Octavian, the founding ruler of the Roman Empire, who took the name Augustus (Baudot 1973: 73–75). Tigellius sang and played the *tibia*, a reeded wind instrument like the Greek *aulos* (Bélis 2001; McKinnon & Anderson 2001; cf. present work: Chapter 3, "Pronomos"), when entertaining his prestigious audiences during evening banquets. Tigellius is sometimes confused with another musician, Tigellius Hermogene, who may have been Tigellius's freed slave (Meloni 1947; Treggiari 1969: 269–270; Ullman 1915; Wille 1967: 329–334).

Despite some uncertainty about Tigellius's background, he seems to have become a professional musician before emigrating from his homeland toward the middle of the first century BCE (Baudot 1973: 23). At this time, Rome had already become rich and powerful, and the city was on its way to rivalling Alexandria and Athens as a Mediterranean cultural center (Fleischhauer 2001: 606–614). It was the place to go to make a career in music, and especially so if you lived in a nearby province.

Tigellius's origins were in the city of Carales (now Cagliari) on the south coast of the island of Sardinia (Mastino 2005: 189). This ancient settlement had experienced several different civilizations before Rome took the island from Carthage in the aftermath of the First Punic War (264–241). Together with Corsica, Sardinia became a province of Rome, and by Tigellius's day, the well-to-do residents in Carales were probably already enjoying the privileges of Roman citizenship (Boatwright, Gargola, Lenski, & Talbert 2012: 95–100; Bouchier 1917: 102). Nevertheless, Sardinians were still often looked down upon in Rome as laughing-stocks or worse, which makes Tigellius's success there the more remarkable.

Tigellius had a rich Sardinian uncle, or perhaps grandfather, named Phamea. Phamea was sufficiently prominent to interact with Cicero, the distinguished Roman attorney, orator, philosopher, and statesman. Such high-level family connections may have proven useful to Tigellius in his career, though wit and talent were undoubtedly fundamental to his success. He became a favorite of Cleopatra, the Queen of Egypt, when Julius Caesar brought her and their infant son Caesarion to Rome in 46. Following Caesar's assassination on the Ides of March, 44, his adopted son Octavian—the future emperor—retained Tigellius in his entourage (Baudot 1973: 73–74; Cazzona 2005: 115; Congia 2012: 23–24; Rowland 1972 457–458).

Even though Tigellius was 'just a musician,' his close relations with the supreme political leadership commanded respect. In 45, Cicero became quite concerned when he learned that Tigellius was openly accusing him of having broken an agreement with Phamea. It seems that Phamea had supported Cicero's candidacy for the consulship in 64 and then, in 52 or 51, had wanted Cicero to represent him in a legal case. The trial date interfered with another of Cicero's legal commitments, and so he backed out of the arrangement, saying, however, that he would represent Phamea if another date were chosen. Phamea was angered, and the bitterness simmered, apparently, for several years (Rowland 1972: 457–458; Treggiari 1969: 186).

Tigellius's airing of the dispute in 45 led to a flurry of correspondence between Cicero and his associates, in which Cicero adopted a stance of indifference. He made fun of the musician and called him "more pestilential than his native climate" (*Letters to Friends*, 260 [VII.24]). However, the affair most certainly absorbed his attention. He wrote to Atticus: "I wonder you have not yet had any talk with Tigellius. I am just dying to know …" (348 [XIII.50]) and "Send me all about Tigellius, and don't waste time, for I'm all agog" (348 [XIII.51]). In the end, the matter probably had no serious repercussions. When the Second Triumvirate officially sanctioned Cicero's murder in 43, revenge, rather than Tigellius's gossip, was the probable cause: In 44 Cicero had urged the Senate to eliminate Marc Antony, a potential dictator. Antony managed, however, to escape and then became one of the triumvirs (Boatwright et al. 2012: 261– 262).

The Phamea affair probably lay behind an attempt by Cicero to put down Tigellius in his correspondence as "a pretty performer on the flute and a tolerable singer" (*Letters to Friends,* 260 [VII.24]). Tigellius was certainly a more accomplished musician than this damnation with faint praise would imply, for he captured the ear of the most powerful of Romans, who had the means to select the very best artists available.

No specific indications have survived of the kind of songs that Tigellius performed, but some information can be gleaned from the eclectic musical environment in which he operated. Rooted in domestic liturgical and military tradition, Roman music had enriched itself for centuries through cultural interactions with neighboring countries and vanquished rivals. The musical traditions of Etruria, Greece, the Hellenistic kingdoms, and other Asian societies had all left their marks. Oriental and Greek influences intensified after the Punic Wars in the third and second centuries, and, in the aftermath of the destruction of Corinth in 146, vast numbers of Hellenistic artists, including actors, poets, and musicians, migrated to Rome, or arrived there as slaves. Thereafter, in the late second and first centuries, Hellenistic art song came into vogue, with settings of the Latin poetry of Virgil, Catullus, and others. Greco-Roman music continued to flourish during the Augustan

Principate (27 BCE–14 CE) and subsequent imperial dynasties (Fleischhauer 2001: 606–614).

Tigellius, who died around the year 39 BCE, can thus be presumed to have sung musical settings of Latin poems. Tigellius Hermogene might very well have been trained by Tigellius, and Horace associates Hermogene with performance of the works of Calvus and Catullus (*Satires* 1.10.16–19; see also Baudot 1974: 76). Cecilia Cazzona has speculated that Sardinian folk music might also have had an influence on Tigellius's songs (2005: 115).

It is possible, and perhaps even likely, that Tigellius brought with him to Rome the characteristic wind instrument of Sardinia, the *launeddas*. Sometimes called a 'triple clarinet,' the *launeddas* has three pipes, whereas the more-common style of Roman *tibia* had only two (Lallai & Selis: 1997). The *launeddas* is an ancient instrument, having been dated to the eighth or seventh century BCE (Bernardini 1997; Lortat-Jacob 2000 & 2001). In Roman times, it was especially prevalent in the southern part of Sardinia, from which Tigellius originated (Paulis 1997). Performing on this instrument would have set Tigellius apart from other Roman pipers and helped him to pique the interest of his high-level patrons. Sergio Congia has hypothesized that the *launeddas* may have been the key to Tigellius's extraordinary success (Congia 2012: 46–50).

Tigellius had what is called nowadays an artistic temperament. He refused to perform on cue, but only when the mood struck him, even if a Julius Caesar were giving the cue. However, when the mood did strike him, he would sing, as Horace notes, "from the first course through to the dessert, now in the highest treble, now in the lowest register which the lyre commands" (*Satires* 1.3.1–9). Horace paints Tigellius to be the model of inconsistency: Sometimes he would rush about madly; at other times, he would walk with measured step. Sometimes he would keep 200 slaves; at other times, ten. Sometimes he would talk of kings and potentates;

at other times, of the simple life. Sometimes he would be frugal; at other times, spendthrift. Tigellius might sleep during the daytime and stay up all night. "Never," Horace writes, "was there such a mass of contradictions" (*Satires* 1.3.9–19).

Horace implies that Tigellius masked his reluctance to support friends in need by giving freely to street people:

> The worshipful Companies of Flute-girls, the pedlars of potions, mendicants, mime-actresses, buffoons and all of that ilk are sadly distressed at the death of Tigellius, the singer. He was so generous! This fellow, on the other hand, afraid of being called a spendthrift, would refuse to give an impoverished friend enough to stave off cold and the pangs of hunger (*Satires* 1.2.1–7).

This sarcastic attack, which brings to light the satirist's illiberal attitude to the lower classes, can be turned about to suggest a positive character trait: even if Tigellius acted inconsistently, concern for less-fortunate fellow entertainers seems to have been part of his make-up.

Few people in the world today would recognize the name of this musician from Sardinia. Tigellius's memory lives on prominently, however, in Cagliari, where tourist pamphlets point visitors to the "Villa di Tigellio," an archeological site once thought to have been his home (cf. Congia 2012: 51–52).

References Cited

Baudot, Alain. 1973. *Musiciens romains de l'antiquité*. Montréal: Presses de l'Université de Montréal.

Bélis, Annie. 2001. Aulos. In *The New Grove Dictionary of Music and Musicians*, edited by S. Sadie and J. Tyrrell. New York: Grove.

Bernardini, Paolo. 1997. L'aulete di Ittiri. In *Launeddas: l'anima di un popolo*, edited by G. Lallai and N. Selis. Cagliari: AM&D; Nuoro: ISRE.

Boatwright, Mary Taliaferro, Daniel J. Gargola, Noel Lenski, and Richard J. A. Talbert. 2012. *The Romans: from Village to Empire*. 2nd ed. New York: Oxford University Press.

Bouchier, E. S. 1917. *Sardinia in Ancient Times*. Oxford & New York: B.H. Blackwell & Longmans.

Cazzona, Cecilia 2005. Il cantante Tigellio. In *Storia della Sardegna antica*, edited by A. Mastino. Nuoro: Edizioni Il Maestrale.

Cicero, Marcus Tullius, Titus Pomponius Atticus, and D. R. Shackleton Bailey. 1999. *Letters to Atticus*. 4 vols, *Loeb Classical Library*. Cambridge: Harvard University Press.

Cicero, Marcus Tullius, and D. R. Shackleton Bailey. 2001. *Letters to Friends*. 3 vols, *Loeb Classical Library*. Cambridge: Harvard University Press.

Congia, Sergio 2012. *Tigellio: Cantore dei due Cesari*. Pescara: Edizioni Tracce.

Fleischhauer, Günter, et al. 2001. Rome. In *The New Grove Dictionary of Music and Musicians*, edited by S. Sadie and J. Tyrrell. New York: Grove.

Horace (Quintus Horatius Flaccus) and P. Michael Brown. 1993. *Satires I*, *Classical Texts*. Warminster, England: Aris & Phillips.

Lallai, Giampaolo, and Nico Selis. 1997. *Launeddas: l'anima di un popolo*. 1st ed. Cagliari: AM&D; Nuoro: ISRE.

Lortat-Jacob, Bernard. 2000. Sardinia. In *The Garland Encyclopedia of World Music, vol.8: Europe*, edited by J. P. Timothy Rice, and Chris Goertzen. New York & London: Garland Publishing, Inc.

———. 2001. Sardinia. In *The New Grove Dictionary of Music and Musicians*, edited by S. Sadie and J. Tyrrell. New York: Grove.

Mastino, Attilio, ed. 2005. *Storia della Sardegna antica, La Sardegna e la sua storia Vol 2*. Nuoro: Edizioni Il Maestrale.

McKinnon, James W., and Warren Anderson. 2001. Tibia. In *The New Grove Dictionary of Music and Musicians*, edited by S. Sadie and J. Tyrrell. New York: Grove.

Meloni, Piero. 1947. Note su Tigellio. *Studi Sardi* 7:115–151.

Paulis, Giulio. 1997. I Romani e le launeddas. In *Launeddas: l'anima di un popolo*, edited by G. Lallai and N. Selis. Cagliari: AM&D; Nuoro: ISRE.

Rowland, Robert J., Jr. 1972. Cicero and the Greek World. *Transactions and Proceedings of the American Philological Association* 103:451–461.

Treggiari, Susan. 1969. *Roman Freedmen During the Late Republic*. Oxford: Clarendon Press.

Ullman, B. L. 1915. Horace, Catullus, and Tigellius. *Classical Philology* 10 (3):270–296.

Wille, Günter. 1967. *Musica Romana: Die Bedeutung der Musik im Leben der Römer*. Amsterdam: Verlag P. Schippers N.V.

Further Reading

Conti, Flavio. 2003. *A Profile of Ancient Rome*. Los Angeles: J. Paul Getty Museum.

Emerit, Sibylle. 2013. *Le statut du musicien dans la Méditerranée ancienne : Égypte, Mésopotamie, Grèce, Rome : Actes de la table ronde internationale tenue à Lyon Maison de l'Orient et de la Méditerranée* (Université Lumière Lyon 2) les 4 et 5 juillet 2008, Lyon, Bibliothèque d'Étude. Le Caire: Institut Français d'Archéologie Orientale.

Pöhlmann, Egert, and Günter Fleischhauer. 1998. Rom (Reich). In
    Die Musik in Geschichte und Gegenwart, edited by L. Finscher.
    Kassel: Bärenreiter.

Emperor Nero (37–68; r. 54–68 CE)

The Roman emperor Nero sang and played *cithara* (concert-lyre), as well as other instruments. During the years in which he was in power (54–68 CE), he performed publicly in costume. He took music and acting seriously, touring Greece for more than a year, while competing as a professional in the Greek music festivals known as *agône*. Nero respected *cithara* performance (*citharôidia*) so strongly that he felt that his victories in Greece should be valued as highly as a successful military campaign. In Rome, he established a new festival of music and athletics known as the Neronia, which was modeled on the Greek *agône*. Some say he took music too seriously, neglecting statecraft for the art, which is one way to interpret the gibe, "Nero fiddled while Rome burned."

Nero was born to a Roman aristocrat named Gnaeus Domitius Ahenobarbus and his wife, Agrippina the Younger, who was Emperor Caligula's sister. Their son, Marcus Domitius Ahenobarbus, the future Nero, came into the world in the year 37. In the year 40, when the boy's father died, Caligula stripped his nephew of his inheritance and sent him to live with his aunt Domitia Lepida. She took care of Nero until Caligula was assassinated in January 41. The new emperor Claudius promptly restored Nero's inheritance and returned him to the care of his mother (Suetonius, *Lives of the Caesars*, "Nero" [abbreviated SN below]: 5–6).

In 48, Claudius had his promiscuous third wife Valeria Messalina executed for conspiracy, and in the following year, Agrippina managed to become her successor. Claudius agreed to give his young daughter Octavia in marriage to Nero. The emperor formally adopted Nero, who now became heir-apparent to the throne, displacing his step-brother, Claudius's biological son Britannicus. Claudius died of food-poisoning in 54, whereupon Nero took over as the supreme leader of the Roman Empire. He was seventeen years old (SN: 7–8).

As a child, Nero had studied singing and poetry. While he was living with his aunt, one of his tutors was a dancer. His uncle Caligula is known to have cultivated singing and instrumental music, which suggests that musical aptitude may have run in the family. Far from becoming absorbed with the affairs of state when he came into power, the young emperor seems to have developed an even stronger passion for music. He brought in a famous citharode named Terpnus to be his music coach and did exercises to strengthen his voice and increase his physical endurance. His regimen included a special diet, enemas and vomiting, and holding a lead tablet on the chest while lying on his back. Although his voice was thin and indistinct, he felt driven to perform in public (SN: 20; Wille 1967: 338– 339).

In the year 59, Nero scandalized conservative Romans by participating in a youth festival, the Juvenalia, on the banks of the Tiber. This was a raucous affair attended by men and women of all classes. Tacitus mentions the sale of food and luxury goods and censures the participants for their indecent behavior. Nero appeared in the full regalia (*skeuê*) of a citharode and sang two airs based on themes from Greek mythology. His claque, the Augustiani, responded with thunderous applause (Tacitus *Annals* [abbreviated TA below]: 14,15,1–5; Wille 1967: 339–340).

The sense of scandal associated with the emperor's participation in such an event was acute in Rome, as a result of the 'infamy' to which theatrical and other performers had traditionally been subjected. From the time of the Republic, music was considered an inferior calling, classed as an art (*ars*), rather than a use of the intellect. To play music as a pastime was respectable, as was serving as a musician in the military or the cults. However, musical entertainers and actors were denied legal rights and barred from citizenship (Baudot 1973: 82–84; Power 2010: 79–80; Vendries 2013).

A similar stigma had been associated with stage performance in the eastern, Hellenic societies. On the other hand, noble contestants suffered no disgrace for taking part in the Greek *agône*, which were of religious origin. To emerge victorious from such an event was considered a great honor. These were the kind of competitions that attracted Nero. In the year 60 he established the quinquennial Neronia, a Greek-style festival, in Rome (Wille 1967: 340).

Eager to transcend private venues and the Juvenalia, Nero decided to launch his formal career at an established theater in Naples. He performed there on several days, singing and acting out traditional Greek pieces (*nomoi*). Although an earthquake struck the theater while he was on stage, providing an odd portent, his debut was enough of a success for him to want to move on in his musical career to Rome (Wille 1967: 342).

In the year 65, Nero had his name entered as a competitor in the Neronia (Wille 1967: 341). Providing a semblance of propriety—even though a victorious outcome was certain from the start—he adhered scrupulously to the prescribed behavior:

> [Nero] entered the theatre obedient to music's rules: no sitting when tired, no wiping sweat except with one's garment, no visible excretions from mouth or nose. Knee bent, he saluted the audience and awaited the judges' decision with pretended anxiety (TA: 14,4,3–4).

The Roman audience responded with "acclamations and pre-arranged applause." Tacitus describes the attendees with some irony: "You would have thought them enjoying themselves—and perhaps they *were* enjoying themselves, careless of public disgrace" (TA: 14,4,3–4).

The country folk, who were at a loss to know what to make of the emperor's performance, received 'guidance' on how to respond by soldiers positioned strategically in the hall. These soldiers delivered harsh blows to anyone who had grown tired of keeping up the steady din of clapping and cheering. Those who too openly showed signs of boredom or committed other improprieties, such as dressing improperly, were dealt with severely, in some cases losing status and property. No one, even the deathly ill, would have dared simply to get up and walk out (Power 2010: 114; SN: 32; TA: 16,5,1–3).

The Achaean cities at which the Greek *agône* were held sent an embassy to Rome. Their emissaries delivered citharodic crowns to Nero and praised a concert that he gave at their request. Flattered, Nero decided to travel to Greece. He ordered a rescheduling of the festivals, so that all of them would take place in one year, and competed in them, one after the other. He left Rome in the latter part of 66 and did not return until December 67 at the earliest. While he was away, the freedman Helius served as imperial deputy in the capital and kept the emperor abreast of important developments (Malitz 2005: 88–98; SN: 22–23).

Nero's repertory included the citharodic *nomos* "Niobe," as well as scenes that he acted out from the Greek tragedies. Wearing masks with features that resembled his own, he sang the roles of heroes and gods and of heroines and goddesses. This Roman emperor even played the part of a woman giving birth (SN: 21).

The Greek judges declared Nero victorious wherever he competed. Who would have dared to rank another contestant above him? Nero won crowns in citharody, tragedy, and proclamation. He emerged victorious in chariot-racing, which was another of his passions. On one occasion, the judges declared him winner of a race in which he had fallen from his chariot and failed to finish. When Nero departed from Greece, he had accumulated a total of 1,808 prizes (Malitz 2005: 90; SN: 22–24; Wille 1967: 344–345).

Upon landing back in Naples, where his musical career had begun, Nero rode triumphantly up the Italian peninsula to Rome. Attired in purple with gold stars and driving the chariot that Augustus had once used, drawn by a team of white horses, he entered the capital city in magnificence. Bearers displayed the crowns he had won and held up placards that announced whom he had defeated and with which songs or dramas. A crowd of applauders followed. They shouted praise and proclaimed their role in his victories. In a fitting variation of the traditional triumph, Nero's parade culminated not on the Capitoline Hill at the shrine of Jupiter Optimus Maximus, as military triumphs had done, but rather at the Palatine Temple, where statues of the lyre-playing god, Apollo Citharoedus, stood (Miller 2000: 415–420; SN: 25).

A biblical maxim holds that "pride goes before destruction, and a haughty spirit before a fall" (Proverbs 16:18). Nero's fall came soon after the celebration of his shameless 'victories.' In the province of Gaul, General Vindex had launched an insurrection. Nero, who was in Naples when the news arrived, showed himself to be incapable of dealing effectively with this problem. After returning to Rome, he learned that the Spanish provinces had also revolted. He held a brief meeting with his war counselors; afterward, he kept them listening for hours to his descriptions of new types of hydraulic organs. He considered traveling with his theatrical baggage and a squad of prostitutes to the battlefront, where, he imagined, his tearful entreaties would bring an end to the conflict (SN: 40–44).

Finally the senate realized that it had to act. Nero was declared a public enemy, subject to execution by being publicly stripped, tied to a stake, and beaten to death. This prospect terrified him. Hesitating fearfully, he at last plunged a dagger into his own neck (SN: 49). While preparing for the end, he kept repeating, *Qualis artifex pereo*, which is usually translated: "What an artist dies in me!" (*ibid.*; but see Champlin 2003, pp. 49–51, for another interpretation). He had survived as emperor for 14 of his 31 years.

Suetonius describes Nero as having been a healthy man, but physically unattractive. His skin was blotchy, his eyes dull, his neck thick, his stomach protruding, his legs spindly. His body stank, and he dressed sloppily. He would appear in public wearing a dinner robe, bare-footed and with his tunic unbelted. In Greece he left his curly, light-colored hair long and hanging down in the back (SN: 51).

Nero's musical efforts led other musicians to emulate them and encouraged the love of the populace for good music. He was a poet, composer, and musician. A recent scholar describes him as the instigator of a sort of Roman *paideia*, or educational program, which was to make "the Hellenic language of *kitharôidia* legible and lovable to Romans" (Power 2010: 102). In addition to 'serious music,' he also created popular works, ribald pieces that caught the imagination of the lower classes, so that even after his death, his songs "belonged to the countrywide repertory" (Wille 1967: 349). However, the inhumanities of Nero's reign besmirched his reputation and overshadow any and all of his purported musical accomplishments.

To stay in power, Nero carried out a reign of terror, continually eliminating both real and suspected enemies. He did not shy from killing anyone whom he saw as a threat, including—among others—his stepbrother; his first wife, who was also his cousin and stepsister; and even his own mother. He forced others to take their own life, including Seneca the Younger, who had been Nero's tutor and adviser. While on tour in Greece, he summoned three of his generals, including Gnaeus Domitius Corbulo, whose campaign in Armenia had been crowned with success, and made them kill themselves (Boatwright, Gargola, Lenski, & Talbert 2012: 324–327).

Many Romans suspected Nero of having started the great fire of 64 in order to clear a hilly section of the city, where he was building a palatial "Golden House." Rumor had it that he was seen watching the blaze and playing the *cithara*—'fiddling,' as the modern expression has it—while dressed in his citharodic *skeuê* and singing his own composition about the fiery demise of Troy (Power 2010: 166–168; SN: 38; TA: 15,38–44).

To divert blame for the fire onto others, Nero is reported to have made scapegoats of Christians. According to the story that has come down to us (which, however, some scholars have questioned—see Dando-Collins 2010: 1–16; Walter 1957: 159–174), the Christians were subjected to gruesome tortures, such as being burned alive to light Nero's way as he drove his chariot among them (Champlin, pp. 121–126; Malitz, pp. 68–71; TA: 15,44).

Gunter Wille follows his acknowledgement that Nero raised the social standing of musicians with a denunciation:

> Nero's contempt for the worthiness of the ruler, his infamous cruelty, his excess paired with half-measure demand condemnation of him as human being, ruler, and artist. He can in no way be understood, as often has happened, as the prototype of Roman musical activity (p. 350, my translation from the German).

As William Shakespeare has noted, "The evil that men do lives after them; the good is oft interred with their bones" (*Julius Caesar*,

III.2). Nero's actions displayed little in the way of 'good' even during his own lifetime. His death unleashed among fellow Romans an outpouring of great public joy (SN: 57).

References Cited

Baudot, Alain. 1973. *Musiciens romains de l'antiquité.* Montréal: Presses de l'Université de Montréal.

Boatwright, Mary Taliaferro, Daniel J. Gargola, Noel Lenski, and Richard J. A. Talbert. 2012. *The Romans: from Village to Empire.* 2nd ed. New York: Oxford University Press.

Champlin, Edward. 2003. *Nero.* Cambridge & London: Belknap Press of Harvard University Press.

Dando-Collins, Stephen. 2010. *The Great Fire of Rome: The Fall of the Emperor Nero and His City.* Cambridge: Da Capo Press.

Malitz, Jùrgen. 2005. *Nero.* Translated by A. Brown, *Blackwell Ancient Lives.* Malden: Blackwell Publishing.

Miller, John F. 2000. Triumphus in Palatio. *The American Journal of Philology* 121 (3):409–422.

Power, Timothy Conrad. 2010. *The Culture of Kithardidia, Hellenic Studies Series.* Washington, DC: Center for Hellenic Studies (distributed by Harvard University Press, Cambridge, Mass., and London, England).

Suetonius. 2000. *Lives of the Caesars.* Translated by C. Edwards, *Oxford World's Classics.* Oxford & New York: Oxford University Press.

Tacitus, Cornelius. 2012. *Annals.* Translated by C. Damon, *Penguin Classics.* London: Penguin Books.

Vendries, Christophe. 2013. Considérations sur le statut du musicien dans la Rome antique: Critères de distinction sociale et de hiérarchie. In *Le statut du musicien dans la Méditerranée ancienne : Égypte, Mésopotamie, Grèce, Rome : Actes de la table ronde internationale tenue à Lyon Maison de l'Orient et de la Méditerranée (Université Lumière Lyon 2) les 4 et 5 juillet 2008, Lyon*, edited by S. Emerit. Le Caire: Institut Français d'Archéologie Orientale.

Walter, Gérard. 1957. *Nero*. London: Allen & Unwin.

Wille, Günter. 1967. *Musica Romana: Die Bedeutung der Musik im Leben der Römer*. Amsterdam: Verlag P. Schippers N.V.

Further Reading

Anderson, Warren, and Thomas J. Mathieson. 2001. Nero. In *The New Grove Dictionary of Music and Musicians*, edited by S. Sadie and J. Tyrrell. New York: Grove.

Balsdon, J. P. V. D. 1969. *Life and Leisure in Ancient Rome*. 1st ed. New York: McGraw-Hill.

Conti, Flavio. 2003. *A Profile of Ancient Rome*. Los Angeles: J. Paul Getty Museum.

Fleischhauer, Günter. 2001. Rome [Ancient]. In *The New Grove Dictionary of Music and Musicians*, edited by S. Sadie and J. Tyrrell. New York: Grove.

Pöhlmann, Egert. 2008. Greek Music and Greek Musicians for Rome. *Philomusica On-Line* 7 (2):29–37.

Pöhlmann, Egert, and Günter Fleischhauer. 1998. Rom (Reich). In *Die Musik in Geschichte und Gegenwart*, edited by L. Finscher. Kassel: Bärenreiter.

Bishop Ambrose (339–397 CE)

Ambrose, who was bishop of Milan from 374 to 397 CE, introduced Eastern religious musical practices such as antiphonal singing to his Roman Catholic congregation. He himself was a composer, and his hymns, several of which have survived to the present day, have continued to prove accessible and moving to churchgoers. His inspirational music played a crucial role in keeping up the spirits of his congregation, when it was under siege by elements of the Roman imperial army during a period of doctrinal religious strife. Thanks in part to the role that music played in this confrontational episode, the practice of hymn-singing spread to other Catholic dioceses (McGuire 2003).

Late in the third century, Christians had been split by a doctrinal dispute concerning the nature of Jesus Christ. So-called Nicenes, who believed that Jesus was eternal and of the same substance as God the Father, faced off against Arians, who followed the ideas of a Libyan priest named Arius (ca. 250–336) in asserting that Jesus was subordinate to and a creation of the Father. Historian Neil McLynn has characterized the conflict between Arians and Nicenes as "the great fault line that cut through the church of the fourth century" (1994: 3). This "fault line" ran right through Milan, Italy. In the years 385–386, religious tensions in this city, which were growing steadily, set off dramatic confrontations, from which a faction headed by the Nicene bishop Ambrose emerged victorious. Ambrose's hymns helped to strengthen and maintain the resolve of his congregation during their struggle.

Ambrose came from the city of Augusta Treverorum (now Trier, Germany) in the Roman province of Belgic Gaul, where his father, who was also called Ambrose, served as praetorian prefect.

Young Ambrose was born ca. 339 as the third and youngest child in the family; he had an elder brother named Satyrus and an elder sister named Marcellina. Sometime after Ambrose's birth, his father died, and his mother moved with her children to Rome, where the boys received their education. Marcellina "took the veil" before Pope Liberius (McGuire 2003: 337).

The boys were educated in the liberal arts and law. As young lawyers from a prominent Roman family, they both received civil-service appointments as advocates in ca. 365. About five years later, Satyrus and Ambrose were promoted to provincial governorships. Ambrose became *consularis* of the province of Liguria and Aemilia, with headquarters in Milan, which at that time was also a Roman imperial residence (*ibid.*).

Milan had an Arian bishop named Auxentius, who died shortly after Ambrose's arrival. In his capacity as *consularis*, Ambrose spoke impressively at a stormy meeting that was to choose Auxentius's successor. According to a biography of Ambrose by his contemporary Paulinus (translated in Ramsey 1997: 195–218), during the meeting a small child cried out "Ambrose for bishop!" whereupon the tone of the gathering changed, and the crowd acclaimed Ambrose as its bishop.

In what may have been a formality, Ambrose raised objections to the idea of his selection. However, the people were insistent, and the emperor ratified their choice of Ambrose. Through the course of a mere eight days, this unbaptized Christian lawyer and government official underwent the baptismal ceremony and passed through various stages of clerical advancement. He was consecrated as bishop on December 7, 374 (McGuire 2003: 337).

If the Milanese Christians had expected Ambrose to keep the peace between Arians and Nicenes, they would find themselves mistaken, for Ambrose proved himself to be an inflexible defender of the Nicene faction. Situated across from him on the other side of the doctrinal "fault line," the emperor Valentinian II (b. 371; r. 375–392) and his mother Justina were Arians. In the mid-380s, when the religious conflict came to a head, Valentinian was a teenager, and his mother was serving as regent. They were based in Milan.

Even in the absence of an agreed chronology, historians high-light three prominent aspects of the Milanese religious conflict: an edict issued by Valentinian in January 386 that guaranteed freedom of assembly for both major religious factions in the city; a request by the imperial court to make use of one of the churches under Ambrose's control; and a summons for Ambrose to take part in a doctrinal debate with an Arian bishop before the emperor and consistory (McGuire 2003: 338; McLynn 1994: 158–219; More-head 1999: 137–155; Ramsey 1997: 25–27).

Valentinian's edict of 386 was contrary in spirit to the famous *Cunctos populos* decree of 380, in which Emperor Theodosius I (r. 379–395) proclaimed orthodox Catholicism as the only allowable faith (Mitchell 2015: 265). However, many Goths were now serv-ing in the Roman army, and they had been granted exemption to Theodosius's proclamation (*ibid.*: 311–312). Valentinian included in his edict a stern warning that any "turbulent" opposition to the principle of free assemblies was to be considered treasonous and a capital offence (McLynn 1994: 181).

Ambrose declined the summons to debate. He based his re-fusal on the grounds that the debaters' beliefs were to be judged by laymen, whereas only clerical authorities should pass judgment on matters of faith (Ramsey 1997: 27). He also refused categorical-ly to permit Arian worship in the churches of his diocese. He turned down requests by the imperial court to use either the Por-tian Basilica outside the city limits or the grand New Basilica in the city center. He contended that "a bishop could not hand over the temple of God" and that "sacred objects are not subject to the jurisdiction even of the emperor" (*Letters* 1954: 365–367).

Both the refusal to debate and the refusal to allow use of a Milanese basilica brought Ambrose in direct conflict with the court. Especially after Valentinian's edict of 386, the bishop had good reason to fear that he would be arrested. Troops were sent on different occasions to surround the Portian and New Basilicas, most famously over an Easter holiday. As described by Ambrose himself in a letter to his sister (No. 60 in *Letters* 1954; cf. Augustine *Confessions* IX,7,15), he responded by retreating with his followers into a church, where they observed round-the-clock vigils of religious music and prayer. These vigils, which may have unnerved the military guards, were early, successful examples of nonviolent protest against civil authority. Faced with public opposition and Ambrose's intransigence, Valentinian gave way. He may also have been rattled by a letter from a potential rival, the usurper Magnus Maximus (r. 383–387), who noted ominously that the religious upheavals in Milan might play into his hands, if he were Valentinian's enemy (cited in McLynn 1994: 208).

Hymnody as an expression and reinforcement of religious faith was one of the keys to success of Ambrose's protest. Augustine of Hippo (354–430), whose mother had taken part in the vigils, reports that the chanting of religious music had sustained the congregation's enthusiasm:

> It was then that the practice was established of singing hymns and psalms in the manner customary in the regions of the East, to prevent the people losing heart and fainting from weariness (IX,7,15).

In addition to encouraging Ambrose's followers, hymn-singing also helped to unite them under his religious leadership.

Ambrose had brought Augustine into the Church. When the younger man became bishop of Hippo, he recalled how the hymns (which were undoubtedly Ambrose's) had overwhelmed him at the time of his baptism:

> How copiously I wept at your hymns and canticles, how intensely was I moved by the lovely harmonies of your singing Church! Those voices flooded my ears, and the truth was distilled into my heart until it overflowed in loving devotion; my tears ran down, and I was the better for them. (IX,6,14)

After hymn-singing was introduced in Milan, many Catholic churches—"nearly all of them," Augustine writes— imitated the practice (IX,7,15).

Ambrose's hymnody touched Augustine deeply, lastingly. In 387, his life had been "rent apart" by the death of his mother, he reports, but he would not, or could not, allow himself to weep at her passing. He felt that "plaintive protests and laments" would be unfitting, because she had "neither died in misery nor died altogether." Remembering Ambrose's hymn *Deus creator omnium* (God, creator of all things), he overcame his inhibition and eased his sorrow through the shedding of tears (IX,12,29–33). In Maria Boulding's translation, this hymn refers to "mourners find[ing] release from pain" (Augustine 1997: 233).

As many as fourteen surviving hymns are considered to be authentically Ambrosian. They are meant to be sung at particular times of the day and for celebrating the major church holidays and feast days (Ambroise; J. Fontaine et al. 1992; Moorhead 1999: 140–143; Ramsey 1997: 65). Even though Ambrose emphasized doctrine, his lyrics are simpler, and therefore more readily appreciated by ordinary churchgoers, than those that were composed earlier in the fourth century by Hilary of Poitiers (McKinnon 2001).

Ambrose enhanced the musical quality of his compositions by careful attention to structure: The words are divided into eight stanzas of four verses, nearly all of which comprise eight syllables. The meter is iambic, and there is a tendency for the stanzas to be grouped thematically in pairs, as if antiphonally, though not rigidly so. The four pairs of stanzas in each hymn create what Jacques Fontaine has termed a "beautiful tetraptych." In the best of Ambrose's hymns, form relates symbiotically to content, providing support for Fontaine's assertion, that the music is not an addition, but rather "it is already inherent in the clearly melodic composition of [...] these hymns" (Ambroise; J. Fontaine et al. 1992: 64–65).

It is unclear whether Ambrose created original melodies or whether, as recent scholarship suggests, he made use of traditional tunes (McKinnon 2001). Notated copies of the hymns are available only from the 12th century, long after their composition (Weakland 2003: 341).

The hymn *Intende, qui regis Israel* (Hearken, you who rule Israel), which was composed for use during the Christmas holiday, provides an example of the doctrinal nature of Ambrose's compositions. In eight stanzas, the text moves forward from the invocation of a messiah in the Old Testament ("Hearken, you who rule Israel, / ... rouse up your power and come!") to the arrival of Jesus at the start of the Christian era. The second to fifth stanzas describe the Christ child's miraculous conception and his mother's pregnancy and intact virginity ("not by man's seed ... [t]he virgin's womb swells / but the door of chastity remains shut"). Stanzas 6 and 7 foreshadow Jesus's later merging again into the godhead ("[H]is return is to the throne of the God"). Stanza 8, with an allusion to his early infancy ("May your crib now shine forth / and the night produce a new light."), completes the arc of the Nativity (Ramsey 1997: 166–167 & 172–173).

This hymn relates directly to the Milanese religious conflicts in which Ambrose was embroiled:

> In contrast to Arianism, the hymn concentrates exclusively on the divine nature of Jesus and presents him as the Son equal to the Father in his immortality (J. Fontaine in Ambroise; J. Fontaine et al. 1992: 266).

The weight given to the description of the virgin birth, to which Ambrose devotes four stanzas, drives home the huge dogmatic significance of this portion of the Nativity story.

Ambrose, who died in 397, is revered as a Christian saint and as one of the Fathers and Doctors of the Western Church (McGuire 2003). During his lifetime, he acted forcibly against Paganism and schismatic Christian doctrine (Ramsey 1997: 23–34). After his victory over the Arians in the mid-380s, the imperial court never again posed a threat to the Catholic orthodoxy in Milan (*ibid.*: 27).

In the secular realm, Ambrose held his own with several Roman emperors, including Gratian (r. 375–383), whom he supplied with doctrinal guidance; Valentinian II, whom he outmaneuvered in the Easter standoff; Magnus Maximus, whom Ambrose persuaded to put off (temporarily) an invasion of Italy; and Theodosius I, whom Ambrose forced into public penance (Delaney & Tobin 1954; cf. McLynn 1994, *passim*). Ambrose was "the first of the Fathers and Doctors of the Church to deal formally with the relations of Church and State" (McGuire 2003: 339). His involvement in this arena provided a model for the Medieval Period (Brown 2015).

Ambrose wrote eloquently in Latin (Ramsey 1997: 55–68), and, of course, he introduced and composed hymns and led his congregation in the performance of religious music. Three of Ambrose's compositions are part of the Tridentine Roman Breviary, which was still in use in the 20th century (Hueller et al. 2003: 259; O'Brien 2003: 182). Ambrose's musical involvement earned him "the title 'father of liturgical hymnody' in the West" (McGuire 2003: 339).

References Cited

Ambroise; Jacques Fontaine et al. 1992. *Hymnes texte établi, trad. et annot. sous la dir. de Jacques Fontaine,... [introd. par J. Fontaine et Marie-Hélène Jullien] [publ. par le Centre Lenain de Tillemont de l'Université de Paris IV]*, Patrimoines Christianisme. Paris: Les Éditions du Cerf.

Ambrose. 1954. *Saint Ambrose Letters [1–91]*. Translated by M. M. Beyenka, *Fathers of the Church*. New York: The Catholic University of America Press.

Augustine. 1997. *The Confessions*. Translated by with introduction and notes by Maria Boulding, *The Works of Saint Augustine, A Translation for the 21st Century*. Hyde Park: New City Press.

Brown, Peter R. L. 2015. "Saint Ambrose". *Encyclopædia Britannica. Encyclopædia Britannica Online Academic Edition*, <http://www.britannica.com/EBchecked/topic/19014/Saint-Ambrose> (accessed May 11, 2015).

Delaney, John J., and James Edward Tobin. 1954. Ambrose, St. In *Dictionary of Catholic Biography*. Garden City: Doubleday & Co.

Hueller, M. M., M. A. Bischsel, and E. J. Selhorst / Eds. 2003. Hymns and Hymnals, I: Historical Developments. In *New*

Catholic Encyclopedia. Detroit & Washington, D.C.:
Thomson/Gale & Catholic University of America

McGuire, M. R. P. 2003. Ambrose, St. In *New Catholic Encyclopedia*.
Detroit & Washington, D.C.: Thomson/Gale & Catholic
University of America.

McKinnon, James W. 2001. Ambrose. In *The New Grove Dictionary
of Music and Musicians*, edited by S. Sadie and J. Tyrrell.
New York: Grove.

McLynn, Neil B. 1994. *Ambrose of Milan: Church and Court in a
Christian Capital, The Transformation of the Classical Heritage*.
Berkeley: University of California Press.

Mitchell, Stephen. 2015. *A History of the Later Roman Empire, AD
284–641*. 2nd ed, Blackwell History of the Ancient World.
Chichester & Malden: Wiley Blackwell.

Moorhead, John. 1999. *Ambrose: Church and Society in the Late Roman
World*. London & New York: Longman.

O'Brien, T. / Eds. 2003. Tridentine Mass. In *New Catholic
Encyclopedia*. Detroit & Washington, D.C.: Thomson/Gale
& Catholic University of America.

Ramsey, Boniface, O.P. 1997. *Ambrose, The Early Church Fathers*.
London & New York: Routledge.

Weakland, R. G. 2003. Ambrosian Chant. In *New Catholic
Encyclopedia*. Detroit & Washington, D.C.: Thomson/Gale
& Catholic University of America.

Further Reading

Bailey, Terence. 2001. Ambrosian Chant. In *The New Grove
Dictionary of Music and Musicians*, edited by S. Sadie and J.
Tyrrell. New York: Grove.

Haas, Max. 1999. Ambrosius. In *Die Musik in Geschichte und
Gegenwart. Personenteil*, edited by F. Blume and L. Finscher.
Kassel: Bärenreiter; Stuttgart: Metzler.

Musicians of Western Asia BCE

Regimes in ancient Mesopotamia and the Levant built impressive musical establishments and vaunted the musical abilities of their rulers. Use of the lyre and an emphasis on religion were elements in much of the region's music.

The Akkadian princess **Enheduanna (fl. ca. 2300 BCE)** was named high priestess (or '*en*-priestess') in the Sumerian city of Ur by her father, Sargon the Great (r. ca. 2334–2279 BCE). She composed temple hymns and poetry, and is considered to have been the first named author of record in history.

Dada (fl. ca. 2040 BCE) served as a *gala* or *gala-mah* ('chief *gala*') for at least twenty-three years under three of the kings in the Mesopotamian dynasty known as Ur III (ca. 2112–2004 BCE). *Galas* (lamentation- or prayer-singers) were religious functionaries, who placated the gods with their hymns, in order to keep adversity at bay.

Risiya (fl. ca.1790 BCE) was head of music in Mari, a city just to the north of the present Syrian-Iraqi border. He had broad responsibilities for the organization of musical life in the court. His situation approximated to that of a civil servant in the twenty-first century, providing an early example of careerist professionalism in music.

The Bible associates **King David (1040–970; r. 1010–970 BCE)** of Israel and Judah with four types of musical activity: lyre-playing, singing, composing, and the organization of cultic music. As a young man, he played on his lyre to calm the ailing King Saul (r. ca. 1010 BCE). David composed psalms and a lamentation on the deaths of Saul and Saul's son Jonathan. David's music is honored even today in the three principal monotheistic religions of the world.

∞

Six of Merriam's ten functions of music can be associated with these musicians:

THE FUNCTION OF EMOTIONAL EXPRESSION

Mesopotamian lamentation priests such as the *gala* **Dada** sang of the emotional stress of the population in times of natural disaster and war.

THE FUNCTION OF COMMUNICATION

The Akkadian *en*-priestess **Enheduanna** and the Sumerian *gala* **Dada** composed and/or sang texts for communicating with the gods. Enheduanna's temple hymns of praise may have been designed for antiphonal performance in a cultic assembly. *Galas* used music to calm the gods and allay their anger.

THE FUNCTION OF PHYSICAL RESPONSE

After **King David** had taken Jerusalem from the Jebusites and made it his capital, he brought the Ark of the Covenant into the city. Thousands of people accompanied the holy vessel on its way, while instrumentalists sounded percussive and melodic instruments. The music provoked exuberant dancing. When the procession arrived in town, David was leaping about at its head in an unrestrained performance that shocked his wife Michal.

THE FUNCTION OF VALIDATION OF SOCIAL INSTITUTIONS AND RELIGIOUS RITUALS

Enheduanna composed temple hymns that validated the merging of Sumerian and Akkadian cults in the Mesopotamian empire ruled by her father, King Sargon of Akkad. Although **Dada** is primarily known for his religious role, he is thought to have reported directly to King Shulgi of Ur, who embraced the musical art as a way of validating his rule. **Risiya** held a prestigious position as head of music in Mari, a city on the Euphrates River in the Ancient Near East. His principal charge was that of organizing music at court. The superior musical establishment, for which he was responsible, added to the prestige of the Mariote monarchs, thereby helping to validate their rule. **King David** composed religious psalms that helped to validate the Judaic religion.

THE FUNCTION OF CONTRIBUTION TO THE CONTINUITY AND STABILITY OF CULTURE

The poetry and hymns that **Enheduanna** composed appear to have had a substantial impact on later generations. Archeological studies have identified copies of her works from as recently as the Old Babylonian period, which suggests that her theological insights continued to be respected and that her hymns continued to be performed for hundreds of years. The psalms attributed to **David** have been part of Near-Eastern and Western religious observances through three millennia, which is a striking example of long-term cultural continuity. Their influence has extended far beyond ancient Israel and Judah. The three principal monotheistic religions of the world venerate this ancient religious leader and honor his hymns.

THE FUNCTION OF CONTRIBUTION TO THE INTEGRATION OF SOCIETY

In the twenty-fourth century BCE, after King Sargon had created an empire centered on his capital in Akkad, he named his daughter **Enheduanna** to the position of high-priestess in the Sumerian city of Ur, which he now ruled. The temple hymns that she composed helped to underpin political unity in the empire and encouraged the integration of Akkadian and Sumerian peoples.

Enheduanna (fl. ca. 2300 BCE)

Enheduanna, an Akkadian princess of the third millennium BCE, is held to be the first named author of record in the history of the world. While serving as a priestess in the Sumerian city of Ur, which her father Sargon the Great (r. ca. 2334–2279 BCE) had brought under Akkadian control, she composed 42 temple hymns and a cycle of three poems in praise of the goddess Inanna (McIntosh 2005: 203; Meador 2009: 2 & 18).

Enheduanna was Sargon's only daughter. He had risen to power in the Semitic city of Kish before building or renovating Akkad to serve as his capital. After he subjugated the city states of Sumer, he named Enheduanna to her high religious position, which was known as *en*-priestess, in Ur. Ur was near the mouth of the Euphrates River on the Persian Gulf, 150 miles, or so, southeast of the presumed location of Akkad (Meador 2000: 45; Hallo & Simpson 1971: 54–60).

Enheduanna's hymns and poems are of a religious nature, but both her appointment as *en*-priestess and the contents of her poetry also served the interests of her father's statecraft. Her presence in a city that had been a center of Sumerian power provided visible evidence of Akkadian dominance. The temple hymns that she composed linked the cults of Sumer and Akkad, establishing syncretism between Inanna, Sumerian patroness of love and fertility, and Ishtar, who was Sargon's personal deity. The furtherance of religious unity helped to underpin political unity in Sargon's empire (Hallo and Simpson 1971: 59).

Enheduanna's hymns and poems are written in Sumerian. Her fluency in this language suggests that her mother may have been one of Sargon's concubines rather than his Akkadian wife. From an image on a limestone disc (Meador 2009: 12–14), it appears that Enheduanna had an aquiline nose and prominent brows, and that she wore her hair long and braided. Her ceremonial garb consisted of a floor-length tufted robe and a headband. Her expression in the image is stern, the look of a woman of authority.

Enheduanna had to travel from Akkad to Ur to assume her position as *en*-priestess. This voyage undoubtedly took several days on the canals and rivers of Mesopotamia. Once there she had to lead religious observances and also take charge of a large staff within the temple and on the croplands, fisheries, and livestock centers that it controlled (Meador 2000: 49–51). Of course an entourage of advisers, guards, and servants must have accompanied her on this journey, but still, the prospect of assuming the supreme religious position—and a position of considerable economic significance—in a distant, subjugated city, where resentment against her father's rule may have smoldered, might have discouraged a timid individual. The assertive tenor of much of Enheduanna's poetry shows that she was not of such a mold. She was the daughter of a king; she had inherited his strong will and character.

Although information with respect to the performance of Enheduanna's hymns has not come down to us, there is reason to believe that they were recited or sung during religious observances and accompanied by musical instruments. The surviving texts of other Sumerian and Akkadian hymns display musical instructions (Kilmer and Lawergren 1997: 137–139). Temple personnel included *galas*—lamentation singers—who were accompanied by drum or lyre (Meador 2000: 102; cf. Gabbay 2014: 153 and present work: next profile). Enheduanna's Temple Hymn 24, "The Kinirsha Temple of Dumuzi-Abzu," describes antiphonal singing during a religious service:

> O house Kinirsha   created for its Lady
> rising from the platform   a verdant mountain

> O house   joyful cries erupt deep in your interior
>
> house
>   your princess
> a storm wind astride a lion
> lifting holy song and countersong
> loud voices constantly singing (Meador 2009:
> 160)

Moreover, as Janet Roberts emphasizes in a 2004 study, Enheduanna refers explicitly to "her harp of lamentation." Alluding to the "music-making role" of this priestess, Roberts asserts that Enheduanna "sings songs of praise [...] and plays a musical instrument, probably a lyre, as several are found buried at Ur." If Roberts's assertions are correct, Enheduanna's hymns were an early example indeed of 'lyric' song, predating compositions of the poet Sappho of Lesbos by some 1700 years.

Enheduanna's appointment was in fact to a double priestess-ship, one which linked the cities of Ur and Uruk, two traditional centers of power in Sumer. She served Nanna, the god of the moon, at Ur and An, the god of the heavens, at Uruk. Her residence was in a religious complex known as the *gipar* in Ur, where she cared for the statue of Ningal, Nanna's consort. Enheduanna played the role of this goddess during an annual fertility ritual. Her connection with An is manifest in the Inanna poems, for Inanna was An's divine consort (Hallo & Simpson 1971: 59).

The Inanna poems are theological in nature. They depict conflict in the realm of the gods and exalt Inanna to a position of primacy in the pantheon of the times. They also contain autobiographical information. During a period of political upheaval, a usurper named Lugalanne temporarily banished Enheduanna from her temple. She complains of this treatment in her third poem, *The Exaltation of Inanna*:

You of the radiant heart
[…]
you drew me toward
my holy quarters
[…]
There I raised the ritual basket
there I sang the shout of joy

but *that man* cast me among the dead
I am not allowed in my rooms
gloom falls on the day
[…]
he wipes his spit-soaked hand
on my honey sweet mouth
my beautiful image
fades under dust

what is happening to my fate
O Suen
what is this with Lugalanne (Meador 2000: 174–175)

(Suen was the Akkadian equivalent of the moon god Nanna.) Apart from this episode, Enheduanna remained in office as *en*-priestess throughout the reigns of her two brothers and into that of her nephew, the powerful Naram-Sim, who was Sargon's grandson. Subsequent kings followed Sargon's lead by naming their daughters to life occupancy of the *en*-priesthood in Ur. Like Enheduanna, many of these later priestesses outlived their fathers, helping to ensure continuity through periods of unrest (Hallo & Simpson 1971: 59).

Enheduanna was the most prominent of the *en*-priestesses at Ur, and her works appear to have had a substantial impact on later generations. As recently as the Old Babylonian period (ca. 2000–

1600 BCE), students at Sumerian scribal schools practiced their art by copying Enheduanna's texts; as a result, many copies of the Inanna poems and temple hymns have been preserved on clay tablets (Meador 2000: 67). From this evidence, we can infer that her theological insights continued to be respected and that her hymns continued to be performed for hundreds of years. This is a remarkable legacy for a collection of songs.

References Cited

Gabbay, Uri. 2014. *Pacifying the Hearts of the Gods: Sumerian Emesal Prayers of the First Millennium BC, Heidelberger Emesal-Studien.* Wiesbaden: Harrassowitz Verlag.

Hallo, William W., and William Kelly Simpson. 1971. *The Ancient Near East: A History.* New York: Harcourt Brace Jovanovich.

Kilmer, Anne Draffkorn, and Bo Lawergren. 1997. Mesopotamien. In *Die Musik in Geschichte und Gegenwart (Sachteil)*, edited by L. Finscher. Kassel: Bärenreiter.

McIntosh, Jane R. 2005. *Ancient Mesopotamia: New Perspectives.* Santa Barbara: ABC-CLIO.

Meador, Betty De Shong. 2000. *Inanna, Lady of Largest Heart: Poems of the Sumerian High Priestess Enheduanna.* 1st ed. Austin: University of Texas Press.

———. 2009. *Princess, Priestess, Poet: The Sumerian Temple Hymns of Enheduanna.* 1st ed. Austin: University of Texas Press.

Roberts, Janet. 2004. Enheduanna, Daughter of King Sargon: Princess, Poet, Priestess (2300 B.C.). *Transoxiana: Journal de Estudios Orientales*, http://www.transoxiana.org/0108/roberts-enheduanna.html.

Further Reading

Hallo, William W., and J. J. A. van Dijk. 1968. *The Exaltation of Inanna*. Yale Near Eastern researches. New Haven: Yale University Press.

Kilmer, Anne, and Sam Mirelman. 2013. Mesopotamia. *Grove Music Online. Oxford Music Online, accessed February 25, 2015*, http://www.oxfordmusiconline.com/subscriber/article/grove/music/18485.

León, Vicki. 1995. *Uppity Women of Ancient Times*. Berkeley: Conari Press.

Dada (fl. ca. 2040 BCE)

The musician Dada served as a *gala* for at least twenty-three years (ca. 2052–2029 BCE) in the ancient Sumerian city of Ur. *Galas*, who are also known variously as lamentation- or prayer-singers and priests, had a long-standing presence in the region around the Tigris and Euphrates Rivers. They performed hymns of mourning and praise in order to placate the gods and keep adversity at bay. String and percussion instruments provided instrumental accompaniment. Most *galas* were affiliated with temples, but some were attached directly to palaces, cities, or states (Gabbay 2014: 63–79; Kilmer & Mirelman 2013; Michalowski 2006; Mirelman 2009).

The first attested mention of Dada as a *gala* (Michalowski 2006: 50) is in a document dated in the forty-second year of the reign of King Shulgi (r. ca. 2094–2047). This ruler has been described as the greatest of the kings in the century-long Third Dynasty of Ur, or Ur III (McIntosh 2005: 341). In addition to expanding his kingdom and strengthening its economy, Shulgi also invested in infrastructure, built temples, and established academies. His respect for music is revealed in a self-laudatory poem known as *Shulgi B*, in which he brags of his ability to tune and play lyres, lutes, dulcimer, and double-oboe (Krispijn 1990).

Dada remained active through the end of Shulgi's tenure and during the rule of his successors, Amar-Sin (r. ca. 2046–2038) and Shu-Sin (r. ca. 2037–2029). This musician's career lifted him into a position of influence, prominence, and wealth. From late in the reign of Amar-Sin, surviving documents refer to him not as a simple *gala*, but rather as a *gala-mah* ('chief *gala*'). He seems to have functioned as "the official state impresario, a manager and organizer of various ceremonial events" and as the "chief musical organizer for the crown" (Michalowski 2006: 50 & 59).

Galas were active in Sumeria as early as 2600 BCE, some 500 years prior to Shulgi's reign (Cooper 2006: 42). Associated from the start with funereal rites, they may have taken over the role of lamentation singer from earlier female practitioners (*ibid.*, p. 45). Sumerian myth tells how the powerful god Enki created *galas* in order to assist the goddess Inanna, when she became trapped in the underworld. He fashioned them out of the clay left under his fingernails after his earlier creation of humanity (Gabbay 2014: 68 & 76–78; Kramer 1981). Inanna, who was associated with sexuality and war, is imagined to have had both male and female character traits, together with the ability to transform men into women and *vice versa* (Bachvarova 2008: 20). Similarly, early Mesopotamian *galas* are also thought to have been sexually ambiguous. They wore special garments and suffered the opprobrium of their 'third-gendered' nature (Cooper 2006: 44–45; Gabbay 2014: 74–75; Roscoe 1997: 65–68). A recent study has suggested that at least up to the century prior to Ur III, *galas* may have been hermaphrodites or eunuchs (Gabbay 2014: 67).

Transgendering represents a kind of boundary-crossing within human society and may have added credibility to attempts by the third-millennium *galas* to navigate a perceived boundary between humans and gods (Gabbay 2014: 19). A similar connection between transgendering and spiritual interactions occurs among Siberian shamans (Bachvarova 2008: 35 and references therein).

Galas performed several types of hymns that were sung in a dialect or 'register' of Sumerian known as Emesal. One such work names five types of musical instruments:

> The gala sings a song for him,
> The gala sings a song of lordship for him,
> The [gala] (sings) a song with the *balaĝ* for (him),
> He (plays) the holy *ùb* and the holy *li-li-ìs* (for him),

> He (plays) the *šem*, *me-ze*, and holy *balaḡ* (for him).
> (cited by Gabbay 2014: 81; cf. Cohen 1988: 418–422)

Here *ùb* and *li-li-ìs* refer to large drums; *šem* is the word for cymbals or frame drum; and a *me-ze* was a rattle or sistrum (Gabbay 2014: 86). The meaning of *balaḡ* has been hotly contested (Franklin 2015: 531–534; Heimpel 2015). It is widely thought to have been a string instrument or a drum, but the meaning may have changed through the centuries. During the Third Dynasty, *balaḡ* almost certainly referred to a string instrument, and probably a lyre (Franklin 2005: 43; cf. Heimpel 2015, 631). The words *balaḡ* and *šem* found their way into the names of two important genres of Emesal hymns, *Balaḡ* and *Eršema*, which were prominent during Dada's lifetime. It is likely, therefore, that these instruments accompanied hymnic performances.

In addition to music, Sumerian cultic rituals also involved offerings, animal sacrifices, and libations. These rituals aimed to appease the gods during natural disasters and military losses, and to keep them happy during periods of calm. Appeasement of the gods, known as "heart pacification," is therefore a common feature of Emesal hymns (Gabbay 2014: 5–17), as illustrated in the following excerpt:

> Lord of the nation, Enlil, unfathomable one, how long will your heart not be soothed?
> Father Enlil, who gazes about, how long will your eyes not be tired?
> […]
> Father Enlil, you have smitten the land until you have (completely) destroyed it.
> Lord of the nation, the ewe has abandoned (her) lamb. The goat has abandoned (her) kid.
> […]
> Lord Enlil, may heaven and earth calm you!

> Hero Asarluhi, may haven [*sic!*] and earth calm
> you!
> Lord of the nation, may your majestic heart be
> calmed!
> May the Anunna-gods stand before you in prayer
> (to calm) your heart!
> (Cohen 1988: 166)

This *Balaĝ* to Enlil, one of a triad of supreme gods in Mesopotamia, survives from the so-called Old Babylonian period (ca. 1850–1530 BCE) and is likely similar to prayers performed by galas during Dada's lifetime.

Dada is thought to have reported directly to the crown, and he had responsibilities in both the cultic and non-cultic musical realms. He supervised other *galas*, and aspects of the manufacture and care of musical instruments fell under his purview. According to a "treasury" document from the era, he officiated when two individuals delivered musical instruments (or perhaps while they played on them) for the king's entertainment at a party at the house of a certain general Niridagal (Michalowski 2006: 50). Dada was in charge of sinew for (presumably) string instruments (Gabbay 2014: 72). He took receipt of nine pairs of copper cymbals after they had been repaired (Mirelman 2010). Remarkably, he also took receipt of two bear cubs, which were to be trained as dancing bears (Michalowski 2006: 50).

Even if the *galas* whom Dada supervised may have lived as outsiders, he, like other exceptions to the stereotype (Cooper 2006: 44), fitted comfortably into the upper levels of society. He was married and had several children, which is consistent with the image of the *gala* later on in Mesopotamian history (Gabbay 2014: 288–289). Two of Dada's children performed as musicians in front of the king; two were named sycophantically after the ruling monarchs Amar-Sin and Shu-Sin. A daughter became the bride of the royal Prince Amir-Shulgi (Michalowski 2006: 50). On the occasion of the inauguration of Su-Shin's successor Ibbi-Sin (r. ca. 2028–2004), the new king sent a gift of five fattened sheep to Dada (Sollberger 1956).

Like other favorites of the crown, Dada was rewarded generously for his efforts. He and his family had the use of properties to the north and east of Ur, where the Third Dynasty had acquired vast tracts of land during its establishment and expansion (McIntosh 2005: 130). His holdings included an estate in Nippur or in nearby Sagdana, fields in Girsu near the city of Lagash, and orchards in various settlements (Maekawa 1996). His official residence may have been in Girsu, but he was also associated with Urua, which lay farther to the east, and he definitely had a residence in Ur (Michalowski 2006: 50). When Dada died in ca. 2029, the king confiscated many of the musician's properties and shifted his laborers to other duties. Dada's wife was allowed to keep her flock of sheep, a dispensation that would have provided her with independent means during widowhood (Maekawa 1996: 142).

References Cited

Bachvarova, Mary R. 2008. Sumerian Gala Priests and Eastern Mediterranean Returning Gods: Tragic Lamentation in Cross-Cultural Perspective. In *Lament: Studies in the Ancient Mediterranean and Beyond*, edited by A. Suter. New York: Oxford University Press.

Cohen, Mark E. 1988. *The Canonical Lamentations of Ancient Mesopotamia*. 2 vols. Potomac: Capital Decisions Ltd.

Cooper, Jerrold S. 2006. Genre, Gender,and the Sumerian Lamentation. *Journal of Cuneiform Studies* 58:39–47.

Franklin, John Curtis. 2005. Lyre Gods of the Bronze Age Musical Koine. *Journal of Ancient Near East Religions* 6:39–70.

———. 2015. *Kinyras: The Divine Lyre. With a Study of Balang Gods by Wolfgang Heimpel and Illustrations by Glynnis Fawkes.* 1st ed, Hellenic Studies. Washington, D.C.: Center for Hellenic Studies.

Gabbay, Uri. 2014. *Pacifying the Hearts of the Gods: Sumerian Emesal Prayers of the First Millennium BC, Heidelberger Emesal-Studien.* Wiesbaden: Harrassowitz Verlag.

Heimpel, Wolfgang. 2015. Balang-Gods. In *J. C. Franklin. Kinyras: The Divine Lyre. With a Study of Balang Gods by Wolfgang Heimpel and Illustrations by Glynnis Fawkes.* 1st ed, Hellenic Studies Series. Washington, D.C.: Center for Hellenic Studies. Pages 571–632.

Kilmer, Anne, and Sam Mirelman. 2013. Mesopotamia. *Grove Music Online. Oxford Music Online, accessed February 25, 2015,* http://www.oxfordmusiconline.com/subscriber/article/g rove/music/18485.

Kramer, Samuel Noah. 1981. BM 29616: The Fashioning of the *gala. Acta Sumerologica* 3:1–12.

Krispijn, T. J. 1990. Beiträge zur altorientalischen Musikforschung, I: Šulgi und Musik. *Akkadica* 70:1–27.

Maekawa, Kazuya. 1996. Confiscation of Private Properties in the Ur III Period. *Acta Sumerologica* 18:138–144.

McIntosh, Jane R. 2005. *Ancient Mesopotamia: New Perspectives.* Santa Barbara: ABC-CLIO.

Michalowski, P. 2006. Love or Death? Observations on the Role of the Gala in Ur III Ceremonial Life. *Journal of Cuneiform Studies* 58:49–61.

Mirelman, Sam. 2009. New Developments in the Social History of Music and Musicians in Ancient Iraq, Syria, and Turkey. *Yearbook for Traditional Music* 41:12–22.

———. 2010. The Gala Musician Dada and the Si-im Instrument. *Nouvelles Assyriologiques Brèves et Utilitaires* (2):40-1, no.33.

Roscoe, Will. 1997. Precursors of Islamic Male Homosexualities. In *Islamic Homosexualities: Culture, History, and Literature*, edited by S. O. Murray and W. Roscoe. New York & London: New York University Press.

Sollberger, Edmond. 1956. Selected Texts from American Collections. *Journal of Cuneiform Studies* 10 (1):11–31.

Further Reading

Hallo, William W., and William Kelly Simpson. 1971. *The Ancient Near East: A History*. New York: Harcourt Brace Jovanovich.

Heimpel, Wolfgang. 1997. A Famous Harpist. *Nouvelles Assyriologiques Brèves et Utilitaires* (4):126, no.137.

Kilmer, Anne Draffkorn, and Bo Lawergren. 1997. Mesopotamien. In *Die Musik in Geschichte und Gegenwart (Sachteil)*, edited by L. Finscher. Kassel: Bärenreiter.

Mieroop, Marc Van De. 2007. *A History of the Ancient Near East, ca. 3000–323 BC*. 2nd ed, Blackwell History of the Ancient World. Malden: Blackwell.

Risiya (fl. ca.1790 BCE)

In the early part of the 18th century BCE, Risiya served as head of music in Mari, a city on the Euphrates River at a site a few miles north of the present Syrian-Iraqi border. The city had recently been captured by the Assyrian conqueror Shamshi-Adad, who integrated Mari into his territorial kingdom of Upper Mesopotamia. He put his younger son Yasmah-Addu on the throne in Mari, replacing a member of the local dynasty. Although the Upper Mesopotamian kingdom is no longer well-known, it loomed large for 30 years, or so, until Shamshi-Addad died in ca. 1776 BCE (Mieroop 2007: 106–111).

This was an era of volatile political change, in which allegiances were quickly sworn and as quickly dissolved, in which kings and kingdoms rose up and vanished in short order. After Shamshi-Addad died, his domain was torn apart by its neighbors. In Mari, an exiled member of the earlier ruling dynasty, a man named Zimri-Lim, recaptured the throne for his clan. Zimri-Lim worked hard to secure his position in Mari, forming alliances with Qatna, Aleppo, and Babylon. However, in ca. 1761 Hammurabi broke faith. His troops roared out of Babylon and put an end to Zimri-Lim. Two years later Hammurabi destroyed the palace and razed the city walls (*ibid.*, pp. 103–107).

In an ironic twist of history, the destruction of Mari led to the preservation in its ruins of a remarkable treasure trove that has served to illuminate the lives of the people and to characterize the city's relations with its neighbors. Some 20,000 letters on clay tablets have been discovered since 1933, when excavations were begun by French archeologists (*ibid.*, p. 87). The story of Risiya's tenure as head of music has emerged in a study of some of these letters, as collated and interpreted by the Assyriology scholar Nele

Ziegler (Ziegler 2007: 1–146; cited simply by page numbers in the following).

Risiya was appointed head of music by Yasmah-Addu after he took over as regent in ca. 1795. The position was important, because music was highly regarded and because the size and quality of the city's musical establishment were seen as measures of royal prestige. The head of music would need to have been an accomplished musician, certainly, but performance virtuosity might not have been required. The head of music needed to have pedagogical, administrative, and management skills (pp. 9–11). Risiya's situation could be approximated to that of a civil servant of the present day, and his tenure therefore provides a very early example of careerist professionalism in music.

Risiya was charged with the organization of musical life in the court. He had to train musicians, collect people at the right place and time, keep up to date with musical developments in other places, and take part in the quest for fresh human resources (p. 84). Heads of state would sometimes trade or barter for capable performers who might enrich the musical life of their courts, and they also acquired musicians as booty during successful military campaigns (p. 37). In addition, musicians in other cities occasionally emigrated or fled to Mari (pp. 28–31). Musicians were not marginalized and appear to have enjoyed comfortable lives. Men were provided with land, livestock, and servants (pp. 24–25).

An assistant to the head of music was in charge of music instruction, which began in infancy and extended through to the most advanced level (pp. 15–20). Children in the harem were likely candidates, and private individuals could give up their children for musical training (p. 134). Both Risiya and the head of music instruction exercised control over distinct groups of performers, whose selection became a source of friction between the two men (pp. 83–86).

Separate facilities were available for teaching. The *bit tegetum* was a conservatory for young female string players from the palace. The *mummum* was a conservatory for men. In domestic situations, there were installations called *wartum* for use in playing or teaching music in a private setting (p. 79).

Although the principal responsibility for the music of worship appears to have rested with religious authorities, Risiya also had some responsibilities in this area. He arranged for lamentation singers (*kalum*) to be present at religious ceremonies, rehearsed the orchestra, and probably decided whom to employ on which occasion (pp. 64–65).

By the start of the 18th century BCE, musical life was already sophisticated in Mesopotamia. Individuals, choruses, and instrumental ensembles sang or performed on a variety of instruments. Harps, lyres, and lutes; flutes and other winds; drums; and a variety of idiophones (cymbals, bells, scrapers, etc.) were typical of the era. The presence in religious services of a "divine" lyre (*ninigizibara*) illustrates the seriousness with which music was viewed (p. 56). This and the giant drum *alum* are the most notable instruments attested in archeological finds at Mari. An *alum* made of bronze and hide, and perhaps as tall as a person, was sent from Mari to Aleppo. The man in charge of the transport complained of the task, writing (with, perhaps, some exaggeration) that 16 or more men were needed to transport it (pp. 74–76).

Most of the court musicians in Mari were women in the royal harem. Twenty-four women made up a "grand orchestra," which may have included both instrumentalists and singers (p. 14). Ziegler reports that there were 270 female musicians in the palace during the reign of Zimri-Lim, half of them children or adolescents, as compared with around 50 male musicians of whom she is aware in the kingdom of Mari (p. 48). Risiya may have had access to the harem, and in any case he taught girls and young women and organized the activities of older female musicians and teachers. The fact that he was allowed to interact closely with female musicians suggests that he may have been a eunuch (p. 23).

The head of music made the travel arrangements when female musicians were being transferred from one place to another. On longer trips they went in caravans, closely guided and guarded. At the start of Zimri-Lim's reign, Risiya was given a further assignment, one that had nothing to do with music but which also involved the transportation of women: he was required to undertake matrimonial missions to other capitals. On the first of these missions, Zimri-Lim sent his sister to become a wife of the king of the Benjamites; on the second, a princess in Aleppo was brought back to Mari to be wedded to Zimri-Lim (pp. 86–87).

The head of music would appear to have led an upper-class life. Risiya kept a country estate for his subsistence, with servants to manage it, and probably also had a residence at the music conservatory, which he headed, in town. At one point, because of poor management, the estate had become run-down, and Risiya asked the king for a new property of 100 arpents (ca. 85 acres) to replace it. As a compromise, he was offered 60 arpents of good land, which met with Risiya's satisfaction (pp. 88–89).

Risiya had the good fortune to serve under Yasmah-Addu, who had been tutored as a child by his father's head of music and retained an appreciation for the art. Yasmah-Addu seems, moreover, to have taken a personal liking to Risiya. His father Shamshi-Adad was, however, aghast when he learned that his son intended to appoint this man. "You have named Risiya," he wrote, "the musician who is absolutely incapable of leading 'soloists,' to the position of head of music! Music has been ruined in Mari! Come on: name Gumul-Dagan as head of music" (p. 100; my translation from Ziegler's French). Although Yasmah-Addu had a reputation for weakness, he dug in his heels in the face of his father's demand

and persisted with the nomination of Risiya. Later, when Risiya was ill, Yasmah-Addu drafted an urgent letter to summon a doctor:

> I have recently written to ask Adda to send Meranum, the physician, here. At present he has not yet arrived. Risiya risks losing his life; he is very ill. If it pleases Adda, Meranum should come quickly so as to save Risiya's life. He must not die!

Evidently, the letter was never sent, and Risiya did recover, but the king's words reveal his fondness for the man (p. 83; my translation from Ziegler's French).

Even though he benefited from the good will of the king, Risiya did, of course, face difficulties during his tenure. Rivals in Shamshi-Addad's court at Subat-Enlil may have been behind the pressure put on Yasmah-Addu to choose Gumul-Dagan over Risiya. Risiya later sought to travel to Subat-Enlil in order to defend himself against slandering by this rival (pp. 99–100). The father of some children whom Risiya was training accused him of teaching indecencies (pp. 134–138). His assistant Ilsu-ibbisu, the head of music instruction at Mari, competed with him for the king's favor and for control of musicians. According to one document, Risiya had 49 female musicians in his service while Ilsu-ibbisu had 94 (p. 113).

Although these difficulties presented serious challenges, they are of the sort that government officials might expect to experience during their careers. When Zimri-Lim seized power from Yasmah-Addu, Risiya was faced with a challenge of another order: his new master was more aggressive militarily and less focused on music than his predecessor. Zimri-Lim kept Risiya on, but the attention that the king paid to matrimonial statecraft suggests that securing the reins of power was his primary concern. After the matrimonial missions, Risiya's name no longer appears in the Mari documents. He may have retired or passed away at this time (pp. 90–92).

References Cited

Mieroop, Marc Van De. 2007. *A History of the Ancient Near East, ca. 3000–323 BC.* 2nd ed, Blackwell History of the Ancient World. Malden: Blackwell Pub.

Ziegler, Nele. 2007. *Les musiciens et la musique d'après les archives de Mari, Florilegium marianum.* Paris: SEPOA.

Further Reading

Dalley, Stephanie. 1984. *Mari and Karana: Two Old Babylonian Cities.* London & New York: Longman.

Hallo, William W., and William Kelly Simpson. 1971. *The Ancient Near East: A History.* New York,: Harcourt Brace Jovanovich.

Kilmer, Anne. 2001. Mesopotamia. In *The New Grove Dictionary of Music and Musicians*, edited by S. Sadie and J. Tyrrell. New York: Grove.

Kilmer, Anne Draffkorn, and Bo Lawergren. 1997. Mesopotamien. In *Die Musik in Geschichte und Gegenwart (Sachteil)*, edited by L. Finscher. Kassel: Bärenreiter.

Soden, Wolfram von. 1988. Musikinstrumente in Märi. *Nouvelles Assyriologiques Brèves et Utilitaires* Note Brève #59.

Ziegler, Nele. 2006A. Introduction: "La Musique au Proche-Orient Ancien". *Les Dossiers d'Archéologie* 310:2–3.

———. 2006B. Les musiciens de la cour de Mari. *Les Dossiers d'Archéologie* 310:32–38.

King David (1040–970; r. 1010–970 BCE)

David was born in the ancient town of Bethlehem late in the eleventh century BCE. According to the Bible (following the Revised Standard Version throughout), he was the eighth son of a shepherd named Jesse, and he rose from his lowly position as a shepherd to become ruler of the United Kingdom of Israel and Judah. Early on, he achieved fame as a musician and a military hero (McKinnon 2001: 44; Rylaarsdam 2014). When the biblical account was being written, musical proficiency and success in combat would have been seen as evidence that David enjoyed the favor of Yahweh, god of the Israelites (Bright 2000: 197; Franklin 2011).

The musical and military aspects of David's complex persona, together with his special religious status, are evident from the outset of the biblical treatment of his life. In 1 Samuel 16, the Israelite king Saul (r. ca. 1010 BCE), who has been suffering from "an evil spirit," is advised to take on a skilled player of the lyre (*kinnôr* in Hebrew; often mistranslated as 'harp'), because listening to the music of this instrument would relieve his condition. A servant suggests that the shepherd David might fit the bill, for the young man is *"skillful in playing,* a man of valor, *a man of war,* prudent in speech, and a man of good presence; and *the Lord is with him"* (italics added). Saul summons David and brings him into the royal entourage. David's lyre-playing counteracts the evil spirit in Saul, and David defeats Goliath, champion of the Philistines, on the field of battle (1 Samuel 17). Both these episodes are afforded comparable weight; indeed, the texts are ambiguous about which of the two situations first brings David to Saul's attention.

The first book of Samuel reports that while David was still in the service of King Saul, he led the Israelite army to numerous victories over the Philistines. In the biblical account, after breaking with the king, David flees into the wilds of his native Judah, where he survives for a time as a warlord. Saul's troops make life uncomfortable for him, and so he seeks refuge in Gath, a stronghold of his former enemies, the Philistines. They set him up as their vassal at a city in Judah, but do not trust him enough to take him along in a major campaign against the Israelite army. In the course of this campaign, Saul and three of his sons die, including Jonathan, with whom David had formed a close friendship.

Still a vassal of the Philistines, David and his private army move to Hebron, where at age thirty he is acclaimed king of Judah (2 Samuel 2 & 5). Here he rules for seven and a half years, making war against the forces of Ish-bosheth, another of Saul's sons, who has become his father's successor. After Ish-bosheth is murdered by two of his own soldiers, David takes his place on the throne. He reigns over the United Kingdom of Israel and Judah for thirty-three years. During this time, he transforms his domain into a sizeable empire (2 Samuel 2–12). In the words of a recent historical study, under David, Israel became "the foremost power of Palestine and Syria [… and] probably as strong as any power in the contemporary world" (Bright 2000: 204).

In contrast with this tale of violence and swashbuckling adventure, the Bible also associates David with four types of musical activity: lyre-playing, singing, composing, and the organization of cultic music. He is said to have had instruments built for use in the religious sanctuary, and to have danced.

As described in 1 Samuel 16, David's rise from obscurity begins, when as a young and inexperienced shepherd he is called upon to perform on the lyre before the ailing king. This passage represents early written documentation of music therapy. Contextually, it foreshadows in religious terms a shift in political leadership away from the house of Saul. In 1 Samuel 10, the Lord anointed Saul as king, but now, in 1 Samuel 16, "the spirit of the Lord" has departed from him, whereas for David, "the Lord is with him."

Although the lyre was the dominant musical instrument in Israel during David's lifetime (Braun 2002: 16–19 & 145–164), his identification with this instrument may be especially significant (Franklin 2011). In areas of the Ancient Near East, the lyre was believed to facilitate prophesy and communicating with the gods, and in some societies, it had acquired divine status (Franklin 2015). The biblical depiction of David as a lyrist places him squarely within this regional context (*ibid.*, pp. 149–184).

David's melodies have not survived, but texts have come down to us. He is said to have written a lamentation on the deaths of Saul and Jonathan:

> Saul and Jonathan, beloved and lovely!
> In life and in death they were not divided:
> They were swifter than eagles,
> They were stronger than lions.
>
> [...]
>
> How are the mighty fallen,
> And the weapons of war perished!
> (2 Samuel 1)

Preceding the lamentation text is a description of David's violent response when an Amalekite refugee reports that he delivered the *coup de grâce* to King Saul, who was dying: David has the young man killed.

The extent of David's compositional activity is controversial. His name appears in the headings on close to half the 150 songs and hymns in the Psalter, but he is now believed to have written far fewer than this. Seidel asserts that the majority of the texts were written after 587 BCE, when the Israelites' exile in Babylon started and long after David's life had ended (Braun & Cohen 1996: col. 1857). Even so, David's significance as a religious figure continued to grow in this period, and more and more hymns and poems came to be attributed to him. A document probably written in the first century BCE, and discovered at Qumran in Palestine, claims that David composed a total of 4050 songs (col. 1859). By way of contrast, a recent discussion dismisses as an exaggeration the attribution of 73 psalm texts to David, while acknowledging that "it is possible that David wrote at least some psalms, since he seems definitely to have composed the moving laments over the deaths of Saul and Jonathan" (McKinnon 2001: 44).

The Psalter is rich in references to singing, songs, and musical instruments—often strings, but also winds and percussion—and to the instrumental accompaniment of songs. Psalm 144 has David playing a ten-stringed lyre, which, it has been suggested, David may have invented. The lyre might have been tuned symmetrically in a pair of identical pentatonic scales, when accompanying choirs that were to perform responsorially "in a single voice" (Sillamy 2006: 73). Several of the psalm headings also appear to specify musical modes or melodies. However, the headings may be a late addition, and the musical information they contain has not yet been clearly deciphered (Sillamy 2006: 72–73; Smith, Bailey, Troelsgard, Doe, Planchart, & Boyd 2001: 449–450).

After David had taken Jerusalem from the Jebusites and made it his capital, he brought the Ark of the Covenant into the city and installed it in a tented sanctuary. Retrieving this relic from Kiriath-Jearim, where it had lain neglected during Saul's reign, was a way to make Jerusalem the religious as well as the political center of the land and to present David's kingdom as the legitimate heir to Israel's ancient order. Uniting Ark and priesthood in an official national shrine would also provide a sacred focus to attract and sustain the loyalty of the disparate Israelite tribes. The move has been described as "a masterstroke" (Bright 2000: 200–201).

In the biblical description, David leads a procession of thousands of people, who accompany the Ark on its way to the shrine. They sing, play music, and dance:

> David and all the house of Israel were making merry before the LORD with all their might, with songs and lyres and harps and tambourines and castanets and cymbals (2 Samuel 6).

In a later, revised version of the event, 1 Chronicles 13 substitutes trumpets for the castanets. The procession is interrupted by the death of one of the drivers of the oxcart on which the Ark is being carried, but after a three-month hiatus, it starts up again with Levites in charge of the transport.

Braun has found the depiction of the procession in 2 Samuel, which McKinnon deems "entirely credible" (McKinnon 2001: 44), to be "brimming with pagan intoxication" (Braun 2002: 20). The music would have been "loud" and "orgiastic," according to Braun and Cohen, who argue that it was likely influenced by Canaanite tradition (1996: col. 1521). A recent study presents a strain of scholarship according to which the transfer of the Ark was a key step in a process by which David adapted and merged into Judaism the cult of the Jebusites on Zion, who were Canaanites and had previously controlled the city (Rylaarsdam 2014).

Whatever the political and religious implications of the transfer may have been, it was clearly a raucous affair. In 2 Samuel 6, the procession arrives in town to the sound of rejoicing and horns, with David leaping and dancing at its head. David's exuberant performance shocks his wife Michal, the daughter of King Saul, who was not with David during his rough existence in the wilderness. She scolds her husband for his lack of dignity, and he responds testily. Following the spat, she has no children—at least not with David: in Josephus's interpretation of 2 Samuel 21, she rejoins a former husband and has five children with him (VII: 87–89).

In 1 Chronicles 23 & 25 and 2 Chronicles 7, David establishes the Levitical orders of temple musicians and makes musical instruments for them. These passages illustrate David's central importance in Jewish music and are revealing of ancient religious practice. They are, however, thought to be largely a reading of later events into the original history, for it was David and Bathsheba's son, King Solomon, who constructed the first temple (McKinnon 2001: 44).

David's musical influence has extended far beyond ancient Israel. As a musician—and in other ways also—the Judeo-Christian tradition venerates this ancient king (McKinnon 2001: 44–45). For all three principal monotheistic religions of the world, David's hymns are "an ideal model of religious song and singing across subsequent generations" (Shiloah 2010: 21). Islam honors David for having "the most beautiful voice that God created" (*ibid.*, p. 26).

References Cited

Braun, Joachim. 2002. *Music in Ancient Israel/Palestine: Archaeological, Written, and Comparative Sources.* Translated by D. W. Stott, Bible in Its World. Grand Rapids & Cambridge: William B. Eerdmans.

Braun, Joachim, and Judith Cohen. 1996. Jüdische Musik. In *Die Musik in Geschichte und Gegenwart. Sachteil,* edited by F.

Blume and L. Finscher. Kassel: Bärenreiter; Stuttgart: Metzler.

Bright, John. 2000. *A History of Israel*. 4th ed, Westminster Aids to the Study of the Scriptures. Louisville: Westminster J. Knox Press.

Franklin, John Curtis. 2011. Sweet Psalmist of Israel. In *Strings and Threads: A Celebration of the Work of Anne Draffkorn Kilmer*, edited by W. Heimpel. Winona Lake: Eisenbrauns.

———. 2015. *Kinyras: The Divine Lyre. With a Study of Balang Gods by Wolfgang Heimpel and Illustrations by Glynnis Fawkes*. 1st ed, Hellenic Studies. Washington, D.C.: Center for Hellenic Studies.

Josephus, Flavius. 1958. Jewish Antiquities. In *Josephus, With an English Translation by H. St. J. Thackeray and Ralph Marcus*. Cambridge & London: Harvard University Press & W. Heinemann.

McKinnon, James W. 2001. David. In *The New Grove Dictionary of Music and Musicians*, edited by S. Sadie and J. Tyrrell. New York: Grove.

Rylaarsdam, J. Coert. David. *Encyclopædia Britannica Online Academic Edition* (23 May 2014), <http://www.britannica.com/EBchecked/topic/152497/David>.

Shiloah, Ammon. 2010. King David and the Devil, Initiators of Two Kinds of Music. In *Across Centuries and Cultures: Musicological Studies in Honor of Joachim Braun*, edited by K. C. Karnes and L. Sheptovitsky. Frankfurt: Peter Lang.

Sillamy, Jean-Claude. 2006. David, roi musicien. *Les Dossiers d'Archéologie* 310:72–76.

Smith, John Arthur, Terence Bailey, Christian Troelsgard, Paul Doe, Alejandro E. Planchart, and Malcolm Boyd. 2001.

Psalm. In *The New Grove Dictionary of Music and Musicians*, edited by S. Sadie and J. Tyrrell. New York: Grove

Further Reading

Avenary, Hanoch, and Jeffrey Dean. Jewish Music. In *The Oxford Companion to Music. Oxford Music Online*, edited by A. Latham: Oxford University Press, accessed May 22, 2014. http://www.oxfordmusiconline.com/subscriber/article/opr/t114/e3564.

Seidel, Hans, Joseph Dyer, and Ludwig Finscher. 1997. Psalm. In *Die Musik in Geschichte und Gegenwart. Sachteil*, edited by F. Blume and L. Finscher. Kassel: Bärenreiter; Stuttgart: Metzler.

Seroussi, Edwin, et al. 2001. Jewish Music. In *The New Grove Dictionary of Music and Musicians*, edited by S. Sadie and J. Tyrrell. New York: Grove.

Musicians of Western Asia CE

As the Islamic Empire expanded during the seventh and eighth centuries CE, aspects of Persian music entered into the culture of the Arabian Peninsula. The musical art flourished in centers such as Medina and Baghdad, but Islamic musicians had to negotiate a treacherous path around religious restrictions. Emigrants carried the cultural achievements of Baghdad to places as far away as the western reaches of the Mediterranean.

The lutenist, singer, composer, and music theorist **Bārbad (fl. ca. 600 CE)** served under King Khosrow II Parviz (r. 591–628 CE) toward the end of the Sasanian Dynasty in Persia. Bārbad played an early form of silk-stringed lute known as a *bārbat*. He devised an elaborate musical framework, the *dastānat*, which was still being used in the tenth century, well after the Arab conquest of Persia in 652 CE.

The singer, lutenist, and music teacher **Jamīla (d. ca. 715 CE)** rose from lowly origins as a *mawala* ('client') of an Arab tribe to a position of prominence and wealth in the city of Medina. She staged elegant entertainments for literati and ran a profitable music school for slaves.

Ibrāhīm al-Mawṣilī (742–804 CE) was born into a family of Persian refugees in the city of Kufa, Iraq. As a young itinerant musician, he acquired extensive knowledge of Persian and Arab songs. His talent carried him to Baghdad, where, after a rocky start, he became the chief court musician and boon companion of Caliph Harun al-Rashid (r. 786–809 CE). Ibrāhīm al-Mawṣilī composed prolifically and coauthored a collection of 100 songs. He lived handsomely on an enormous salary plus income from land-holdings and a music school for young female slaves.

Ibrāhīm's son **Isḥāq al-Mawṣilī (767–850 CE)** excelled as a lutenist and was admired for his extensive knowledge and writings on music. When Ibrāhīm died in 804, Isḥāq took over as chief court musician. He is said to have composed 400 songs and nearly 40 works of prose. He developed a new way to classify rhythmic modalities. He had many pupils and is considered to have been one of the greatest Islamic musicians. Both he and his father are featured in the *Arabian Nights*.

The lutenist and singer **Ziryāb (ca. 790–850 CE)**, whose name refers to his dark complexion, was likely of black-African heritage. In the face of prejudice and discouraging setbacks, he advanced beyond lowly beginnings in Syria and Arabia to become the leading musician at the Umayyad emirate in Córdoba on the Iberian Peninsula and an intimate of its ruler, 'Abd al-Raḥmān II (r. 822–852). He founded a school for freemen and slaves that influenced the development of Andalusian music. Ziryāb commanded a large repertory of songs and made technical improvements to the lute. After he died, his children carried on his music teachings.

∞

Seven of Merriam's ten functions of music can be associated with these musicians:

THE FUNCTION OF EMOTIONAL EXPRESSION

In Medina on the Arabian Peninsula, **Jamīla** staged elegant entertainments (*majalis*), at which music and poetry transported her guests in episodes of collective catharsis. At one such event, many listeners succumbed under the emotional impact, when she sang erotic verses by a renowned Arab poet. They clapped, stamped, swayed their heads, shouted ecstatically, and even tore their clothing.

THE FUNCTION OF AESTHETIC ENJOYMENT

The Persian **Bārbad** devised an elaborate musical framework, the so-called *dastānat*, which incorporates seven 'royal' and thirty derivative musical modes for the creation of distinctive melodies. His *dastānat*, which was adopted by Islamic musicians, is the earliest known systematization of tonalities in the region of Western Asia. **Ibrāhīm al-Mawṣilī** and his son **Isḥāq al-Mawṣilī** dominated the musical scene in Baghdad during their lifetimes. The aesthetic they promoted derived from traditional Persian and Arabic song. Both musicians represented the conservative or classical wing in a lengthy debate with modernists at the court in which they served.

Trained by Isḥāq al-Mawṣilī in Baghdad, the lutenist and singer **Ziryāb** carried Middle Eastern aesthetics to the Emirate of Córdoba on the Iberian Peninsula. He established a conservatory that influenced musical taste in Al-Andalus.

THE FUNCTION OF ENTERTAINMENT

The following musicians composed and/or performed entertainment music at court: **Bārbad** in Ctesiphon, **Ibrāhīm** and **Isḥāq al-Mawṣilī** in Baghdad, and **Ziryāb** in Córdoba. **Jamīla** held musical entertainments at her home in Medina.

THE FUNCTION OF COMMUNICATION

A story attributed to the life of the Persian lutenist and singer **Bārbad** illustrates the indirect communication of information through music: The Persian king Khosrow II, under whom Bārbad served, had a favorite horse called Šabdēz. The king swore death to anyone who would report that the animal had died. When the horse did die, the Grand Equerry feared for his life and asked Bārbad to intercede. Bārbad composed a song that contained subtle allusions to the event. Grasping the song's meaning, the king cried out: "Šabdēz is dead!" "Yes, and the king himself has announced it!" the musician responded, thereby averting the ultimate penalty.

THE FUNCTION OF SYMBOLIC REPRESENTATION

Jamīla in Medina, **Ibrāhīm al-Mawṣilī** and **Isḥāq al-Mawṣilī** in Baghdad all had to contend directly or indirectly with influential Moslem clerics, who believed that musical entertainment symbolized evil.

THE FUNCTION OF VALIDATION OF SOCIAL INSTITUTIONS AND RELIGIOUS RITUALS

The music of the outstanding musicians **Ibrāhīm** and **Isḥāq al-Mawṣilī** created a culturally rich environment at court, which added to the impression of validity of the social institution of government.

THE FUNCTION OF CONTRIBUTION TO THE CONTINUITY AND STABILITY OF CULTURE

The musical framework known as the *dastānat*, which **Bārbad** created in Persia around 600 CE, was in use by Arabian musicians during several centuries after his passing. To obtain firsthand knowledge of traditional Arabian music, **Ibrāhīm al-Mawṣilī** traveled to the town of Medina in the Hijaz, a region in the west of present-day Saudi Arabia. He interviewed elderly inhabitants and gathered popular songs to be integrated into his own musical repertory. At the behest of Caliph Harun al-Rashid, he and two other musicians created a collection of one-hundred songs, which was later revised by Ibrāhīm's son **Isḥāq al-Mawṣilī**. Preserving these pieces represented a contribution to the continuity and stability of musical culture in the Islamic Empire. When **Ziryāb** arrived in Al-Andalus from Baghdad, he brought the glittering cultural heritage of the eastern city to his new home in Córdoba. He established a school for transmitting his musical precepts to Andalusian musicians.

Bārbad (fl. ca. 600 CE)

Lutenist, singer, composer, and music theorist Bārbad served under Khosrow II Parviz (r. 591–628 CE), one of the later kings of Persia's Sasanian Dynasty (Daniel 2012: 56–66). Khosrow's palace was in the ancient city of Ctesiphon on the Tigris River near the site of the present city of Baghdad. This dynasty lasted more than 400 years, from 224 to 651 CE, during which time Persia dominated much of western and central Asia. Khosrow II, whose epithet means 'victorious,' expanded Sasanian rule to its greatest expanse (if temporarily), while indulging in an extravagant lifestyle at home. An ardent admirer of the musical arts, he created what has been termed "a veritable Golden Age of Iranian music" (Lawergren, Farhat, & Blum 2001: 528).

Among the half-dozen Golden Age musicians whose names have come down to us, Khosrow's favorite Bārbad takes clear precedence (During, Mirabdolbaghi, & Safvat 1991: 106; Miller 1999: 6). He has been described as "the most distinguished and talented minstrel-poet of his epoch" (Tafażżolī 1988: 757) and the "founder of Persian music" (cited by Lawergren, Farhat, & Blum 2001, p. 529). In addition to composing and performing, Bārbad devised an elaborate musical framework, which was later absorbed into the culture of the Islamic Empire, ensuring widespread and persistent significance for his musical achievements (Blum 2001: 365; Farhat 1990: 3–4; Lawergren, Farhat, & Blum 2001: 530; Miller 1999: 6–11).

Bārbad played an early form of lute known as *bārbat*, which probably originated around the start of the first millennium CE in what was eastern Persia and is now Tajikistan. This pear-shaped instrument had a short neck and a rather flat belly, both of which were carved out of a single piece of wood. A wooden sounding-board covered its belly and supported a bridge, to which four silk strings were tied. They ran along the fretted neck to adjustable pegs on a bent-back section at the top. The *bārbat* was tuned in fourths and played with the aid of a large plectrum. It was in use until the tenth century, when the closely related *'ūd*, with four or five double gut strings, supplanted it (During, Mirabdolbaghi, & Safvat 1991: 106).

The musical framework that Bārbad devised is the earliest known systematization of tonalities in the Middle East. His seven heptatonic structures, the so-called "royal modes" (*khosrovāni*), were to be combined with thirty derivative modes (*lahn*) in the creation of distinctive melodies (*dastānat*), of which he is said to have composed 360. His framework was thus in correspondence respectively with the number of days in the week, month, and year (apart from intercalary days) of the Zoroastrian calendar. Bārbad's *dastānat* was in common use into the tenth century, well after the Arab conquest of Persia in 652 CE. Sources from the Islamic period list the names of some 170 of his pieces (Braune 1999; Lawergren, Farhat, & Blum 2001: 529–530).

Bārbad performed his songs on various state occasions including festivals, banquets, and celebrations of military victories (Tafażżolī 1988: 757). His *Bāġ-e nakjīrān* ("Garden of the Game") marked the completion of the great gardens at Qaṣr-e Šīrīn (*ibid.*). Other song titles give evidence of thematic diversity: For example, "The Vengeance of Iraj" and "The Throne of Ardešir" seem related to historical topics; "Sovereign's Garden" and "The Seven Treasures" may have sung praises of Khosrow's court; and "Green Spring" and "Moon over the Mountains" would possibly have depicted the glories of nature (Farhat 1990: 3; Tafażżolī 1988: 757).

Unfortunately, only the song titles have survived from the past. Bārbad's melodies and poetry are lost, apart from a fragment in Middle Persian of a panegyric, which an Arabian author had quoted (Tafażżolī 1988: 758). However, in the 1930s a poem titled *Khvarshēdh ī rōshan* ("The Shining Sun") surfaced within a collection of Manichaean manuscripts in Xinjiang Province, China:

> The shining sun, the beaming full moon
> resplendent and beaming behind the trunk of a tree;
> the eager birds strut about it full of joy,
> the doves and the colorful peacocks strut about.
> (Lawergren, Farhat, & Blum 2001: 529)

The scholar A. Christensen is reported to have suggested that Bārbad may have composed and sung these lines (*ibid.*).

Bārbad's appearances as a musician and gifts as a composer have remained alive in numerous stories and legends. He emerges from such accounts as an individual of intellectual agility, who became influential at court and possessed outstanding creative talents.

One such story relates how Bārbad first came to the king's attention. Having been kept away from the court out of jealousy by the chief minstrel Sargīs, he performed while hidden in foliage during an outdoor banquet at the palace. The music so delighted the king that he granted Bārbad an audience and made him chief minstrel in Sargīs's place (Tafażżolī 1988: 757).

Another account describes how Bārbad foiled the nefarious scheme of a rival, who had secretly detuned Bārbad's *bārbat* prior to a performance. Bārbad played so well on the corrupted instrument that the king, who disliked having musicians tune their instruments in his presence, was oblivious to the problem (*ibid.*).

The tale most often told about Bārbad relates to a black horse called Šabdēz (Color of the Night), which belonged to the king

(Blum 2001: 365; Caron & Safvate 1997: 213; During, Mirabdolbaghi & Safvat 1991: 154; Miller 1999: 6; Tafażżolī 1988: 757). This was Khosrow's favorite steed, and he swore death to any messenger who would report that the animal had died. When Šabdēz did die, the Grand Equerry asked Bārbad to intercede. Bārbad composed a song that the king interpreted correctly: "Šabdēz is dead!" Khosrow cried out. "Yes, and the king himself has announced it!" the wily musician responded, thereby averting the ultimate penalty.

Bārbad interceded with the king on behalf of courtiers and even for Khosrow's favorite wife Šīrīn. For her, he reminded the sovereign of his promise to build her a palace. She rewarded Bārbad by giving him an estate near Isfahan, where he settled with his family (Tafażżolī 1988: 757).

The end of this musician's life is the subject of contradictory accounts. When the king died, Bārbad is said to have cut his fingers, recited elegies, and burned his instruments. Other stories claim that he was poisoned or even that he himself poisoned a rival (*ibid.*).

References Cited

Blum, Stephen. 2001. Central Asia. In *The New Grove Dictionary of Music and Musicians*, edited by S. Sadie and J. Tyrrell. New York: Grove.

Braune, Gabriele. 1999. Bārbad. In *Die Musik in Geschichte und Gegenwart. Personenteil*, edited by F. Blume and L. Finscher. Kassel: Bärenreiter; Stuttgart: Metzler.

Caron, Nelly, and Dariouche Safvate. 1997. *Musique d'Iran, Collection Les Traditions Musicales de l'Institut International d'Études Comparatives de la Musique*. Paris: Buchet/Chastel.

Daniel, Elton L. 2012. *The History of Iran*. Edited by F. W. Thackeray and J. E. Findling. 2nd ed, *The Greenwood Histories of the Modern Nations*. Santa Barbara: Greenwood.

During, Jean, Zia Mirabdolbaghi, and Dariush Safvat. 1991. *The Art of Persian Music*. Washington: Mage Publishers.

Farhat, Hormoz. 1990. *The Dastgāh Concept in Persian Music, Cambridge Studies in Ethnomusicology*. Cambridge & New York: Cambridge University Press.

Lawergren, Bo, Hormoz Farhat, and Stephen Blum. 2001. Iran. In *The New Grove Dictionary of Music and Musicians*, edited by S. Sadie and J. Tyrrell. New York: Grove.

Miller, Lloyd. 1999. *Music and Song in Persia: The Art of Āvāz, Persian Art and Culture Series*. Richmond: Curzon.

Tafażżolī, A. 1988. Bārbad. In *Encyclopaedia Iranica*, edited by E. Yarshater. London and New York: Routledge & Kegan Paul.

Further Reading

Huart, Clément. 1927. *Ancient Persia and Iranian Civilization*. Translated by M. R. Dobie, *The History of Civilization*. New York: Knopf.

Zonis, Ella. 1973. *Classical Persian Music: An Introduction*. Cambridge: Harvard University Press.

Jamīla (d. ca. 715 CE)

S inger, lutenist, and music teacher Jamīla flourished around the turn of the eighth century CE in the city of Medina, in the Hijaz region on the western side of the Arabian Peninsula. She was revered by her audiences and admired by subsequent generations of Islamic musicians. The monumental *Kitāb al-Alghānī* ('Book of Songs') by the Arabian scholar Abū al-Faraj al-Iṣfahānī presents her in glowing terms:

> Jamīla was the most gifted of all creatures in the art of song. Ma'bad, for his part, affirmed that she was the tree of which we were the branches: without her, we would not be singers (al-Iṣfahānī, Mestiri, & Mestiri 2004: 94).

Her pupil Ma'bad, who is quoted here, became one of the most famous teachers and musicians of the following century, earning his sobriquet, "the prince of singers" (Jargy 1971: 30–33; Sawa 2000: 294).

Jamīla was a *mawala* (literally, 'client') of the Banu Sulaim, one of the Arab tribes in the Hijaz. During the Umayyad era, in which she lived, this term was applied to freed slaves and recent converts to Islam, who had to be accepted by Arabian patrons to gain recognition within Islamic society. Even though the *mawali* did not enjoy full equality with other members of the Muslim community, talented individuals could rise to fame and respectability. Jamīla was one of these individuals (Farmer 1967: 85; Kennedy 2004: 106–107 & 394).

Jamīla was at least partly self-taught. She claimed—according to an account in the *Kitāb al-Alghānī*—to have learned to sing by listening to her neighbor Ṣā'ib Khāthir (d. 683), a freed slave and music teacher, who is said to have introduced the Persian *'ūd* (a type of lute) to Medina. Absorbing his melodies by ear, Jamīla surprised her mistress one day by singing not only his songs, but also those of her own composition (Farmer 1967: 53–54 & 85; Islamic Arts 2010: 67; Sawa 2000: 294).

During Jamīla's lifetime, the holy cities of Medina, where she lived, and nearby Mecca were, ironically, the leading musical sites in the Islamic Empire (Farmer 1967: 67; Islamic Arts2010: 67; Ribera 1929: 40; Shiloah 1994: 695). "Ironically" because of a religiously based proscription of musical entertainment, which the *mullahs* persistently attempted to enforce, with varying degrees of success. The Umayyad caliphs, who came to power in 660, were, however, less pious than the first four 'orthodox' caliphs and more relaxed in terms of enforcing abstinence with respect to music and wine. Moreover, a greater knowledge of foreign musical traditions, notably in Persia, had arisen out of the Islamic conquests, while the spoils of war had brought considerable wealth and many slaves, some of whom were talented musicians, back to the homeland. Male and female slave musicians formed the nucleus of a musical renaissance, which found first expression privately in the homes of the wealthy. Of this era it is said that "no house could be without its [enslaved] singing-girl" (Farmer 1967: 67).

News of Jamīla's musical ability spread and brought her into her own as a teacher. She married and moved into a fine residence, where she established a school for teaching slaves how to sing and play instruments. Supporting a growing demand for *qainat* (singing-girls), schools of this sort sprang up and thrived in both Medina and Mecca (Farmer 1967: 85–86; Jargy 1971: 24; Ribera 1929: 41).

Jamīla's home became a center of attraction for musicians, poets, and lovers of music. She staged elegant entertainments (*majālis*), at which music and poetry transported her guests, while fine food and wine delighted their palates. At one of these events, she sang erotic verses by the poet ʿUmar Ibn Abī Rabīʾa, who was in attendance (Jargy 1971: 24–26):

> Then she says to her companions
> Frolicking around her like does:
> Catch hold of my shadow, I am afraid it might
> follow me:
> Then she ran towards his tent.
> Never before did she embrace a man:
> A child still tender and fresh in her dress!
> Never do his arrows miss their target:
> Anyone struck by one
> Cannot escape …
> (*ibid.*, pp. 25–26; my translation from the French)

Her singing charmed the audience, many of whom succumbed under the emotional impact, known as *tarab*, that Arabian music is reputed to provide (Farmer 1945: 11–14; Shiloah 1994: 698). They clapped, stamped, swayed their heads, and shouted ecstatically. ʿUmar, who had fainted and torn his clothing at a similar event hosted by ʿAzza-t al Maylā, another famous singer of the era, not only collapsed at this concert but also ripped his garments from head to toe, so deeply was he moved (Jargy 1971: 23–24 & 26).

ʿUmar's loss of self-control would certainly have disturbed orthodox Muslims. Published accounts of two other *majālis* hosted by Jamīla seem designed to prove the moral acceptability of musical entertainment.

In one of these accounts, a legal expert utters explicit praise of music. He is present when Jamīla informs her invited guests, that on the basis of religious scruples, she has decided to give up singing. Her listeners express different opinions as to whether she should do this, but after a doctor of law declares singing to be a legitimate pleasure, the day is won for music. He says that "only stupid and ignorant people" would consider music sinful, where-upon Jamīla performs her songs to the delight of the audience (Ribera 1929: 37).

The protagonist of the second account is the Prophet's cousin 'Abdullah Ibn Ja'far, whom other sources describe as an active patron of music in Medina. 'Abdullah accepts Jamīla's entreaty to attend a concert in his honor. She prepares for his arrival by dressing her singing-girls in jewels and colorful silks and arranging their hair in long clusters, which tumble to the base of the back. On seeing the brilliant display, 'Abdullah exclaims, "Oh Jamīla, you have assembled for me all that the earth has made of great beauty," to which she responds, "Beauty is only suitable for beauty, and this assembly is for you." She arranges her singers with their lutes in two rows, taking her position in the middle, and sings a panegyric in honor of the Holy Family (Jargy 1971: 22 & 24–25; my translation from the French).

Jamīla's name has been associated with a musical pilgrimage from Medina to Mecca. If this event actually took place as record-ed (and this has been called into question—see Schaade 1965), it was an enormous undertaking, involving all the professional male and female musicians in Medina, several well-known poets, many singing-girls, and a group of amateur lovers of music. After return-ing to Medina, they staged a three-days-long festival of music. During the first two days, individuals or small groups of singers and instrumentalists performed, while on the third day, fifty lute-playing *qainat* accompanied Jamīla and other singers. In his *History of Arabian Music*, Farmer writes that this was an event "the like of which had not been experienced in Al-Hijaz before" (1967: 57–58, 68, & 74–75).

Although progress in the musical arts in Medina and Mecca had benefited at the start of the Umayyad era from a period of relative calm on the Arabian Peninsula, this situation changed after twenty years, or so. By the fourth quarter of the seventh century, the administrative center of the empire was firmly established in faraway Damascus, Syria, whereas many civilian Umayyad families were still living comfortably in Medina and its surroundings. Opposition developed to the agricultural policy of the Umayyad rulers, who were drawing revenue, like absentee landlords, from large-scale agricultural development in the Hijaz. In addition, Caliph Mu'awiya (r. 661–680) upset traditionalists in the region by having his own son Yazid (r. 680–683) appointed as his successor. Matters came to a head during Yazid's caliphate. Local forces drove the Umayyads out of the Hijaz, and the caliph responded by sending in a Syrian army, which sacked Medina in 683. In a separate incident, Mecca suffered bombardment in 692 (Kennedy 2004: 82–90 & 98).

Jamīla's teacher Ṣā'ib Khāthir lost his life in 683, an innocent victim of the attack on Medina (Farmer 1967: 54). Details of Jamīla's passing are lacking. She is thought to have died around 715–720 (Farmer 1967: 85; Sawa 2000: 294; Shiloah 1994: 696).

References Cited

Abū al-Faraj al-Iṣfahānī, Mohammed Mestiri, and Soumaya Mestiri. 2004. *La femme arabe dans le Livre des chants: une anthologie, Bibliothèque Maktaba*. Paris: Fayard.

Farmer, Henry George. 1945. *The Minstrelsy of "The Arabian nights": A Study of Music and Musicians in the Arabic "Alf Laila wa Laila"*. Bearsdon, Scotland: [issued privately].

———. 1967. *A History of Arabian Music to the XIIIth Century*. London: Luzac & Co.

Islamic Arts. 2010. In *The New Encyclopædia Britannica*. Chicago & London: Encyclopædia Britannica.

Jargy, Simon. 1971. *La musique arabe*. Paris: Presses universitaires de France.

Kennedy, Hugh. 2004. *The Prophet and the Age of the Caliphates: The Islamic Near East from the Sixth to the Eleventh Century.* 2nd ed. Harlow: Longman.

Ribera, Julián. 1929. *Music in Ancient Arabia and Spain, Being La música de las Cantigas.* Translated by E. Hague and M. Leffingwell. Stanford: Stanford University Press (reprinted 1970 by Da Capo Press, New York).

Sawa, Suzanne Meyers 2000. Historical Issues of Gender and Music. In *The Garland Encyclopedia of World Music, vol. 6: The Middle East*, edited by S. M. Virginia Danielson, and Dwight Reynolds. New York and London: Routledge.

Schaade, A.-[Ch. Pellat]. 1965. D̲jamīla. In *The Encyclopaedia of Islam*, edited by B. Lewis, C. Pellat and J. Shacht. Leiden: E. J. Brill and London: Luzac & Co.

Shiloah, Amnon. 1994. Arabische Musik. In *Die Musik in Geschichte und Gegenwart. Sachteil*, edited by F. Blume and L. Finscher. Kassel: Bärenreiter; Stuttgart: Metzler.

Further Reading

Farmer, Henry George. 1965. Ghinā'. In *The Encyclopaedia of Islam*, edited by B. Lewis, C. Pellat and J. Shacht. Leiden: E. J. Brill and London: Luzac & Co.

Ibrāhīm al-Mawṣilī (742–804 CE) & Isḥāq al-Mawṣilī (767–850 CE)

Musical arts of the Islamic Empire had their "golden age" during the reign of Caliph Harun al-Rashid (r. 786–809 CE) and his immediate successors. Two of the most prominent golden-age musicians were Ibrāhīm al-Mawṣilī (742–804)—born Ibrāhīm ibn Mahan—and his son Isḥāq al-Mawṣilī (767–850). Both these men were outstanding singers, instrumentalists, and composers. Whereas Ibrāhīm gained prominence by virtue of his magnificent voice, Isḥāq excelled as a lutenist and was admired for his extensive knowledge and writings on music (Farmer 1967: 90–136; Kennedy 2005: 113–129; Ribera 1929: 43–55).

Ibrāhīm's parents were refugees living in the city of Kufa, Iraq. His father, of noble birth, and his mother had left their homes in the Persian province of Fars, which was under the thumb of an oppressive Umayyad governor. Shortly after Ibrāhīm came into the world, the first of the Abbasid rulers overthrew the Syrian-based Umayyad caliphate and moved the administrative center of the Islamic Empire from Damascus to Kufa. It remained there until ca. 762, when Caliph al-Mansur (r. 754–775) founded a new capital in Baghdad (Abu al-Faradsch & Rotter 1997: 152–153; Kennedy 2004: 134–135 and 2005: 126).

While Ibrāhīm was still a young boy, his father died in a plague, and his maternal uncles took charge of the child. The arrangement proved difficult. Ibrāhīm was a poor student, who learned very little and received numerous beatings at school. Later on, he began to make friends with musicians, behavior that the family found untenable (Abu al-Faradsch & Rotter 1977: 153–154; Kennedy 2005: 127).

Leaving his unsympathetic relatives behind, Ibrāhīm embarked on a traveling musical apprenticeship. He spent a year in Mosul, where he is thought to have associated with the local musicians. His stay in this city gave rise to the sobriquet, al-Mawṣilī. Near Mosul, according to varying reports, he was either kidnapped by or joined with a group of highwaymen. The experience allowed him to learn their songs during celebrations of successful robberies (Abu al-Faradsch & Rotter 1977: 153–154; Farmer 1967: 116; Fück 1971; Ribera 1929: 48).

Ibrāhīm went to Rayy (now part of Tehran) in northern Iran, where he learned more about Persian and Arabic music. In Rayy he also acquired two wives: Dushar and Shahak. His earliest surviving poem is dedicated to Dushar:

> Oh Dushar, oh my mistress,
>   oh my purpose, oh my good fortune,
> Oh my joy above all,
>   bring me back my slumber!
> (al-Faradsch & Rotter 1977: 154; my translation
> from the German)

His second wife Shahak gave birth to Isḥāq while in Rayy (Fück 1978).

A large gift from a eunuch, who was traveling through Rayy on assignment from Caliph al-Mansur, provided Ibrāhīm with the means to move to Ubulla, on the northern tip of the Persian Gulf. In Ubulla he had expected to study with a Zoroastrian singing teacher. However, Ibrāhīm told his son later that his own knowledge had already outclassed that of the local musicians (Abu al-Faradsch & Rotter 1977: 154–155; Kennedy 2005: 128).

Ibrāhīm acquired firsthand knowledge of old Arab music by traveling to the town of Medina in the Hijaz, a region in the west of present-day Saudi Arabia. Medina is the place to which the Prophet Mohammad had migrated from Mecca in 622, marking the beginning of the Islamic era, and where he died in 632. This significant history made Medina the second most holy city after Mecca for Muslims; however, despite an interdiction of light entertainment in the Qur'an (Surah Luqman 31:6), Islamic Medina soon became a center of musical activity (Braune 1996; Islamic Arts 2010: 67; Jargy 1971: 21–34). In this city and its surroundings, Ibrāhīm gathered popular songs and gleaned information from elderly Arab inhabitants (Ribera 1929: 48).

Ibrāhīm's growing reputation earned him entry into the entourage of a wealthy Abbasid prince in Basra. This time, it was a visiting eunuch-emissary of Caliph al-Mahdi (r. 775–785) who found Ibrāhīm's singing impressive. When this messenger reported back to the caliph, the potentate ordered the musician brought into the imperial court in Baghdad. At an age of approximately forty, Ibrāhīm had arrived at the center of Islamic power. His career seemed to be made (Abu al-Faradsch & Rotter, 1977: 155; Kennedy 2005: 128).

Ibrāhīm soon suffered a severe setback. It seems that two of the caliph's sons, Harun and al-Hadi, enjoyed his singing. However, to avoid scandal and discourage the princes from carousing with wine and music, the caliph had barred professional singers from the princes' apartments. Having been caught disobeying this order, Ibrāhīm and another talented musician, Ibn Jami', were arrested and punished. Ibrāhīm received 300 strokes of the lash and a prison sentence, while Ibn Jami', who could claim nobility, was simply banished. When Prince al-Hadi ascended briefly to the throne (r. 785–786), he rehabilitated both these men, making them court musicians and awarding Ibrāhīm compensation totaling 150,000 pieces of gold (Farmer 1967: 93 & 115–116).

Al-Hadi's brother Harun al-Rashid, who ruled from 786 to 809, elevated Ibrāhīm to the foremost rank among his musicians. Ibrāhīm came to be al-Rashid's *nadīm* (boon companion), which gave rise to another of Ibrāhīm's sobriquets, al-Nadim (Farmer 1967: 116; Neubauer 2001: 165).

Ibrāhīm became fabulously wealthy, pursuing additional riches even while receiving a monthly salary of 10,000 pieces of silver plus income from his landholdings. He and a partner established a lucrative music school. They bought young female slaves, taught them music, and sold them at a profit. The training of such 'singing-girls' had been practiced for many years in Medina and elsewhere. Ibrāhīm's innovation was to train white girls, who were deemed more beautiful than black or yellow girls and therefore fetched a higher price. The music school yielded a lifetime profit of some 24 million pieces of silver (Abu al-Faradsch & Rotter 1977: 160; Farmer 1967: 116–117; Fück 1971).

Several eminent male musicians benefited from Ibrāhīm's training. Among these were his son Isḥāq, of course, as well as Zalzal, Mukhariq, and others, including both singers and instrumentalists (Farmer 1967: 117; Ribera 1929: 60).

While pursuing riches for himself, Ibrāhīm dispensed gifts willingly and entertained generously. At his luxurious mansion in Baghdad, he always kept three sheep on the ready for guests: one butchered and ready for cooking, one skinned and hanging on a hook, and one living. His brother once sent him 80 slave girls to be trained. Ibrāhīm clothed and fed them, and when they left, he sent them back with presents and gowns. Isḥāq said that his father's fortune was reduced at the time of his passing to the comparatively small sum of "3000 dinars, from which 700 dinars were withdrawn to pay off his debts" (Abu al-Faradsch & Rotter 1977: 158–159).

With a superb voice and excellent instrumental technique, Ibrāhīm commanded the respect of musicians and the nobility. Having acquired extensive knowledge of Persian and Arab song, he came to personify the syncretism of early Islamic music. He sang typically in a descending melodic line:

> [H]e started most of his compositions with high tones where he held the melody for a moment, then proceeded to descend progressively down to the low register, arriving at the tonic; next he climbed again toward the high register and moved down again, passing from loud (*forte*) to soft (*piano*), and like this until the end (cited by Jargy 1972: 38; my translation from the French).

Ibrāhīm is credited with the composition of 600–900 songs and with the introduction of new musical modes, although details of these achievements have, apparently, not survived (Farmer 196: 117; Jargy 1971: 38 & 45; Ribera 1929: 48–50).

The caliph ordered Ibrāhīm to make a collection of 100 songs in collaboration with Ibn Jami' and another prominent musician, Fulaih ibn Abi'l-'Aura'. This collection formed the basis for a monumental study, *Kitāb al-Aghānī*, by the tenth-century savant Abū l-Faraj al-Iṣfahānī. At court, Ibrāhīm and Ibn Jami' led rival camps, the latter seeking to modernize music while Ibrāhīm held on to what he considered to be the classical style of Hijaz. These differences marked the start of a long-lasting dispute between classicists, led by Ibrāhīm's son Isḥāq, and modernists, led by Prince Ibrāhīm ibn al-Mahdi, who was himself a prestigious musician. It culminated in the days of Caliph al-Mutawakkil (r. 847–861), when the classicists achieved a temporary victory (Farmer 1967: 146–147; Fück 1971; Shiloah 1994: 713–714).

In Baghdad, Ibrāhīm had been able to provide Isḥāq with an excellent education. The boy began his day with the study of the Qur'an and the Islamic traditions (*hadiths*) and etiquette (*adab*). His music teachers included, in addition to his father, his uncle Zalzal, who provided instruction on the lute and on the rhythmic modes, and a famous female singer named 'Ātika bint Shu'ba, who taught him her vocal art. His daily schooling ended with the study of history and *belles lettres* (Farmer 1967: 124; Fück 1978).

As soon as Isḥāq was old enough, he joined the circle of court singers under Harun al Rashid. He served as a court singer under all the subsequent rulers until his death in 850, during the reign of Caliph al-Mutawakkil. When his father passed away in 804, Isḥāq took over as the chief court musician (Farmer 1967: 124; Neubauer 2001: 155).

The respect that Isḥāq enjoyed was based on his profound musical knowledge, on his own contributions to music, and, as well, on the extent of his scholarly engagement. He was a dedicated savant with an impressive personal library, who not only took books with him while traveling but even paid an annual stipend to a philologist. He composed 400 songs and wrote nearly forty works of prose, many of them about music, dancing, and musicians. On order of Caliph al-Wathik (r. 841–847), he revised the collection of 100 songs that his father and colleagues had assembled (Farmer 1967: 125; Fück 1978; Jargy 1971: 44).

Isḥāq knew old songs from the days of the singer Tuwais (632–710). He was better than other contemporaries at distinguishing the melodies of various Islamic artists, and he also had a substantial familiarity with foreign music. It is said that he modified the traditional melodic line to include an ascending element, thereby revolutionizing his father's own method. He augmented the classification of rhythms with a new system of modalities related to tab-lature on the lute (Farmer 1967: 105; Jargy 1971: 41; Ribera 1929: 51–52).

Isḥāq's voice has been described as "magnificent" (Fück 1978). He made effective use of the 'head voice,' but his introduction of singing in the male soprano register left him open to satire, even though other singers soon emulated this practice (Jargy 1971: 41):

> His own special device, as singer and composer, consisted in passing gradually and smoothly from the fortes to the pianos, as demanded by the music. Most of his best songs began with a high and loud note, even to the point of giving him a con-temporaneous   depreciatory   nickname—"the scorpion-bitten one." He held the forte until the melody gradually dropped in pitch, with an alternating balance of loud and soft, and this was the most exquisite characteristic of his art. The historians describe to us one of his ramels, conform-ing with this style, which began on the highest note of the octave, and gradually descended to end on the lowest note of the octave in the final cadence (Ribera 1929: 54).

Isḥāq's compositions, though deemed excellent, were reportedly better appreciated when sung by others (Ribera 1929: 53).

It was as a lutenist that Isḥāq astonished his contemporaries. Like the Persian Barbad, who is profiled earlier in this chapter, he could play beautifully even if an instrument had been mistuned or the strings had been rearranged from their normal positions (first string in place of the third, etc.). Caliph al-Mu'taṣim (r. 834–842) exclaimed, "Was there ever his equal?" (Ribera 1929: 52–53).

Isḥāq had many pupils. One of these was the singer and lute-nist Ziryāb (789–857), who emigrated from Baghdad to Córdoba, where he contributed seminally to the development of Iberian music (see the following profile). Another of Isḥāq's pupils, ʿAlī b. Yaḥyā Ibn al-Munajjim, wrote a book about his master. Isḥāq also taught the gifted poetess Danānīr al-Barmakiyya and a well-known singer and poetess named Mutayyim al-Hāshimiyya (Farmer 1967: 128–130 & 135; Fück 1978; Ribera 1929: 101–102).

The eminent Middle-Eastern scholar Henry George Farmer wrote that "[a]s an all-round musician, Isḥāq was the greatest that Islam had produced." Others may have had better voices, but Isḥāq reigned supreme as an instrumentalist, and he possessed the intellectual acumen needed to reduce the practice of music to a definite system (Farmer 1967: 125).

The rulers served by Isḥāq seemed determined to outdo one another with their praises. Honoring Isḥāq's erudition and up-rightness, Caliph al-Ma'mun (r. 813–833) said:

> Were Isḥāq not so publicly known as a musician, I would have appointed him a judge (*qadi*), for he is more deserving of it than any of the judges that we now have, and he surpasses them all in virtu-ous conduct, piety and honesty (cited in Farmer 1967: 124).

During sessions at court, this caliph allowed Isḥāq to wear the robes of a legal specialist and to stand with savants of a higher rank than that of ordinary musicians (Farmer 1967: 124).

Caliph al-Wathiq (842–847) framed his homage to Isḥāq in terms that would arouse the envy of any other professional musi-cian:

> Never has Isḥāq sung in my presence without making me feel that he added new splendor to my monarchy; never have I heard him perform

the songs of Ibn Surayj without my feeling that I have seen that singer brought to life again. I have come to admire other singers, but since Isḥāq has come in his turn, I see the others shrink, while he rises above them. For Isḥāq is one of the charms of the monarchy. If youth and health could be bought, I would have procured them for him at the price of half of my kingdom! (cited in Jargy 1971: 41; my translation from the French).

Al-Wathiq could speak of Isḥāq's accomplishments with some authority, for he was himself an accomplished musician.

Finally, in 850, when Isḥāq died from the results of the Ramadan fast, Caliph al-Mutawakkil noted: "With the death of Isḥāq my Empire is deprived of an ornament and a glory" (cited in Farmer 1967: 125).

Ibrāhīm and Isḥāq al-Mawṣilī have entered into the canon of Arabian literature: They are prominent among the musicians featured in the *Arabian Nights* (Farmer 1945). In Nights 687 and 688, Scheherazade relates a story in which the Devil visits Ibrāhīm in order to teach him some songs. In contrast to the uncanny setting of this story, one of the songs has an erotic tenor:

> Men say that when the lover is near his love,
> He grows bored, and that distance is a cure for passion.
> I have tried both, and neither one cured me,
> > But to be near is better than to be far,
> > Though how can nearness be of help
> > When the beloved feels no love?
> (Lyons, Lyons, & Irwin 2010: II 778)

A similar description of the Devil's visit to Ibrāhīm had appeared earlier in the *Kitāb al-Aghānī*. The tale reflects an early Arab belief, which held that musical inspiration came from other-worldly spirits, or *jinn* (Farmer 1967: 7; Shiloah 1994: 723). A satanic connection arose with the advent of Islam: The sayings and deeds attributed to the Prophet Muhammad, which are known as the *hadiths*, censure song and musicians as being "inspired by the Devil" (Jargy 1971: 20).

References Cited

Abu al-Faradsch and Gernot Rotter. 1977. *Und der Kalif beschenkte ihn reichlich: Auszüge aus dem Buch der Lieder.* Tübingen & Basel: Horst Erdmann Verlag.

Braune, Gabriele. 1996. Islam. In *Die Musik in Geschichte und Gegenwart. Sachteil,* edited by F. Blume and L. Finscher. Kassel: Bärenreiter; Stuttgart: Metzler.

Farmer, Henry George. 1945. *The Minstrelsy of "The Arabian nights": A Study of Music and Musicians in the Arabic "Alf Laila wa Laila".* Bearsdon, Scotland: [issued privately].

———. 1967. *A History of Arabian Music to the XIIIth Century.* London: Luzac & Co.

Fück, J. W. 1971. Ibrāhīm al-Mawṣili. In *The Encyclopaedia of Islam,* edited by B. Lewis, V. L. Ménage, C. Pellat and J. Shacht. Leiden: E. J. Brill and London: Luzac & Co.

———. 1978. Isḥāḳ b. Ibrāhīm al-Mawṣilī. In *The Encyclopaedia of Islam,* edited by E. van Donzel, B. Lewis and C. Pellat. Leiden: E. J. Brill.

Islamic Arts. 2010. In *The New Encyclopædia Britannica.* Chicago & London: Encyclopædia Britannica.

Jargy, Simon. 1971. *La musique arabe.* Paris: Presses universitaires de France.

Kennedy, Hugh. 2004. *The Prophet and the Age of the Caliphates: The Islamic Near East from the Sixth to the Eleventh Century.* 2nd ed. Harlow: Longman.

————. 2005. *When Baghdad Ruled the Muslim World: The Rise and Fall of Islam's Greatest Dynasty*. 1st De Capo Press ed. Cambridge: Da Capo Press.

Lyons, Malcolm C., Ursula Lyons, and Robert Irwin. 2010. *The Arabian Nights: Tales of 1001 Nights*. 3 vols. London: Penguin Classics.

Neubauer, Eckhard. 2001. Mawṣilī, al-. In *The New Grove Dictionary of Music and Musicians*, edited by S. Sadie and J. Tyrrell. New York: Grove.

Ribera, Julián. 1929. *Music in Ancient Arabia and Spain, Being La música de las Cantigas*. Translated by E. Hague and M. Leffingwell. Stanford: Stanford University Press (reprinted 1970 by Da Capo Press, New York).

Shiloah, Amnon. 1994. Arabische Musik. In *Die Musik in Geschichte und Gegenwart. Sachteil*, edited by F. Blume and L. Finscher. Kassel: Bärenreiter; Stuttgart: Metzler.

Further Reading

Bennison, Amira K. 2009. *The Great Caliphs: The Golden Age of the 'Abbasid Empire*. New Haven: Yale University Press.

Farmer, Henry George. 1943. The Minstrels of the Golden Age of Islam. *Islamic Culture* (XVII):273–281.

————. 1944. The Minstrels of the Golden Age of Islam (Continued from Issue No. 3. July 1943). *Islamic Culture* (XVIII):53–61.

————. 1965. Ghinā'. In *The Encyclopaedia of Islam*, edited by B. Lewis, C. Pellat and J. Shacht. Leiden: E. J. Brill and London: Luzac & Co.

Pacholczyk, Josef M. 1980. Secular Classical Music in the Arabic Near East. In *Musics of Many Cultures: An Introduction*, edited by E. May. Berkeley - Los Angeles - London: University of California Press.

Ziryāb (ca. 790–850 CE)

The musician Abū 'l-Ḥasan 'Alī ibn Nāfi' (ca. 790–850 CE), who was called Ziryāb ('black songbird'), acquired a huge reputation after his death. His abilities as a lutenist and singer became amplified, and his biographers began to describe him as a polymath and an arbiter of societal fashion and taste (Reynolds 2008; Davila 2009). Though likely overblown, his acquired reputation was anchored on a remarkable career trajectory. In the face of prejudice and discouraging setbacks, he had advanced beyond lowly beginnings in Syria and Arabia to become the leading musician at the Umayyad emirate in Córdoba on the Iberian Peninsula and an intimate of its ruler, 'Abd al-Raḥmān II (r. 822–852). Ziryāb became "the single most famous figure in the history of Andalusian music" (Davila 2009: 155), who "has for centuries been considered the apogee of medieval Muslim musicianship and an icon of the golden age of Muslim Spain" (Reynolds 2008: 249).

Despite an absence of hard evidence about Ziryāb's origin and birth, it seems clear that he came from an underclass of Middle-Eastern society. Several historical references mention his "dark-" or even "jet-black" skin, which indicates a black-African heritage (Reynolds 2008: 167 n.14). The name ibn Nāfi' suggests that he was the son of a recent convert to Islam (*ibid.*, p. 166). A tenth-century source (cited in Davila 2009, p. 127) asserts that he was a slave of Ibrāhīm al-Mawṣilī's, the leading musician at the court of the Abbasid caliph Harun al-Rashid, who ruled from 786 to 809.

In 796, Harun al-Rashid moved his capital to Raqqa in Syria, while leaving the administrative center in Baghdad (Shaban 1976: 30–31). Upon Harun's death, his son and successor, Caliph al-Amin (r. 809–813), re-established Baghdad as the capital. Ziryāb may thus have spent portions of his youth in these two places.

During a terrible civil war, which broke out after al-Amin took power, Ziryāb took flight. The war started as a succession conflict between al-Amin and his half-brother, ʿAbd Allāh. After Al-Amin was killed in 813, ʿAbd Allāh assumed power as the seventh Abbasid caliph, with the regnal name of al-Maʾmūn (r. 813–833). However, fierce fighting persisted for six more years, until al-Maʾmūn finally entered Baghdad in 819 (Kennedy 2016: 128–135).

During the war, Baghdad and its surroundings were especially hard hit. The historian Hugh Kennedy describes conditions in the city:

> [P]alaces were looted and burned and talented poets turned out on the streets. Among these was one ʿAlī b. Nāfiʿ, called Ziryāb (1996, p. 46).

No doubt the violence and chaos provided ample reason for Ziryāb to depart. A further motivation, as noted without further explanation by the tenth-century historian Ibn al-Qūṭiyya (d. 977), was that Caliph al-Maʾmūn "reproached Ziryāb for various things" (Ibn al-Qūṭīyah and Nichols 1975: 149–150).

One often-cited account links Ziryāb's departure from Baghdad to a breakdown in his relations with Ibrāhīm al-Mawṣilī's son Isḥāq, to whom he was apprenticed. Isḥāq supposedly felt threatened in his position by the young man's outstanding musical abilities and forced him out of town (al-Maqqarī & Gayangos 1984: 1411–412). Like fanciful descriptions of Ziryāb's supposed trendsetting later on in diverse realms of Andalusian life, including hair style, clothing, cuisine, dining habits, and hygiene (Lévi-Provençal 1948: 72–73; Piquet 1945: 29; Read 1974: 65), this account of his departure from Baghdad should be considered "exaggerated, or perhaps even apocryphal" (Davila 2009: 133).

When Ziryāb left Baghdad, he headed westward, stopping first in Syria, where oral tradition places him for several years among the musicians of the city of Aleppo (Davila 2009: 126–127). He moved subsequently along the coast of North Africa to the Aghlabid emirate at Qayrawān on the Tunisian plain. Initially, Emir Ziyādat Allāh I (r. 816–837) provided Ziryāb with shelter and support, but eventually the musician fell into disgrace by singing a song that the emir found offensive. The song, which was based on a poem by the half-black pre-Muslim hero called 'Antara, began with the verse, "If my mother were as black as a crow." It seems that the Ziyādat Allāh's mother was a black woman, and he became so angry that he had Ziryāb struck on the back of the neck and gave him just three days, on pain of beheading, to get out of Ifrīqiyya (Davila 2009: 128; Farmer 1967: 129). The episode as reported is fraught with irony in view of Ziryāb's apparent black-African heritage.

Ziryāb resumed his westward journey, hoping to get a position with the Umayyad emir al-Ḥakam in Córdoba (r. 796–822). Córdoba is in the portion of the Iberian Peninsula then known as Al-Andalus. Al-Ḥakam was also a poet; he encouraged music and wanted to add cultural sophistication to his court (Immamudin 1965: 178; Kennedy 1996: 41). Ziryāb sailed with his family to the Andalusian port city of Al-Jazīra Al-Khadrā' (present-day Algeciras), where they learned that al-Ḥakam had just died. Al-Ḥakam's son 'Abd al-Raḥmān II (r. 822–852) was the new ruler. Fortunately, he proved enthusiastic about receiving a gifted new musician and sent one of his court musicians, a Jew named al-Mansūr, to meet Ziryāb. Ziryāb and his family arrived in Córdoba at the end of May 822 (Davila 2009: 121).

'Abd al-Raḥmān accepted Ziryāb into his court. The Easterner embodied the glittering cultural reputation of Baghdad, with its lavish court life and music. He would have been viewed by Cordovans as a *ẓarīf*, a man of refinement and taste, who was in a position to enrich their heritage with his first-hand knowledge of the leading musicians in the world of Islam, Ibrāhīm and Isḥāq al-Mawṣilī. He became a central personage at court, and he founded a school that influenced the development of Andalusian music.

'Abd al-Raḥmān provided Ziryāb with more than ample support. According to a seventeenth-century source, he received a monthly pension of 200 pieces-of-gold (*dinars*) per month for himself and 20 *dinars* per month for each of his four sons; and in addition, gratuities totaling 3000 *dinars* yearly at certain festivals. But this was not all; Ziryāb was also to receive annual provisions of grain, a portion of the produce raised in Córdoba and environs, the use of several houses, and lands. The package of benefits is said to have "brought him in a clear revenue of forty thousand *dinars*" (al-Maqqarī & Gayangos 1984: II117–118).

Even if these figures are exaggerated, anecdotal evidence suggests that Ziryāb's contemporaries considered his earnings to have been impressively large. Reynolds cites an anecdote from an eleventh-century source, in which a religious scholar expresses envy of the generous gifts that Ziryāb received for his praise songs. The scholar claims that he himself deserved such gifts because of his "superior dedication to his craft" (2008, p. 161). A ninth-century writer relays an anecdote in which a Middle-Eastern musician named 'Allūyah complains to Caliph al-Ma'mūn about his meagre stipends "by comparing his own starved state to that of Ziryāb, the former client of the 'Abbāsids." 'Allūyah portrays Ziryāb as "living among the Umayyads in al-Andalus, surrounded by hundreds of servants" (cited by Davila 2009, p. 126).

Following an influential study by the historian al-Maqqarī (d. 1632), recent biographers have often emphasized Ziryāb's role as a *nadīm*, or 'boon companion,' to 'Abd al-Raḥmān (al-Maqqarī & Gayangos 1984: II118; cf. Reynolds 2008: 156). An earlier text by Ibn Ḥayyān (d. 1076) provides evidence of this relationship, while also illustrating the somewhat charged racial situation that confronted the black musician in Córdoba. It seems that a poet and astrologer, ʿAbd Allāh ibn al-Shimr ibn Numayr, relentlessly teased and made fun of Ziryāb. At the singer's request, the emir had al-Shimr jailed. When asked later on to relent, Ziryāb did so. But on an outing during which both men were present with the emir, al-Shimr made a crude racist joke about Ziryāb, which the emir liked. Ziryāb bowed to the emir's taste and forgave al-Shimr. The pair then became friends (cited in Reynolds 2008: 162).

If true, the jailing at Ziryab's request demonstrates a remarkable degree of influence by a court musician over an emir. Another version of the story apparently presents the two courtiers as close companions, whose exchange of jokes and insults formed part of their friendship (Reynolds 2008: 168 n.28). Even this second version suggests that Ziryāb's otherness set him apart in a way with which he had to contend.

Ziryāb established a school of music, in which he imbued local talent with the theory and practice of the Mawṣilīs of Baghdād. He trained both freemen and female slaves. The school would have yielded a considerable source of income, just as similar establishments had for Jamīla in Medina and Ibrāhīm al-Mawṣilī in Baghdad (present work: previous profiles). 'Singing-girls' fetched higher prices when the owner could certify their music credentials. Ziryāb reportedly trained or owned thirty-eight such women at ʿAbd al-Raḥmān's court. In later years, musicians would reportedly turn to one of the female slaves named Shanīf for guidance on the performance of his songs (Davila 2009: 133). When ʿAbd al-Raḥmān became enamored of Ziryāb's slave Mutʿa, he gave her to the emir (Farmer 1967: 136; Ribera 1929: 106).

The slave-singers known as Ghizlān and Hunayda were professionally important to Ziryāb. They stayed on the ready at nighttime, in case he became musically inspired in his dreams. When this happened, he would communicate the melody and words for the two women to memorize. In the morning, they would replay the song for him, and he would revise the new composition (Ibn Ḥayyān, as cited by Davila 2009: 134).

Four verses of Ziryāb's lyrical poetry have survived:

> I became attached to her, a sprig of sweet basil,
>> Slender, fragrant, [and] blossoming.
> Neither plump nor thin,
>> Neither tall nor short.
> What glorious days we had,
>> Spent at Dayr al-Maṭīra
> Their only lack for the lovelorn one
>> Was that they were too few!
> (Reynolds 2008: 167 n.20)

In accordance with the practices of the day, Ziryāb would have delivered this poem in song. Unfortunately, none of his melodies is still available, but Ibn al-Qūṭīyah (d. 977) describes briefly one of Ziryāb's performances. This was of a poem by al-'Abbās ibn al-Aḥnaf, which Ziryāb sang for the emir:

> Said Zulum, namesake of the dark,
>> "My dear, I think you are too lean."
> *I answered her with tears flowing like strung pearls,*
> "O you who aim and pierce my heart,
>> you well know where strikes the dart!"
> (Ibn al-Qūṭīyah & Nichols 1975: 133, emphasis added)

The first line is a play on words: *ẓulm* means 'darkness.' Another poet named 'Abaid Allāh ibn Qarlumān was present at Ziryāb's presentation of this song. When the emir noted that the two parts of the poem seemed unconnected, ibn Qarlumān improvised the verse in italics (*ibid.*, pp. 131 & 133; cf. Ibn al-Qūṭīyah & James 2009: 97–98).

As a singer, Ziryāb followed certain Middle-Eastern practices. When presenting a 'measured' song, that is, a song having a definite meter, he would introduce the piece by singing an 'unmeasured' recitative. During the performance, he would gradually increase the lightness and tempo in both text and melody. These characteristics supported the development of a later musical form, the vocal suite or *nawba* (Farmer-[Neubauer] 1960–2002: 517). Ziryāb's repertory is claimed to have included more than one-thousand songs (al-Maqqarī & Gayangos 1984: II119–120).

At Ziryāb's school, applicants were required to pass several tests before being accepted as his pupils. After acceptance, they followed a structured course of instruction (al-Maqqarī & Gayangos 1984: II121; Ribera 1929: 104; Trend 1926: 18–19).

The testing phase began with applicants sitting on round leather cushions and exerting the full power of their voices. Those with weak voices had to tighten turban cloths around their waists in order to increase the volume. Those whose mouths did not open fully, or who stammered, would be required to hold a piece of wood three fingers wide inside the mouth, day and night, until their jaws expanded. They would then be asked to shout *Ya Hassam* or *Ah!* as loudly as possible and to extend the sound for as long as possible. Only if the words came out clearly, powerfully, and sonorously would Ziryāb accept them as students (al-Maqqarī & Gayangos 1984: II121)

The instructional phase covered the three basic elements of rhythm, melody, and ornamentation:

> [A pupil] began by learning the words and metre; he spoke the words while he beat time with a tambourine, marking the strong and the weak ac-

cents, and the pace of different movements. Then he was taught the melody in its simplest form with no ornaments, and only when he could sing it perfectly was he allowed to study the shakes, vocalizes, scale-passages, and appoggiaturas with which the master embellished the song, and the nuances he introduced to give it the expression and charm (Trend 1926: 19).

Trend writes that Ziryāb's method reveals something of the music of his time: "Before all else came the rhythm; and the rhythm of Arab music was primarily the flow of the words, the duration of the syllables—in fact the metre" (*ibid.*).

Some new musical instruments were introduced in Iberia during the period of Islamic rule. Among them were the *'ūd*, or lute; the *qïtār*, or guitar; and the *rebeck*, a bowed stringed instrument favored by dancers (Imamuddin 1965: 199). Ziryāb reportedly made at least one notable contribution to instrumental technology: He added a fifth string to his lute and chose as his plectrum the talon of an eagle. The new implement is said to have been neater and lighter, and to have had a better edge, than the conventional wooden plectrum (Reynolds 2015: 249; Ribera 1929: 103–104).

Ziryāb's ten children were all musical and helped to prolong his school's teachings. A son named 'Abd al-Raḥmān was the most prominent of his male children. His daughter Hamaduna married the chancellor of the realm. Her younger sister Alya was much sought after as a teacher (Farmer-[Neubauer] 1960–2002: 516; Ribera 1929: 106).

References Cited

Al-Maqqarī, Aḥmad ibn Muḥammad, and Pascual de Gayangos.
        1984. *The History of the Mohammedan Dynasties in Spain; extracted from the Nafhu-t-tíb min ghosni-l-Andalusi-r-rattíb wa*

táríkh lisánu-d-dín Ibni-l-Khattíb, IAD religio-philosophy (reprint) series. Delhi: Idarah-i Adabiyat-i Delli. Original edition, 1840.

Davila, Carl. 2009. Fixing a Misbegotten Biography: Ziryāb in the Mediterranean World. *Al-Masaq (Al-Masaq: Islam and the Medieval Mediterranean)* 21 (2):121–136.

Farmer, H. G., [E. Neubauer]. 1960–2002. Ziryāb. In *The Encyclopaedia of Islam*, edited by H. A. R. Gibb et al. Leiden: Brill.

Farmer, Henry George. 1967. *A History of Arabian Music to the XIIIth Century.* London: Luzac & Co.

Ibn al-Qūṭīyah, Muḥammad ibn 'Umar, and David Lewis James. 2009. *Early Islamic Spain: The History of Ibn al-Qūṭīya; A Study of the Unique Arabic Manuscript in the Bibliothèque Nationale de France, Paris, with a Translation, Notes, and Comments.* Culture and Civilization in the Middle East. London & New York: Routledge.

Ibn al-Qūṭīyah, Muḥammad ibn 'Umar, and James Mansfield Nichols. 1975. *The History of the Conquest of Al-Andalus by Ibn al-Qūṭīyah the Cordovan.* Thesis (Ph.D.), University of North Carolina at Chapel Hill.

Imamuddin, S. M. 1965. *Some Aspects of the Socio-Economic and Cultural History of Muslim Spain 711–1492 A.D.* Leiden: E. J. Brill.

Kennedy, Hugh. 1996. *Muslim Spain and Portugal: A Political History of al-Andalus.* London & New York: Longman.

———. 2016. *The Prophet and the Age of the Caliphates: The Islamic Near East from the Sixth to the Eleventh Century.* 3rd ed. Abingdon & New York: Routledge.

Lévi-Provençal, Evariste. 1948. *La civilisation arabe en Espagne; vue générale.* Nouvelle ed. Paris: G. P. Maisonneuve.

Piquet, Victor. 1945. *L'Espagne des Maures; esquises historiques.* Paris: E. de Boccard.

Read, Jan. 1974. *The Moors in Spain and Portugal.* London: Faber and Faber.

Reynolds, Dwight F. 2008. Al-Maqqarī's Ziryāb: The Making of a Myth. *Middle Eastern Literatures* 11 (2):155–168.

————. 2015. North Africa and the Eastern Mediterranean: Andalusian Music. In *The Other Classical Musics: Fifteen Great Traditions,* edited by M. Church. Woodbridge: The Boydell Press.

Ribera, Julián. 1929. *Music in Ancient Arabia and Spain, Being La música de las Cantigas.* Translated by E. Hague and M. Leffingwell. Stanford: Stanford University Press (reprinted 1970 by Da Capo Press, New York).

Shaban, M. A. 1976. *Islamic History: A New Interpretation.* 2 vols. Cambridge: Cambridge University Press.

Trend, J. B. 1926. *The Music of Spanish History to 1600.* Oxford: Oxford University Press.

Further Reading

Dozy, Reinhart Pieter Anne. 1972. *Spanish Islam: A History of the Moslems in Spain.* Translated by F. G. Stokes, Islam and the Moslem World. London: Frank Cass. Original edition, 1913.

Gutiérrez, Carmen Julia, et al. 1998. Spanien. In *Die Musik in Geschichte und Gegenwart. Allgemeine Enzyklopädie der Musik begründet von Friedrich Blume. Sachteil in neun Bänden,* edited by L. Finscher. Kassel - Basel - London - New York - Prag / Stuttgart - Weimar: Bärenreiter-Verlag / Metzler.

Imamuddin, S. M. 1969. *A Political History of Muslim Spain.* 2nd ed. Dacca: Najmah Sons.

Lévi-Provençal, Evariste. 1950. *Histoire de l'Espagne musulmane.* Nouv. éd. rev. et augm. ed. Paris: Maisonneuve; Leiden: Brill.

Neubauer, Eckhard. 2001. Ziryāb. In *The New Grove Dictionary of Music and Musicians*, edited by S. Sadie and J. Tyrrell. London: Macmillan Publishers Ltd.

Reynolds, Dwight F. 2013. Arab Musical Influence on Medieval Europe: A Reassessment. In *A Sea of Languages: Rethinking the Arabic Role in Medieval Literary History*, edited by S. C. Akbari and K. Mallette. Toronto, Buffalo, & London: University of Toronto Press.

CHAPTER FOUR

The Big Picture

The profiled musicians flourished in the distant past in circumstances far different from those of the present. Their profiles can therefore serve to explore similarities in musical behavior that persist, and differences that arise, as societies mature. To this end, in Chapter 3, information about the musicians' activities was extracted from the profiles and categorized within an established framework of ten functions of music, which Alan P. Merriam formulated in mid-twentieth century (1964: 219–227). The results of this process may be epitomized by bringing together the names of all the musicians associated with each of the ten functions:

∞

THE FUNCTION OF EMOTIONAL EXPRESSION

Dada	Marcabru
Emperor Xuanzong	Walther von der Vogelweide
Jamīla	

THE FUNCTION OF AESTHETIC ENJOYMENT

Amīr Khusrau Delhavī	Otomae
Bārbad	Pronomos
Emperor Xuanzong	Stratonicus
Ibrāhīm al-Mawṣilī	Ziryāb
Isḥāq al-Mawṣilī	

THE FUNCTION OF ENTERTAINMENT

Amīr Khusrau Delhavī	Jamīla
Bārbad	Li Yannian
Dugha	Otomae
Emperor Nero	Pronomos
Emperor Xuanzong	Stratonicus
Fu Niang	Tigellius
Ibrāhīm al-Mawṣilī	Yang Guifei
Isḥāq al-Mawṣilī	Ziryāb
Ipi	

THE FUNCTION OF COMMUNICATION

Bārbad	Enheduanna
Dada	Raia

THE FUNCTION OF SYMBOLIC REPRESENTATION

Akashi no Kakuichi	Ibrāhīm al-Mawṣilī
Amīr Khusrau Delhavī	Isḥāq al-Mawṣilī
Bishop Ambrose	Jamīla
Dugha	Pronomos
Emperor Nero	

THE FUNCTION OF PHYSICAL RESPONSE

King David	Yang Guifei

THE FUNCTION OF ENFORCING CONFORMITY TO SOCIAL NORMS

Akashi no Kakuichi   Pindar

Marcabru

THE FUNCTION OF VALIDATION OF SOCIAL INSTI-TUTIONS AND RELIGIOUS RITUALS

Amīr Khusrau Delhavī   Isḥāq al-Mawṣilī

Balla Fasséké Kouyaté   Jayadeva

Bishop Ambrose   King David

Dada   Li Yannian

Dugha   Marcabru

Emperor Nero   Peripatjauemope

Emperor Xuanzong   Raia

Enheduanna   Risiya

Ibrāhīm al-Mawṣilī   Walther von der Vogelweide

Ipi

THE FUNCTION OF CONTRIBUTION TO THE CONTI-NUITY AND STABILITY OF CULTURE

Akashi no Kakuichi   Ibrāhīm al-Mawṣilī

Balla Fasséké Kouyaté   Isḥāq al-Mawṣilī

Bārbad   King David

Bishop Ambrose   Li Yannian

Dugha   Otomae

Emperor Xuanzong   Ziryāb

Enheduanna

THE FUNCTION OF CONTRIBUTION TO THE INTE-GRATION OF SOCIETY

Bishop Ambrose   Pindar

Enheduanna

∞

All ten categories are represented in the list, but the number of individuals associated with each function varies widely, between two and nineteen. This large range may have resulted, in part, from the limited size of the cohort, in comparison with the total number of ancient musicians. As noted in Chapter 2, the selection of individuals in Chapter 3 illustrates the variety to be found among the lives of ancient musicians but cannot be described as a representational sampling.

The profiles provide explicit evidence of **emotional expression** for five of the musicians. Because of the close association of music and emotion, this function was also satisfied implicitly by many other individuals.

All but one of the musicians in the **aesthetic-enjoyment** category performed professionally. Experiencing audience response in person may have provided the motivation to support or revise traditional styles of music.

That more than half of the profiled individuals made music for **entertainment** is perhaps not surprising, given the universal appeal of this art form. On the other hand, readers may find it surprising that so many of the musicians took part in the **validation of social institutions and religious rituals**. This emphasis on society and religion reflects in part the prevalence of state and religious support. As the saying goes, "Who pays the piper calls the tune."

Devotional music dominates in the **communication** category. However, one of the listed musicians, Bārbad, is said to have used a song to announce subtly to his king that a worldly tragedy had occurred.

The category of **symbolic representation** includes individuals whose physical mimesis reinforced the representational symbolism of their music. Others in this category used music to symbolize community. For still others, their music came to be viewed by orthodox clerics as a symbol of immorality.

The **physical-response** category contains only two names, a religious-cum-political leader and a concubine. This small number should not be taken to mean that physical response was uncommon. As explained in the Preface, dancers have been sidelined in the present study.

Three musicians created works in the category of **enforcing conformity to social norms**. Two of them composed songs about athletes and soldiers. The third criticized immoral sexual relationships.

Thirteen musicians undertook efforts that supported **the continuity and stability of culture**. Three were involved with religious music; the others, in the secular realm. In most cases the focus was on musical culture, but in some instances, broader cultural continuity and stability were impacted.

Three individuals contributed musically to **the integration of society**. Their art helped to unite people who shared religious, political, and class affiliations.

Perhaps the most striking aspect of the categorization process is that it works quite well. All of Merriam's ten functions of music have been identified in the profiles of the ancient musicians, which indicates that musicians' functions in society have remained much the same through a wide range of historical changes. This observation serves in the following discussion as the basis for introducing a new principle to guide historical research in musicology.

The profiles also offer evidence of an additional function of music, which, prosaic though it may be, is nevertheless central to the well-being of societies: stimulation of the economy. In the following text, examples from the profiles validate the addition of such a function.

Work songs and military music, which, like dance, exploit physical responses to music, were prevalent in early civilizations. The uses of music to accompany manual labor and to prepare for and fight battles will be discussed below as applications of the phenomenon known as musical entrainment.

Stimulation of the Economy

The profiles offer considerable evidence that music encouraged economic activity. Music gave employment to composers, performers, and instrument-makers, and the money that they earned would certainly have diffused outward to others in the society. Public performances, moreover, were events that attracted crowds and facilitated sales of food and material items. Thus, music that found one use—for example, in encouraging integration, entertaining, or validating state institutions—also could satisfy a separate societal need, namely that of stimulating the economy. The situation is analogous to that which Merriam describes in his consideration of love songs: They are *used*, he observes, to attract mates but have the *function* of promoting "the continuity and perpetuation of the biological group" (1964: 210; cf. present work: Appendix B). Analogously, it would seem that 'contribution to the economy' should be viewed as one of the *functions* of music.

In Greece, **Pindar (ca. 520–440 BCE)** composed music that encouraged social conformity and integration. As an aristocrat, he felt perhaps uneasy as an aristocrat for selling his compositions, but he did certainly accept payment. The instrumentalists **Pronomos (ca. 470–390 BCE)** and **Stratonicus (ca. 410–360 BCE)** received income from their performances in the theater and at music competitions. Those events invigorated economic life in the places where they were staged. In Rome, **Emperor Nero (37–68; r. 54–68 CE)** played at a youth festival at which hawkers are known to have sold food and luxury items.

All the court musicians received life support from the rulers, and the level of their compensation was in some instances breathtakingly high. In Baghdad, Caliph Harun al-Rashid paid **Ibrāhīm al-Mawṣilī (742–804 CE)** a monthly salary of 10,000 pieces of silver. This musician had other earnings, as well, including a one-time compensatory payment of 250,000 pieces of gold, but he spent freely throughout his life and had almost nothing left at the end. His earnings as a musician had therefore moved into the economy of his society.

It is a safe assumption that the spending of other highly paid musicians had a similarly beneficial economic effect. In Córdoba, Emir 'Abd al-Raḥmān II is reported to have paid **Ziryāb (ca. 790–850 CE)** a monthly salary of 200 pieces-of-gold (*dinars*) per month for himself and 20 *dinars* per month for each of his four sons, plus other bonuses. In Niani, Mansā Sulaymān rewarded **Dugha (fl. ca. 1352 CE)** for a ceremonial performance one afternoon with a purse of 200 *mithqals* (approximately 1.6 lbs) of gold dust, and he received more gifts the next day from the *farariyya* (imperial military commanders).

Those readers of the twenty-first century who are familiar with the mega-events of contemporary popular culture will have no trouble in accepting the idea that music contributes to the economy. Like other functions of music, the economic function is manifested differently in different societies and at different stages of development. The economic examples that have been extracted from the profiles derive from situations in which money was exchanged. Music has also contributed economically in situations in which money may not have been exchanged: for example, through the singing of work songs to speed the harvesting of crops in a barter economy (cf. Merriam 1964: 217). It is an advantage of identifying societal functions that they facilitate understanding the workings of a wide range of societies.

Musical Uniformitarianism

The ease, with which the activities of the profiled musicians could be fitted into Merriam's categories, as augmented by the function 'stimulation of the economy,' confirms the relevance of his approach for the present study. This observation may be more significant than it would seem at first consideration. Merriam's model was informed by ethnomusicological research on communities of the nineteenth and twentieth centuries CE, whereas the present project has treated musicians in societies from the early historical past. Many religious, political, technological, and economic qualities distinguish the societies considered here from those of the present. For a model to have proven applicable in such diverse settings raises the possibility that the societal functions of music may have stayed essentially the same, or evolved only slowly, throughout history and in various stages of social development. This is to the author's knowledge the first time that such an observation has been grounded in firm historical evidence.

In the eighteenth century CE, a Scottish naturalist named James Hutton (1726–1797) put forward a theoretical basis for understanding how the earth had evolved through its history (Dean 1992: 1–83). Expounded and popularized in the eighteenth century by another Scot, Charles Lyell (1797–1875), Hutton's ideas became the basis for a principle known as uniformitarianism, which has proven seminally important in the field of geology (Bailey 1962; Dean 1992: 202–229; Rudwick 2012a). Expressed in simple terms, uniformitarianism states that because the physical and chemical laws of nature are unchanging, "one can study processes in the present and make reasonable inferences about the past" (Larue 1992: IV117). To understand the mechanism for prehistoric alterations to the surface of the earth, geologists should therefore look first to processes that have been historically verified.

This principle has been encapsulated in the catchphrase: "The present is the key to the past" (Harris & Fairbridge 1988: 848).

It would seem that a similar principle might prove applicable in historical (ethno)musicology. The present study has demonstrated that the social functions of music remain constant or vary only slowly and over a long time scale. This suggests that musicologists who investigate past cultures should try first to interpret their findings on the basis of the recently enumerated functions. Such an approach may be labelled 'musical uniformitarianism.'

The most conservative form of geological uniformitarianism, which is known as 'paleo-conservatism,' insisted that the natural processes in the past were exactly the same as they are today (Harris & Fairbridge 1988: 849). This view of the earth's history was shaken by the discovery of evidence pointing to the occurrence of global catastrophes such as glaciation and mass extinction of the dinosaurs. A looser formulation of the principle, which is known as 'logical rationalism,' provides for greater flexibility:

> [O]ne interprets the evidence of past events on a basis of logical reasoning, a basis of induction, avoiding supernatural or ad hoc hypotheses. Intuitive insight will not be accepted unless it is supported by demonstrable evidence. That evidence will be based on experimental procedures or field observations (*ibid.*).

An analogous flexibility is called for when interpreting past musical practices within the framework of Merriam's functions of music. In the present study, the attempt to fit all the observations into the traditional framework revealed the absence of a function concerning the economic role of music. Far from indicating a theoretical weakness, the recognition that the economic role had been overlooked has enriched our understanding and demonstrates the strength of an uniformitarian approach to the social history of music.

Musical Entrainment

Musical entrainment induces coordinated movement within groups of music participants. Chapter 1 alludes to the possibility that this phenomenon may have contributed to the evolution of human musicality. The role of music and dance—or 'musical entrainment' in the present context—in the facilitation of courting and mating will be familiar to every reader. In 1871, Charles Darwin described this role, in effect, as a *reproductive* benefit, when he wrote that music's "varied tones and cadences" allowed our "half-human ancestors [to arouse] each other's ardent passions, during their courtship and rivalry" (2004 [1871]: 639). In the following discussion, three of the likely *survival* benefits of musical entrainment will be illustrated by drawing on specific examples from the profiles.

The archeologist and evolutionist Iain Morley (2013) sees the linkage between music and movement as so strong, that he would have "music-dance" treated as a single phenomenon. He offers the definition:

> *Music-dance is deliberate metrically-organized gesture*
> (and deliberate metrically-organized gesture is music-dance) (p. 316)

with the lemmas

> Music is the auditory product of deliberate metrically-organized gesture;
>
> Dance is the physical product of deliberate metrically-organized gesture. (p. 317)

Morley's useful concept of 'music-dance' will be adopted in the following discussion.

Morley writes that the experience of musical entrainment "has the potential to allow both 'losing oneself' in the stimulus and/or a profound sense of physical cooperation, and synchronization of arousal level between individuals entrained to the same beat" (p. 314). This potential has played a part in religious ritual and is central to the many situations in which music has served to facilitate manual labor. As outlined in the following paragraphs, entrainment has also contributed during the preparatory stages of warfare and, in some instances, even in the midst of battle.

RELIGION

In religious history, according to McNeill (1997), music-dance "figure[s] largely [...], since from that spring came a perennial strengthening of group identities as well as perennial challenge and renewal" (p. 67). Religious music has existed for millennia, an early example being the hymns composed in Sumer ca. 2300 BCE by the influential priestess **Enheduanna (fl. ca. 2300 BCE)**. Text and melody are important in religious music, but in performance they have often been linked with physical movement or dance.

Desirous of eternal life, the Chinese emperor Wudi (156–87 BCE) staged elaborate nocturnal sacrifices to Heaven and Earth. To invigorate these services, he ordered new music-dance to be adapted from the religious observations of commoners. One of the musicians profiled in this text, **Li Yannian (fl. ca. 100 BCE)**, was in charge of the adaptations.

Followers of the mystical poet Jalāl ad-Dīn Rūmī (1207–1273) founded the Mevlevi order of Sufis in the thirteenth century CE (cf. the epigraph at the front of this book). Adepts of this Muslim order, who are popularly known as Whirling Dervishes, meditate trancelike to music by whirling for lengthy periods around their master (McNeill 1997: 92).

By around 1830 in the USA, a significant portion of the African-American slave population had accepted Christianity and was taking part in Christian revivalist "camp meetings." After the close of all-camp services, the slaves would gather in their quarters and sing repetitive spirituals, while shuffling around in a circle. These lengthy "ring shouts," which might last for hours, are said to have carried participants into a state of ecstasy (Southern 1997: 88–89; Stewart 1998: 21–23; Wilson 1985:13–17). One observer compared a farewell procession at the end of such encampments to the exuberant leaping and dancing of **King David (1040–970; r. 1010–970 BCE)**, when he brought the Ark of the Covenant into Jerusalem (cited by Southern 1997: 88).

Native American cultures associate music strongly with religion. They value music-dance for its ability to integrate society by way of ceremonial and social events and for its supernatural power. In Blackfoot medicine-bundle events, singing the text, "It is spring; let others see you," initiates the unwrapping of sacred objects. As each object is revealed, the celebrant alone or with others performs a specified activity, such as dancing, singing, smoking, eating, or praying. Another Blackfoot ceremony known as the Sun Dance begins with the singing of the phrase, "Sun says to sing." Traditionally, this ceremony extended over four days of preparation and four days of dancing (Nettl 2004).

WORK

In a 1985 article, the composer and musicologist Ollie Wilson discusses both religious and work songs. He notes that in the African-American tradition, body movement is "an integral part of the music-making process" (p. 10). This characteristic is manifest in the ring-shouts described above as well as in songs that arise out of physical labor:

> In the work song, the physical activity of work is incorporated as a means of producing the song; conversely, the song is part of the work. [...] Thus, the music-making activity is also a work activity. Work is an integral part of the music. (pp. 17–18)

The rhythm of the work song follows the repetitive pulsations of the labor. Although Wilson focuses on African-American music-dance, his characterization of the work song would seem to have more general applicability.

The musician and music historian Ted Giola (2006) considers the "inner experience of the field work song" (pp. 58–60). He suggests that work music brings laborers into a "flow state," a condition that has been described and popularized by the psychologist Mihaly Csikszentmihalyi. The characteristics of such a state resemble somewhat those of musical entrainment: people lose themselves in an activity, becoming unaware of externalities and the passage of time (Csikszentmihalyi 2008). Attaining a flow state purportedly enables individuals to perform at high levels for long periods. With respect to labor, Giola characterizes the flow state as one in which "the work becomes effortless and almost seems to happen of its own accord" (p. 59).

Work songs date from the beginnings of written history or possibly even earlier. Surviving tomb inscriptions and illustrations indicate that sowing and harvesting songs were being performed by laborers in the so-called Old Kingdom of Egypt, ca. 2700–2200 BCE. This is the era in which the Egyptian flutist **Ipi (fl. ca. 2600 BCE)** flourished. The texts of the ancient Egyptian work-songs are in the form of questions and answers, which suggests antiphonal performance, possibly by two groups of laborers. Plowing, fishing, digging, and transporting heavy objects also had musical accompaniment in ancient Egypt. In addition to singing, musical instruments such as tambourines, drums, clappers, and flutes also helped to encourage the progress of manual labor (Manniche 1991: 16–23).

The ancient Greeks used music in connection with many different types of economic activity: wool-processing, rope-making, various types of grinding and pounding, harvesting, viniculture, construction, and rowing. In several of these activities, the aulos supported or substituted for voice in the performance of work songs. One striking example of the work-related use of the aulos was to keep ships' oarsmen moving in synchrony (West 1992: 28–29). A contemporary scholar has estimated that Athens needed scores or hundreds of *auletes* to keep time for the rowers of triremes (Wilson 2002: 46).

Recent centuries were marked by the African diaspora, during which black slaves and, later on, their descendents invented and performed songs to facilitate a wide range of farm work. African-American slaves and laborers worked at "cutting sugarcane, shucking corn, picking cotton, turning water through the rice fields, [and] threshing" (Gioia 2006: 44). Gioia notes that cotton-picking songs are rarely mentioned in surviving documentation. In contrast to much "brutal and dehumanizing" labor, "corn shucking offered a marked contrast, with its quasi-festive atmosphere" (Gioia 2006: 44).

The work-song tradition has weakened in areas of the world in which industrial technology has replaced many manual tasks. Music inspired by manual labor is essentially irrelevant to driving a tractor or programming a computer. Recorded music has to some extent filled the void by calming the mind or providing diversion. Where concentration is required for carrying out individual tasks, music delivered through earphones may take on the antisocial function of shutting out interference from others (Radocy & Boyle 2012).

BONDING AND DEFENSE

Hagen and Bryant (2003) suggest that an important *prehistorical* role of music and dance was to signal social cohesion in displays that support the forming of alliances and defending of territories and that such displays "may have formed the evolutionary basis for the musical behaviours of modern humans" (p. 27). They contend that territorial defense has been relatively neglected as a factor in human evolution (pp. 25–26; but see McNeill 2013: 101–150). They downplay the role of music and dance in creating group cohesion, a process that is better served, in their view, by the (presumably vocal) interchange of information about the offered and shared benefits of group membership (p. 25). However, Morley (2013) argues convincingly that such a viewpoint ignores "factors of emotional bonding and loyalty engendered by mutual emotional experience, which could contribute to the perception of shared mutual goals" (p. 283).

In Chapter 3 of the present work, situations described in two of the profiles illustrate the phenomena of musical group-bonding and coalition-signaling. In a stand-off with the civil authorities, **Bishop Ambrose of Milan (339–397 CE)** held a vigil of hymn-singing and prayer that encouraged and strengthened the cohesion of his congregation. By signaling solidarity of purpose, hymn-singing may have helped to keep at bay a contingent of imperial troops, which had surrounded his basilica. After **King David** had taken Jerusalem from the Jebusites and made it his capital, he led a procession that brought the Ark of the Covenant into the city. While parading raucously into town, David and thousands of his followers sang and danced together to instrumental accompaniment. This was an ideal way to cement bonding among the revelers and to announce to any dissenters that they would be facing a united front of people who supported the king and his religion. Those who willingly took no part in the celebration might well have felt themselves outside the 'mainstream' of society, a feeling that could have contributed to the testy reaction of David's wife Michal upon greeting her husband.

With respect to occurrences of martial music-dance, McNeill (1997) presents examples in military-training, preparatory war-dancing and singing, and signaling during battle. Late in the fourth century BCE, a Chinese author named Wei Liao-tzu detailed a procedure for drilling soldiers and assembling them into effective forces of 30,000 men with the help of gongs, drums, bells, and flags. McNeill comments:

> Such passages show that very large infantry armies were taught to handle their weapons in unison and maintain formation by keeping in step while moving about on the battlefield in response to signals (p. 110).

McNeill cites Thucydides and Plutarch on the tactics of the Spartans in the fifth century BCE. They drilled their formidable infantry so effectively that Spartan soldiers would advance calmly and evenly into battle, and without breaking ranks, to the sound of the aulos (p. 116). McNeill also mentions Maori war-dancing in preparation for battle (p. 103), which has inspired the New Zealand All Blacks to perform *haka* (posture dances) at the start of their rugby matches (cf. Morley 2013: 284).

As described by McLean (1996), music-dance served the Maori not only to prepare for warfare but also during their military confrontations. Warriors performed a *peruperu* (war dance) immediately prior to the start of the fighting, at intervals during the battle, and afterwards too, if they were victorious. The *peruperu* was a terrifying spectacle, designed to unite the men in their purpose and demoralize or frighten the enemy. As many as several thousand armed, naked warriors would grimace, extend their tongues, contort their bodies, slap themselves, shout imprecations, and leap high into the air so as to come down with a thud, managing all this with such a remarkable degree of precision that the earth shook and the sound traveled several miles (pp. 47–57). Mclean reports that the Maori sang defensive and offensive incantations, challenges, watch songs, cursing and head-brandishing songs, and songs of triumph (p. 27).

Emotional Redundancy and Survival

Many of the functions of musical behavior, such as those described in Chapter 3, act together with other human capabilities to reinforce our sensibilities. Being able to sing of our love, as well as speak of it, enriches the emotional content. Our aesthetic appreciation expands when we can take in aural as well as visual forms of art. Watching a movie gives us more pleasure when the performance is accompanied by music. Prayer seems to grow more powerful when sung. Music unlocks our grief when we are mourning the loss of a loved one. Visual and other types of symbols, including musical anthems and hymns, remind us of group identities that we have learned about in school. Songs soothe our children while teaching them rules of behavior. Like language, literature, and architecture, the various forms of musical expression preserve and maintain distinctive cultures in the world.

In the *physical* realm, the doubling of human capabilities, or physical redundancy, represents a kind of survival benefit for individuals, in the sense that it allows life to proceed even after some functions have been lost. We continue to see if we lose an eye, to hear with only one ear, to grasp with nine fingers instead of ten, etc. By way of contrast, the reinforcements listed in the previous paragraph take advantage of doubling into the *emotional* sphere. This is where musical behavior has a major impact, as indicated in the first of the four functions of music that Martin Clayton has recently proposed:

> Regulation of an individual's emotional, cognitive or physiological state (2016: 54; cf. present work: Appendix B).

Doubling into the emotional sphere, or emotional redundancy, can provide resilience during periods of emotional stress. Like physical redundancy, therefore, emotional redundancy also can act as a kind of survival benefit. Nevertheless, the number of situations in which music functions only in *association* with other capabilities may have contributed to its characterization as an 'unnecessary' art.

Musical Entrainment and Survival

One aspect of music-dance that does not seem to be duplicated in other human capabilities is its ability to entrain, i.e., to coordinate the gestures of those who are participating in the music. We can use visual cues if we wish consciously to move in synchrony with others, but simply hearing a musical pulse actually *induces* us to move. The apparent uniqueness of entrainment throws a spotlight on this musical characteristic.

As described in the previous paragraphs, evolutionary scholars have outlined a number of likely benefits of entrainment: in the promotion of group identification and social-bonding; in the signaling of group cohesion and cooperation; and in defending and enlarging territorial control. The identification of these potential aids to survival raises the possibility, or perhaps even the likelihood, that entrainment played a role in human evolution and influenced the early development of musical behavior. Today, if we dance with others at a disco, march to music at a political protest, sway and sing-along at a pop concert, or simply tap our fingers while listening to classical music, we are responding to an age-old compulsion that may have influenced the very essence of our being.

References Cited

Bailey, Edward B. 1962. *Charles Lyell.* Edited by Gavin de Beer, British Men of Science. London: Thomas Nelson & Sons.

Clayton, Martin. 2016. The Social and Personal Functions of Music in Cross-Cultural Perspective. In *The Oxford Handbook of Music Psychology. Oxford Library of Psychology,* edited by S. Hallam, I. Cross and M. Thaut. Oxford: Oxford University Press.

Csikszentmihalyi, Mihaly. 2008. *Flow: The Psychology of Optimal Experience.* New York: Harper & Row.

Dean, Dennis R. 1992. *James Hutton and the History of Geology.* Ithaca: Cornell University Press.

Gioia, Ted. 2006. *Work Songs.* Durham & London: Duke University Press.

Hagen, Edward H., and Gregory A. Bryant. 2003. Music and Dance as a Coalition Signaling System. *Human Nature* 14 (1):21–51.

Harris, Stuart A., and Rhodes W. Fairbridge. 1988. Uniformitarianism. In *The Encyclopedia of Field and General Geology. Encyclopedia of Earth Sciences,* edited by C. W. Finkl. New York: Van Nostrand Reinhold.

Larue, D. K. 1992. Sedimentology, Walther's Law of Facies. In *Encyclopedia of Earth System Science,* edited by W. A. Nierenberg. San Diego: Academic Press.

Manniche, Lise. 1991. *Music and Musicians in Ancient Egypt.* London: British Museum Press.

McLean, Mervyn. 1996. *Maori Music.* Auckland: Auckland University Press.

McNeill, William Hardy. 1995. *Keeping Together in Time: Dance and Drill in Human History.* Cambridge: Harvard University Press.

Merriam, Alan P. 1964. *The Anthropology of Music.* Evanston: Northwestern University Press.

Morley, Iain. 2013. *The Prehistory of Music: Human Evolution, Archaeology, and the Origins of Musicality.* 1st ed. Oxford: Oxford University Press.

Nettl, Bruno. 2004. Native American Music. In *Excursions in World Music*, edited by B. Nettl, C. Capwell, I. K. F. Wong, T. Turino and P. V. Bohlman. Upper Saddle River: Pearson/Prentice Hall.

Radocy, Rudolf E., and J. David Boyle. 2012. *Psychological Foundations of Musical Behavior.* 5th ed. Springfield: Charles C Thomas, Publisher, LTD.

Rudwick, Martin. 2012. Charles Lyell: Earth's Present as the Key to its Past (1797–1875). In *The Scientists: An Epic of Discovery*, edited by A. Robinson. London: Thames & Hudson.

Southern, Eileen. 1997. *The Music of Black Americans: A History.* 3rd ed. New York & London: W. W. Norton & Company.

Stewart, Earl L. 1998. *African American Music: An Introduction.* New York & London: Schirmer Books & Prentice Hall International.

West, M. L. 1992. *Ancient Greek Music.* Oxford: Clarendon Press.

Wilson, Olly. 1985. The Association of Movement and Music as a Manifestation of a Black Conceptual Approach to Music-Making. In *More Than Dancing: Essays on Afro-American*

Music and Musicians: Contributions in Afro-American and African Studies, edited by I. V. Jackson. Westport: Greenwood Press.

Wilson, Peter. 2002. The Musicians Among the Actors. In *Greek and Roman Actors: Aspects of an Ancient Profession*, edited by P. E. Easterling and E. Hall. Cambridge: Cambridge University Press.

Further Reading

Fuld, James J. 2017. Patriotic Music. In *Grove Music Online. Oxford Music Online*: Oxford University Press. Web. 26 Jan. 2017. http://www.oxfordmusiconline.com/subscriber/article/grove/music/A2225007.

Jackson, Irene V., ed. 1985. *More Than Dancing: Essays on Afro-American Music and Musicians, Contributions in Afro-American and African Studies*. Westport: Greenwood Press.

McCollum, Jonathan, and David G. Hebert, eds. 2014. *Theory and Method in Historical Ethnomusicology*. Lanham, Boulder, New York, & London: Lexington Books.

McLean, Mervyn. 2006. *Pioneers of Ethnomusicology*. Coral Springs: Llumina Press.

Nettl, Bruno. 2015. *The Study of Ethnomusicology: Thirty-Three Discussions*. 3rd ed. Urbana, Chicago, and Springfield: University of Illinois Press.

CHAPTER FIVE

Closure

This text is built around brief biographies, or 'profiles,' of thirty musicians from the distant past. They lived between approximately 2500 BCE and 1500 CE at locations that span half the globe. They came from a variety of social classes, and the group includes both men and women. These brief biographies provide what may be a unique glimpse into the geographical spread and variety of musical life in earlier civilizations.

In Chapter 3, the activities of the early musicians have been categorized within an established framework of ten functions of music, which Alan P. Merriam formulated in mid-twentieth century. In Chapter 4, two significant conclusions emerge from the analysis: first, that an additional function of music, stimulation of the economy, needs to be added to Merriam's list; and secondly, that all of the now eleven functions of music can readily be identified within the profiles in Chapter 3.

The latter conclusion is striking, for it suggests that the purposes served by music in the distant past closely resembled its societal role in the present. This evidence of constancy in the social functions of music through different historical stages adds support to the view, as presented in Chapter 1, that human musicality is a genetically determined trait, rather than a characteristic that is transmitted culturally from generation to generation. Further studies may be needed to confirm or qualify this assertion. A possibly productive approach in the future would be to focus on a single long-lived music culture, such China's, and look for continuities and differences in musical behavior, as the culture evolves throughout history.

An analogous situation of constancy through the ages holds in geological studies, where a principle known as uniformitarianism expresses the idea that current conditions often are a key to understanding the past. In Chapter 4, a similar principle, labeled 'musical uniformitariansm,' has been described for use in music-related studies. According to this principle, scholars who seek to understand past music cultures should try first to explain their findings as earlier manifestations of present musical practice.

Music often reinforces sensibilities in an associational way, enriching our expressions of affection, triggering emotional catharsis at a funeral, and so on. In Chapter 4, it is argued that this associational role of music can act as a survival benefit. However, because of its secondary, reinforcing nature, it tends to be overlooked. This observation may be helpful in explaining why music has sometimes been viewed as an 'unnecessary' art.

The recently explored phenomenon of 'entrainment' induces coordinated movements in groups of people. Involuntary, or subconscious, entrainment would appear to be uniquely associated with music. In Chapter 4, examples drawn from the profiles and from other sources illustrate the multifaceted benefits of this phenomenon. Entrainment can promote group identification and social-bonding, aid in the signaling of group cohesion and cooperation, and underpin defensive and offensive military actions. The identification of these potential aids to group survival provides evidence that entrainment may have played a part in human evolution and influenced the early development of musical behavior. Perhaps musical entrainment should be viewed as a 'necessary' art.

In this book, a focus on the lives of early musicians has supported the formulation of insights into human musicality. A similar approach could conceivably help to uncover useful information on the human response to other arts, such as literature and painting.

APPENDIX A

Relation to (Ethno)musicology

Since its founding in 1927, the International Musicological Society (IMS), which recently strengthened its global outlook, has concerned itself with the history of musicians and their music (Baumann & Fabris: 2017). As discussed below, *ethno*musicologists are now also setting their sights on historical and biographical topics. The US-based Society for Ethnomusicology (SEM) has even inaugurated an official section on historical ethnomusicology.

Adjustments of Focus

Since 1955, when the SEM was founded, its members have repeatedly questioned both theory and practice of their discipline. Scholars have recognized a need to modify approaches that emphasize distinctions and project insensitivity to the cultures being studied. Comparative studies are considered susceptible to such faults, and as a result, comparative musicology lost ground to other approaches to the subject in the last quarter of the twentieth century. By the 1980s and 1990s, the dominant trend in ethnomusicology was "to carry out detailed, thick ethnography with essentially culture-specific interpretation" (Nettl 2010: 68).

Ethnomusicologists have also had to react to far-reaching social, technological, and political changes. As a result of decolonization, migration, and expanded access to communication resources, ethnic communities that were somewhat isolated have melted into a global amalgam. Distinctive cultural characteristics have become more difficult to tease out:

> Once it was easy to say that a "culture" was the sum of the lived experience and stored knowledge of a discrete population that differed from neighboring groups. Now it seems that there is no one experience and knowledge that unifies everyone within a defined "cultural" boundary or if there is, it's not the total content of their lives (Slobin 1992: 2).

Culture has become, as Martin Stokes describes it, "provisional, reflexive and mediated [...] no longer the semi-invisible ground of being and belonging, but a site of manipulable and malleable self-fashioning" (2001: 390).

Such considerations have given rise to numerous significant changes in the practice of ethnomusicology. Indeed, in the view of the eminent scholar Bruno Nettl, "ethnomusicology has far surpassed other fields of music research in its tendency toward changes of direction wrought by self-criticism—criticism of the practices and procedures of the discipline going far beyond correction of details and culture-specific findings" (2010: 69). For the purposes of the present text, it will not be necessary to review such developments fully in detail. Suffice it to emphasize two of the "changes in direction" that bear directly on this study: a placing of greater emphasis on the lives of individual musicians and an expansion of ethnomusicological research objectives in the direction of the historical past.

Individuals and History

Jonathan Stock notes in a 2001 article "an increasing number of ethnomusicological studies that focus directly on the musical experience of *individual* persons" (p. 5, emphasis added), and he explores the reasons behind this trend (pp. 10–15). Timothy Rice suggests that the field of ethnomusicology move in two directions: toward the study of individuals and small groups of individuals and the investigation of their dynamic context. He seeks "answers to the general question, how do *individuals* experience music in modernity, in modern life, in the modern world system" (2003: 152, emphasis added). Jesse Ruskin and Timothy Rice acknowledged in 2012 that ethnomusicologists are being pulled "toward the study of *individual* musicians." These authors investigate how such scholars "have tried to reconcile the competing poles of social and the *individual* in their musical ethnographic work and in their assessments of the field" (pp. 299–300, emphases added). The author and editor of a best-selling textbook, Jeff Todd Titon, suggests that ethnomusicology be defined as "the study of *people* making music" (emphasis added):

> [A]sking what the life of a musician is like in different societies, and answering in life histories and autobiographies, is essential if we are to know music as a human activity, not just a sequence of organized sound (1992: xxiii).

Titon's book includes biographies of individual musicians in the chapters on regional musics.

Friedrich Blume, long-time editor of the encyclopedia, *Die Musik in Geschichte und Gegenwart*, has said that musical scholarship "deals with the *history* of music and musicians" (1972: 27, emphasis added). Timothy Rice urges ethnomusicologists to attempt answers to a "deceptively simple question":

[H]ow do people *historically* construct, socially maintain and individually create and experience music? (1987: 473, emphasis added).

In a contribution to *Ethnomusicology and Modern Music History*, Christopher Waterman propounds the study of "*historically* situated human subjects who perceive, learn, interpret, evaluate, produce, and respond to music" (1991: 66, emphasis added). Joseph Lam, who has written biographically about the poet-composer Jiang Kui (1155–1279 CE), asserts:

Only when the *biographically individualized* and the *historically unique* in the artist's life and works are gauged will our understanding of what is typical and average in Chinese music history and culture become clearer and more meaningful (2001: 92, emphases added).

Jonathan McCollum and David Hebert urge ethnomusicologists to take up historical studies with a global perspective:

[We] call on fellow music scholars to rethink our position vis-à-vis global musical traditions and to rediscover both the unique role of *historical* insights and the value of an ethnomusicological perspective in attaining new knowledge of our global musical past (2014: 27).

These authors characterize historical scholarship as "a significant emerging subfield of ethnomusicology" (2014: 23).

Ethnographic Universals

Beyond the emphasis on individuality and history, the present work reflects what may prove to be yet another significant change in direction in the discipline: an increasing trend toward the consideration of general or universal concepts in ethnomusicological research. Gabriel Solis detects "a growing dissatisfaction in certain quarters with the notion of discrete 'cultures,' the prevailing mode of thinking in most of the second half of the twentieth century in anthropology and ethnomusicology" (2012: 540). He sees the following as a possible scenario:

> [G]eneral theories of music that draw on recent studies in cognition or on other neurophysiological literature may bring us full circle to music-anthropological notions that privilege our shared biology as humans, while being informed by studies of cultural difference that have made up the bulk of ethnomusicology in the past forty years (*ibid.*).

The present work draws examples from a wide range of historical music cultures for the purpose of generalizing about music in society. To express this thought in another way, learning about 'music,' rather than 'musics,' is the object of the investigation.

Historical Comparisons

The goal in studying musical behavior in earlier times has been to learn whether and how it may have changed throughout history. This is inherently a comparative mission. As noted above, contemporary ethnomusicology tends to shun comparative studies, concentrating instead on the understanding of music cultures in context. Since, in the present work, the cultures being compared are not contemporaneous, there should be little concern about projecting an insensitive bias.

The examination of regional groupings of early musicians bears a formal resemblance to the undertaking of ethnomusicological case studies. This formal resemblance, together with the comparative flavor of the present investigation, makes the use of traditional ethnomusicological methods, as epitomized in Alan P. Merriam's ten functions of music (1964: 219–227), particularly appropriate.

References Cited

Baumann, Dorothea, and Dinko Fabris, eds. 2017. *The History of the IMS (1927–2017)*. Basel, Kassel, London, New York, & Praha: Bärenreiter.

Blume, Friedrich. 1972. Musical Scholarship Today. In *Perspectives in Musicology: The Inaugural Lectures of the Ph.D. Program in Music at the City University of New York*, edited by B. S. Brook, E. Downes and S. Van Solkema. New York: W. W. Norton.

Lam, Joseph S. C. 2001. Writing Music Biographies of Historical East Asian Musicians: The Case of Jiang Kui (A.D. 1155–1221). *The World of Music* 43 (1):69–95.

McCollum, Jonathan, and David G. Hebert, eds. 2014. *Theory and Method in Historical Ethnomusicology*. Lanham, Boulder, New York, & London: Lexington Books.

Merriam, Alan P. 1964. *The Anthropology of Music*. Evanston: Northwestern University Press.

Nettl, Bruno. 2010. *Nettl's Elephant: On the History of Ethnomusicology*. Urbana: University of Illinois Press.

Rice, Timothy. 1987. Toward the Remodeling of Ethnomusicology. *Ethnomusicology* 31 (3):469–488.

———. 2003. Time, Place, and Metaphor in Musical Experience and Ethnography. *Ethnomusicology* 47 (2):151–179.

Ruskin, Jesse D., and Timothy Rice. 2012. The Individual in Musical Ethnography. *Ethnomusicology* 56 (2):299–327.

Slobin, Mark. 1992. Micromusics of the West: A Comparative Approach. *Ethnomusicology* 36 (1):1–87.

Solis, Gabriel. 2012. Thoughts on an Interdiscipline: Music
    Theory, Analysis, and Social Theory in Ethnomusicology.
    Ethnomusicology 56 (3):530–554.

Stock, Jonathan P. J. 2001. Toward an Ethnomusicology of the
    Individual, or Biographical Writing in Ethnomusicology.
    The World of Music 43 (1):5–19.

Stokes, Martin. 2001. Ethnomusicology, §IV: Contemporary
    Theoretical Issues. In *The New Grove Dictionary of Music and
    Musicians*, edited by S. Sadie and J. Tyrrell. New York:
    Grove.

Titon, Jeff Todd, ed. 1992. *Worlds of Music: An Introduction to the
    Music of the World's Peoples*. 2nd ed. New York: Schirmer
    Books.

Waterman, Christopher A. 1991. *Jùjú* History: Toward a Theory of
    Sociomusical Practice. In *Ethnomusicology and Modern Music
    History*, edited by S. Blum, P. V. Bohlman and D. M.
    Neuman. Urbana: University of Illinois Press.

Further Reading

Hindley, Geoffrey, ed. 1971. *Larousse Encyclopedia of Music*. London
    - New York - Sydney - Toronto: Hamlyn.

Kaden, Christian, Dietlef Giese, and Bernhard Schrammek. 1997.
    Musiksoziologie. In *Die Musik in Geschichte und Gegenwart.
    Allgemeine Enzyklopädie der Musik begründet von Friedrich
    Blume. Sachteil in neun Bänden*, edited by L. Finscher. Kassel
    - Basel - London - New York - Prag / Stuttgart - Weimar:
    Bärenreiter-Verlag / Metzler.

McLean, Mervyn. 2006. *Pioneers of Ethnomusicology*. Coral Springs:
    Llumina Press.

Rice, Timothy. 2010a. Disciplining *Ethnomusicology* A Call for a
    New Approach. *Ethnomusicology* 54 (2):318–325.

————. 2010b. Ethnomusicological Theory. *Yearbook for Traditional Music* 42:100–134.

Sachs, Curt. 1943. *The Rise of Music in the Ancient World East and West.* New York: W. W. Norton & Company Inc.

Slobin, Mark. 1993. *Subcultural Sounds: Micromusics of the West.* Hanover & London: Wesleyan University Press : University Press of New England.

Stone, Ruth M. 2008. *Theory for Ethnomusicology.* Upper Saddle River: Pearson Prentice Hall.

APPENDIX B

Explanation of the Functions

Musical functions have been extracted from the profiles in Chapter 3 with the help of an empirical framework, which the anthropologist Alan P. Merriam assembled in the 1960s. Merriam's approach has proven a convenient basis for overviewing the activities of the musicians in this book. This Appendix will describe his list of ten functions of music and their reception by other scholars.

Although Merriam developed the functions in association with his "theoretical research model" (pp. 32–35), they appear not to be dependent on it. Rather, they would seem to have been formulated out of empirical observations made on music cultures of the nineteenth and twentieth centuries.

In his presentation (pp. 219–227), Merriam distinguishes 'function' from 'use.' He contends that the functions of music are of a deeper nature than its uses. The latter are "the ways in which music is employed," that is, "the habitual practice or customary exercise of music either as a thing in itself or in conjunction with other activities" (p. 210). The functions, by way of contrast, identify the purposes that music fulfills in society. He illustrates this distinction with reference to love songs, which are *used* to gain sexual favor and have the *function* of promoting "the continuity and perpetuation of the biological group" (*ibid.*).

Merriam discusses his functions in some detail (pp. 219–227). The following paragraphs describe their import and relevance to the present work.

1. THE FUNCTION OF EMOTIONAL EXPRESSION

Merriam devotes several pages to explaining the function of emotional expression, suggesting examples that, for the most part, refer to the venting of the collective affect of a community. He refers as well to a cathartic or "release" function, which music provides "to the individual who finds himself in particular social situations." He notes that "the creative process itself" can also offer emotional release (pp. 219–223).

Recent studies have emphasized the centrality to music of emotional communication. John Sloboda describes a strong emotional reaction as "one of the most inescapable and characteristic features of music" (Deutsch et al. 2001: 544). Dissanayake discusses the origins of emotion in music, suggesting that "sophisticated musical emotion arises from the manipulation of expectations using the same fundamental structural features (formalization, repetition, exaggeration, elaboration) as in ritualized behaviors in nonhuman animals and in mother-infant interaction" (2006: 43). Emmanuel Bigand points to four large categories of musical emotion: gaiety, anger/fear, sadness, and serenity (2013: 54). Patrik N. Juslin offers a more detailed list, including "calm-relaxation, happiness-joy, nostalgia-longing, interest-expectancy, pleasure-enjoyment, sadness-melancholy, arousal-energy, love-tenderness, and pride-confidence" (2016: 200).

The profiles in Chapter 3 report instances in which music is performed in direct response to emotional stress. These instances have been taken to represent examples of emotional expression in the sense that Merriam intended.

2. THE FUNCTION OF AESTHETIC ENJOYMENT

Several of the profiled musicians concerned themselves with developing and promoting musical styles. In Chapter 3, this activity has been associated with the promotion of aesthetic enjoyment, because, as Jerrold Levinson writes, aesthetic appreciation involves the "appreciation of music for its hearable form and content, rather than for its instrumentality in relation to external purposes" (2015: 18).

3. THE FUNCTION OF ENTERTAINMENT

Listening to or performing music for pleasure is a generally recognized aspect of musical behavior. More than half of the profiled musicians entertained themselves or others in this way. Court musicians performed on command for their noble patrons, whereas concert artists played for a broader public. Musically trained impresarios organized performances for others. In certain instances, entertainment music was played to curry favor with a particular individual or simply for the pleasure of participating in the art.

4. THE FUNCTION OF COMMUNICATION

Merriam relates the communication function to the conveyance of "direct information" through song texts and to the conveyance of "emotion, or something similar to emotion, to those who understand its idiom" (1964: 223). He notes that the texts "provide a vehicle for the expression of ideas and emotions not revealed in ordinary discourse" (p. 219).

Religious music represents an attempt to communicate outside "ordinary discourse." The practice of chanting and singing poetic texts may have come into use as a way to attract the attention of spirits and gods. Because these beings were considered to be different from mortals, it may have been thought that they would be responsive to an extraordinary style of communication. Several of the profiled musicians in Chapter 3 participated in this type of activity. However, another of the profiled individuals used music to communicate sensitive "direct information" implicitly.

5. THE FUNCTION OF SYMBOLIC REPRESENTATION

Although symbolic representation is widely recognized as a musical characteristic, this function is perhaps the least perspicuous of the ten. Merriam devotes a whole chapter to the subject (pp. 259–258). He delineates four levels of musical symbolism: "the signing or symboling evident in song texts, the symbolic reflection of affective or cultural meaning, the reflection of other cultural behavior and values, and the deep symbolism of universal principles" (p.258).

In discussing symbolism in music, Martin Clayton (2016) asserts that "musical sound and action can specify aspects both of affect and of movement more precisely than words." He mentions the "unmatched precision and economy," with which musical signs "can specify their referents in cinema or advertising." He writes that musical signs "tend to be concerned with identity and alterity, bodily motion, and relationships between self and other" (p. 55).

Martin Stokes (2001) argues that music "clearly plays an important role in symbolizing community" (p. 387):

> Communities undoubtedly recognize themselves as such in their music making, and constitute themselves through and around this recognition (*ibid.*).

He cites evidence of African ethnic groups, for which musical gatherings play a central role in the production of community (pp. 387–388).

Merriam asserts that music can play a role in society in which it "is taken to symbolize values and even passions of the most specific yet most general nature" (1964: 241). He clarifies this assertion with reference to jazz. This genre is now universally respected as a form of musical expression and has profoundly influenced other musical forms, but in the 1920s and 1930s, as Merriam explains, it was condemned by many as "a symbol of culturally defined evil." In the USA, jazz was associated with "crime, insanity, feeble-mindedness, and other ills" (p. 242).

In summary, music is a symbolic medium in the sense that it can represent other things, such as human activities and emotions, and even abstractions such as morality and community. Some the profiled individuals who performed in the Classical Greek tradition drew attention to symbolism of their music, when they acted out physical mimicry during its performance. Profiled musicians from India and Western Asia CE performed in an atmosphere of religious intolerance of musical entertainment. Community values were symbolized in the compositions and performances of profiled individuals from Christianized Rome, Mali, and Japan. All these individuals have been associated in Chapter 3 with the function of symbolic representation.

6. THE FUNCTION OF PHYSICAL RESPONSE

Understood today as musical 'entrainment,' the characteristic of inducing synchronized physical movement has contributed to the well-being of society in a variety of ways. Societal benefits have been noted in the interpersonal, religious, economic, religious, and military spheres. Entrainment may even have played a significant role in human evolution. Physical response is recorded for only two of the musicians in Chapter 3, but numerous other examples have been documented throughout history (present work: Chapters 2 & 4).

7. THE FUNCTION OF ENFORCING CONFORMITY TO SOCIAL NORMS

Songs can support social conformity by praising examples of propriety and by pillorying improper behavior. Two of the musicians in Chapter 3 adopted the former approach in composing songs about athletes and soldiers. This functional category also suits a third musician, who criticized immoral sexual relationships.

8. THE FUNCTION OF VALIDATION OF SOCIAL INSTITUTIONS AND RELIGIOUS RITUALS

Merriam provides the following categories for the identification of music that might fulfill the function of validation of social institutions and religious rituals:

> Religious systems are validated, as in folklore, through the recitation of myth and legend in song, as well as through music which expresses religious precepts. Social institutions are validated through songs which emphasize the proper and improper in society, as well as those which tell people what to do and how to do it (1964: 224–225).

He notes that this function needs further study.

Composers of cultic music and performers at religious institutions can readily be associated with the first of these categories. The second category needs sharpening: The emphasis on proper and improper overlaps with the function of enforcing conformity to social norms. More to the point is the role of musicians in praising leaders and creating the kind of pomp-and-circumstance that imbue the social institution of government with an impression of validity.

Nearly two thirds of the musicians profiled in Chapter 3 performed music for the validation of social institutions and religious rituals. Unsurprisingly, most of these individuals were associated with religious or governmental institutions.

9. THE FUNCTION OF CONTRIBUTION TO THE CONTINUITY AND STABILITY OF CULTURE

Songs and other musical works that emphasize social and religious values can support cultural continuity and stability both within and outside the musical realm. Moral guidelines and church dogma can be passed on to future generations through song. The establishment or strengthening of schools of music and state music institutions contributes to the continuity and stability of musical culture. Other efforts that have this effect include the gathering and preservation of folk music and the development of forward-looking music theory. All such endeavors can be associated with contributing to the continuity and stability of culture.

10. THE FUNCTION OF CONTRIBUTION TO THE INTEGRATION OF SOCIETY

Merriam notes that music can provide "a rallying point around which the members of society gather to engage in activities which require the cooperation and coordination of the group" (p. 227). This integrative effect of music has recently been associated with the phenomenon of entrainment, as discussed in Chapters 2 and 4 of the present work. Musicians whose efforts helped to integrate religious, political, and class segments of society are profiled in Chapter 3.

Reservations, Revisions, and Alternatives

Merriam acknowledges that his list of functions "may require condensation or expansion" (p. 227). Several musicologists have addressed this possibility (see the following discussion). An eleventh function, to be appended to Merriam's ten, is proposed in Chapter 4 of the present work.

Bruno Nettl makes the point that Merriam's *functions* and *uses* may be identical in certain cases, such as for entertainment music (Nettl 2015: 262). This caveat concerning the theoretical rigor of Merriam's analysis should be borne in mind, but it is relatively inconsequential in the present context.

Nettl objects as well that Merriam's functions are not music-specific. He asserts that music differs functionally from the other arts and that one should therefore be able to link it to a unique function (p. 262). He provides his own wording of such an entity:

> [T]he most fundamental or significant function of music in human society, what music ultimately does for humans, is to mediate between various forces: to control humanity's relationship to the supernatural, mediating between human and other beings; and to mediate in ways not possible with speech between individuals and of [*sic!*] individuals. It does this by expressing the relevant central values of culture in abstracted form (p. 267).

This articulation might be simplified by saying that music underpins religion and supports the social order. Despite Nettl's reservation about Merriam's functions, however, he is content to embed them within his own "pyramid model" of music (p. 264).

Martin Clayton (2016) has also taken issue with Merriam, arguing that Merriam's list of functions is not "a thoroughly worked out taxonomy" (p. 48). Clayton has developed a list of his own (p.

49), as Ellen Dissanayake had also done somewhat earlier (Dissanayake 2006).

Dissanayake's proposal falls within the context of a discussion how ritual and ritualization guide human emotional responses to music. She presents six "Social functions served by ritual music":

> Display of resources.
> Control and channeling of individual aggression.
> Facilitation of courtship.
> Establishment and maintenance of social identity through rites of passage.
> Relief from anxiety and psychological pain.
> Promotion of group cooperation and prosperity.
> (pp. 43–49)

Dissanayake anchors her list on the social practices of thirty "traditional" societies. Her functions are worded more concretely than Merriam's, which is a very attractive feature, but their formulation reflects her focus on "traditional" musical behavior.

Clayton proposes a concise set of just four functions of music:

> 1. Regulation of an individual's emotional, cognitive or physiological state.
> 2. Mediation between self and other.
> 3. Symbolic representation.
> 4. Coordination of action. (pp. 54–55)

He notes that these functions "are largely concerned with relations between the personal and the social—identity, alterity, and mediation" (p. 56):

Discussing the first of his functions, Clayton explains that music performance has physiological effects, and that these can influence emotional and cognitive states. He observes that musical behavior is used in many cultures to regulate these states. Music can induce "mild effects such a[s] temporary calming or excitation or more dramatic changes such as trance." For individuals, listening to music "can be used in parallel ways as a tool for self-regulation" (p. 54). These influences of music ground the concept of 'emotional redundancy,' which is introduced toward the end of Chapter 4.

With respect to the second function, Clayton notes that music has long been used in situations in which normal speech has proven inadequate:

> Examples include the use of special forms of song or music to communicate with gods, spirits, or ancestors in ritual contexts. More mundane examples might include the use of song to communicate emotional states felt to be beyond the scope of everyday speech, or to communicate intimately with large numbers of people. (*ibid.*)

These situations relate closely to those for which Merriam's functions of "communication" and "validation of social institutions and religious rituals" apply.

Clayton's third function is the same as Merriam's fifth, which has been described above. His coordination-of-action function falls under the rubric of 'entrainment,' which is discussed in Chapters 2 and 4 of this book.

Clayton acknowledges that Merriam's list is "a useful device on which to hang a compilation of numerous case studies" (p. 48). In this connection, it should also be noted that Merriam's ten functions, even if they do not form a "perfect taxonomy," make explicit a broad range of identifiable musical characteristics. Such breadth of coverage adds useful detail to the description of a given music culture and facilitates intercultural comparisons.

Merriam's functions relating to conformity, validation, and integration would likely be approached more psychologically by today's theorists, namely in terms of the creation of individual identities (cf. Rice 2010a). However, the present work has stuck to his original wording, avoiding thereby the pitfall of confusing different theoretical approaches.

The gathering of empirical observations into broadly defined categories, which can be tested for validity in different situations, is a scientific approach to the study of music in society. As such, it flies in the face of much recent ethnomusicological practice. Timothy Rice notes that "most ethnomusicologists no longer regularly employ" scientific theory, which has been "to a large extent supplanted by social theory," since the late 1970s (2010b: 103–104; but see also p. 100 n.2 and McLean 2006: 21). Scientific theory has, however, been applied in this book. By allowing diffuse observations of musical behavior to be systematically categorized, it has provided a framework for understanding the role of music in historical situations.

Although Merriam's model has fallen out of fashion with scholars who favor social theory over science, it maintains a significant presence in ethnomusicology, and it has proven useful in the present study. The prominent social theorist Timothy Rice has acknowledged that Merriam's anthropological framework "still usefully guides a significant portion of our research" (2003b: 151). Keith Howard notes that Merriam's books, like those of Bruno Nettl, "essentially remain current, albeit with theoretical refinements introduced by Rice" (see the preface to McCollum & Hebert 2014: xii).

References Cited

Bigand, Emmanuel. 2013. *Le cerveau mélomane*. Paris: Belin.

Clayton, Martin. 2016. The Social and Personal Functions of
 Music in Cross-Cultural Perspective. In *The Oxford
 Handbook of Music Psychology. Oxford Library of Psychology*,
 edited by S. Hallam, I. Cross and M. Thaut. Oxford:
 Oxford University Press.

Deutsch, Diana, et al. 2001. Psychology of Music. In *The New
 Grove Dictionary of Music and Musicians*, edited by S. Sadie
 and J. Tyrrell. New York: Grove.

Dissanayake, Ellen 2006. Ritual and Ritualization: Musical Means
 of Conveying and Shaping Emotion in Humans and
 Other Animals. In *Music and Manipulation: On the Social
 Uses and Social Control of Music*, edited by S. Brown and U.
 Volgsten. Oxford & New York: Berghahn Books.

Juslin, Patrik N. 2016. Emotional Reactions to Music. In *The
 Oxford Handbook of Music Psychology. Oxford Library of
 Psychology*, edited by S. Hallam, I. Cross and M. Thaut.
 Oxford: Oxford University Press.

Levinson, Jerrold. 2015. *Musical Concerns: Essays in Philosophy of
 Music*. 1st ed. Oxford & New York: Oxford University
 Press.

McCollum, Jonathan, and David G. Hebert, eds. 2014. *Theory and
 Method in Historical Ethnomusicology*. Lanham, Boulder, New
 York, & London: Lexington Books.

McLean, Mervyn. 2006. *Pioneers of Ethnomusicology*. Coral Springs:
 Llumina Press.

Merriam, Alan P. 1964. *The Anthropology of Music*. Evanston:
 Northwestern University Press.

Nettl, Bruno. 2015. *The Study of Ethnomusicology: Thirty-Three
 Discussions*. 3rd ed. Urbana, Chicago, and Springfield:
 University of Illinois Press.

Rice, Timothy. 2003. Time, Place, and Metaphor in Musical Experience and Ethnography. *Ethnomusicology* 47 (2):151–179.

———. 2010. Disciplining *Ethnomusicology*: A Call for a New Approach. *Ethnomusicology* 54 (2):318–325.

———. 2010. Ethnomusicological Theory. *Yearbook for Traditional Music* 42:100–134.

Stokes, Martin. 2001. Ethnomusiology, §IV: Contemporary Theoretical Issues. In *The New Grove Dictionary of Music and Musicians*, edited by S. Sadie and J. Tyrrell. New York: Grove.

Further Reading

Carlin, Richard. 1987. *Man's Earliest Music*. Vol. 1, *The World of Music*. New York: Facts On File Publications.

Herskovits, Melville J. 1956. *Man and His Works: The Science of Cultural Anthropology*. 1st ed. New York: Alfred A. Knopf.

Hindley, Geoffrey, ed. 1971. *Larousse Encyclopedia of Music*. London - New York - Sydney - Toronto: Hamlyn.

Kaden, Christian, Dietlef Giese, and Bernhard Schrammek. 1997. Musiksoziologie. In *Die Musik in Geschichte und Gegenwart. Allgemeine Enzyklopädie der Musik begründet von Friedrich Blume. Sachteil in neun Bänden*, edited by L. Finscher. Kassel - Basel - London - New York - Prag / Stuttgart - Weimar: Bärenreiter-Verlag / Metzler.

Rice, Timothy. 1987. Toward the Remodeling of Ethnomusicology. *Ethnomusicology* 31 (3):469–488.

Sachs, Curt. 1943. *The Rise of Music in the Ancient World East and West*. New York: W. W. Norton & Company Inc.

Stone, Ruth M. 2008. *Theory for Ethnomusicology*. Upper Saddle River: Pearson Prentice Hall.

APPENDIX C

The Musicians Briefly Characterized

Name (Date), Location	Music Specialty	Social Position
Akashi no Kakuichi (ca. 1300–1371 CE), Japan	Voice, *biwa* (lute), composition	*Biwa-hōshi* (itinerant Buddhist musician-priest)
Ambrose (339–397 CE), Italy	Hymn composition	Bishop of Milan
Amīr Khusrau Delhavī (1253–1325 CE), India	Composition, voice	Court poet-composer
Balla Fasséké Kouyaté (fl. ca. 1230 CE), Mali	*Bala* (xylophone), voice, composition	*Djeli* (adviser to the king, spokesman, musician, praise-singer, historian, entertainer)
Bārbad (fl. ca. 600 CE), Persia	*Barbat* (lute), voice, composition, music theory	Court musician

Name (Date), Location	Music Specialty	Social Position
Dada (fl. ca. 2040 BCE), Mesopotamia	Hymns of lamentation, music management	Gala singer and impresario
David of Bethlehem (1040–970 BCE), Israel	Lyre, voice, composition	King of Israel and Judah
Dugha (fl. ca. 1352 CE), Mali	*Bala* (xylophone), voice	*Djeli* (adviser to the king, spokesman, musician, praise-singer, historian, entertainer)
Enheduanna (fl. ca. 2300 BCE), Mesopotamia	Hymn composition	Priestess
Fu Niang (fl. ca. 880 CE), China	Voice	Courtesan
Ibrāhīm al-Mawṣilī (742–804 CE), Arabia	Voice, *ʿūd* (lute), composition	Court musician
Ipi (fl. ca. 2600 BCE), Egypt	Flute	Court musician, priest
Isḥāq al-Mawṣilī (767–850 CE), Arabia	Voice, *ʿūd* (lute), composition, theory	Court musician
Jamīla (d. ca. 715 CE), Arabia	Voice, *ʿūd* (lute), composition, music instruction	Professional musician
Jayadeva (12th century CE), India	Composition	Poet and composer
Li Yannian (fl. ca. 100 BCE), China	Voice, composition, arranging	Court musician

Name (Date), Location	Music Specialty	Social Position
Marcabru (fl. ca. 1130–1150 CE), Occitania/Spain	Voice, composition	Troubadour
Nero (37–68; r. 54–68 CE), Italy	*Cithara* (concert lyre), bagpipe, hydraulus (water organ), voice, composition	Roman Emperor
Otomae (1085–1169 CE), Japan	Voice performance and training	*Kugutsu* entertainer
Peripatjauemope (fl. ca. 1080 BCE), Egypt	Trumpet	Temple musician
Pindar (ca. 520–ca. 440 BCE), Greece	Victory odes and other choral works	Professional poet and composer
Pronomos (ca. 470–390 BCE), Greece	*Aulos* (reed pipes) and composition	Professional musician
Raia (fl. ca.1250 BCE), Egypt	Harp and voice	Chief of temple singers
Risiya (fl. ca.1790 BCE), Mesopotamia	Music management and teaching	Head of music in Mari
Stratonicus (ca. 410–360 BCE), Greece	*Cithara* (concert lyre), music theory	Entertainer and teacher
Tigellius (fl. ca. 50 BCE), Sardinia/Italy	*Tibia* (reed pipes) and voice	Court musician
Walther von der Vogelweide (ca. 1170–1230 CE), Austria/Germany	Voice, composition	Minnesinger

Name (Date), Location	Music Specialty	Social Position
Xuanzong (685–762; r. 712–756 CE), China	Drums, composition, institutional reform	Emperor
Yang Guifei (719–756 CE), China	*Pipa* (lute), *bianqing* (stone chimes), flute, voice, composition	Imperial consort
Ziryāb (ca. 790–850 CE), Arabia and Al-Andalus	Voice and *'ūd* (lute)	Court musician

INDEX